Faith in Nichiren Buddhism

Guidance on Happiness, Health, Wealth, and Harmonious Relationships

The Living Buddha

Nichiren-Buddhism

Copyright © 2022 Nichiren-Buddhism

All rights reserved.

This book is licensed for your personal use only and may not be sold or given away.

For information about permission, to reproduce selections from this book, write to Nichiren-Buddhism

Published by Nichiren-Buddhism

No part of this book may be reproduced by any mechanical, photographic, or electronic process, or in the form of a phonographic recording; nor may it be stored in a retrieval system, transmitted, or otherwise be copied for public or private use other than for "fair use" as brief quotations embodied in articles and reviews without prior written permission of the publisher.

Contents

Acknowledgment	IX
1. The History of Buddhism	1
2. The Origins of Buddhism	10
3. The World of Nichiren Buddhism	21
4. The Life of Nichiren Daishonin	25
5. Introduction to Nichiren Buddhism	33
6. What is Nichiren Buddhism	40
7. What is Myoho-Renge-Kyo	44
8. Nam-myoho-renge-kyo	47
9. The Title of the Lotus Sutra	49
10. The Power of Chanting Nam Myoho Renge Kyo	54
11. The Practice of Prayer in Nichiren Buddhism	58
12. The Limitless Potential of Nam-myoho-renge-kyo	62
13. The Language of Gongyo and Daimoku	64
14. Unlocking the Power of Chanting	66
15. Why Aren't My Prayers Getting Answered?	68
16. Finding Fulfillment Within	70
17. Profound Realization of 'Myo' and 'Ho'	72

18.	The Transformative Power of Faith and Prayer	76
19.	Chanting Can Benefit Our Entire Family	78
20.	The Complexity of Changing Someone Else's Karma	80
21.	Transforming Misfortune into Great Good Fortune	82
22.	Changing Problems into Springboards for Growth	85
23.	The Significance of Faith in Every Situation	88
24.	The Power of Words: The Essence of the Lotus Sutra in Nam-myoho-renge-kyo	92
25.	How 'Nam-Myoho-Renge-Kyo' Differs from Chanting Other Words?	95
26.	The Use of Bells in Nichiren Buddhism's Gongyo Practice	100
27.	The Prime Point of Faith: Daimoku First	103
28.	The Role of Faith and Effort in Achieving Happiness	111
29.	A Powerful Tool for Achieving Your Deepest Desires	116
30.	Transforming Our Attitude in Faith for Positive Change	119
31.	The Unwavering Faith of Nichiren Daishonin	123
32.	Prayer is the Key	126
33.	The Eternity of Life	136
34.	The Eight Winds	140
35.	Changing Your Destiny	144
36.	Living True Buddhism	147
37.	The Seed of Buddhahood	150

38.	Essentials of Individual Guidance	153
39.	The Great Blessing of the Gohonzon	156
40.	Helping Others with Individual Guidance	160
41.	The Role of Leaders	163
42.	Treasuring Each Individual	168
43.	One's Way of Living	173
44.	Understanding the True Benefits of Faith	178
45.	A Mother's Journey from Blame to Apology: A Lesson in Parenting	181
46.	Achieving a Work-Life-Buddhism Balance	183
47.	Overcoming Grief: A Family's Journey to Kosen-rufu	185
48.	Being a Representative of Nichiren Buddhism	187
49.	From Busy to Balanced: Buddhism into Your Daily Life	189
50.	How Problems Help us Grow	194
51.	Financial Problems as Opportunities	196
52.	The Gohonzon: The Only Reliable Support in Life	200
53.	A Story of Triumph Over Adversity	202
54.	The Correct Way to Practice Faith	204
55.	Don't Wait for the Perfect Time	206
56.	The Warning Signs of Faith	208
57.	Inspiring Inactive Members to Return	211
58.	The Power of Home Visits	214
59.	Building Unity in Your District	217

60.	The Art of Giving Guidance	220
61.	The Dangers of Complaining	224
62.	Understanding the Causes of Suffering	226
63.	Inconspicuous Benefits of Faith	230
64.	Supporting Each Other	233
65.	The Relationship Between Problems & Happiness	235
66.	Conquering Devilish Functions	239
67.	Deepening Faith for Effective Guidance	241
68.	Strengthening Faith to Overcome Illness	244
69.	Great Misfortune Followed by Great Good Fortune	246
70.	The Dichotomy of Benefit and Loss	250
71.	Our Lives Contain The Universe	253
72.	Chanting Daimoku – Fueling the Engines Of Our Lives	255
73.	Excuses and Complaining	258
74.	Becoming Someone Your Husband Can Trust	261
75.	Breaking Free from Negative Cycles	263
76.	The Significance of Posture in Gongyo	266
77.	Chanting for Personal Happiness	268
78.	The Law of Cause and Effect	270
79.	The Nine Consciousness in Buddhism	273
80.	Simultaneity of Cause and Effect: Understanding the Lotus	277
81.	Choosing a Marriage Partner	281

82.	The Significance of Reciting Gongyo	286
83.	The Strategy of The Lotus Sutra	289
84.	The Three Proofs	291
85.	Finding Happiness through Faith, Practice, and Study	294
86.	Practice for Oneself and Others	296
87.	The Power of Buddhist Study	298
88.	Managing Your Karmic Bank Account	300
89.	The Two Types of Happiness	304
90.	Life Changing Experience	307
91.	Using Bad Karma for Good Fortune	310
92.	Turning Poison into Medicine	312
93.	The Illuminating Effect of Daimoku	316
94.	Embracing Nam-myoho-renge-kyo	319
95.	Nichiren Daishonin's Doctrine of Changing Destiny	321
96.	Nichiren Daishonin's Call to Kosen-rufu	326
97.	Empowering Others: The Essence of Compassion	330
98.	The Key to Increasing Good Fortune	334
99.	The Relationship between Knowledge and Wisdom	338
100.	From Basic Needs to Spiritual Fulfillment	343
101.	The Gohonzon: A Blueprint of Inner Potential	345
102.	Human Revolution: Path to Inner Transformation	348
103.	Nichiren's Controversial Message	352
104.	Living Confidently in the Present Moment	358

105.	Activating the Inherent Buddha Qualities	362
106.	The Oneness of Body and Mind	366
107.	The Middle Way in Buddhism	370
108.	The Optimistic Philosophy of Buddhism	374
109.	The Power of Interconnectedness	378
110.	The Heart of Buddhist Practice	382
111.	Beyond Cause and Effect: Karma and Choice	387
112.	Manifesting Buddhahood in Everyday Life	391
113.	Funi: The Idea of 'Two, but Not Two'	395
114.	From Hell to Buddhahood: Exploring the Ten Worlds	399
115.	A Path to Buddhahood	405

Acknowledgment

THROUGHOUT THE CREATION OF this book, our focus has been entirely on the transcripts of Nichiren Daishonin's writings. Our aim has been to present his words in their original form to the best of our abilities. However, we would like to draw your attention to some important points to consider.

Firstly, the translations have undergone multiple revisions to enhance clarity and conciseness. While we have made every effort to preserve accuracy, it is worth noting that not all sources are primary, and we cannot guarantee the authenticity of every excerpt.

Secondly, it is essential to acknowledge that concepts and interpretations can evolve over time and vary in different contexts. We strongly encourage readers to cross-reference phrasing with primary sources when citing Nichiren Daishonin from this text and to approach interpretations with openness and generosity.

Please be aware that everything presented in this book is extracted from its original context, and interpretations may evolve over time.

The original intentions behind Nichiren's words may differ from your interpretation in a different era, medium, format, or context.

While we have made sincere efforts to maintain the original intent, errors can occur as the content has transcended time, space, and different mediums. Moreover, older texts have been edited and rearranged to enhance readability. We acknowledge the contributions of Nichiren Daishonin, Dr. Daisaku Ikeda, Richard Causton, Satoru Izumi, Josei Toda, Tsunesaburo Makiguchi, and others, but any mistakes that may arise are solely our responsibility.

We sincerely appreciate your understanding and hope you derive great enjoyment from the book!

The History of Buddhism

BUDDHISM, ONE OF THE world's major religions, traces its origins back to ancient India in the 5th century BCE. It emerged as a spiritual path that sought to alleviate suffering and attain enlightenment. Over the centuries, Buddhism spread across Asia, adapting to various cultures and giving rise to different schools and traditions. One of these prominent schools is Nichiren Buddhism, which has gained recognition for its relevance and applicability to the modern age. This chapter delves into the history of Buddhism, its spread across the world, and the emergence of Nichiren Buddhism as a potent form of Buddhist practice.

The Birth of Buddhism

Buddhism was founded by Siddhartha Gautama, later known as the Buddha, who lived in the 5th century BCE. Born into a royal family in present-day Nepal, Siddhartha renounced his privileged life to seek enlightenment and understand the nature of suffering. After years of rigorous meditation, he achieved enlightenment under the Bodhi tree, becoming the Buddha, or "the awakened one."

The Buddha spent the remainder of his life teaching the Dharma, his profound insights into the nature of reality and the path to liberation. His teachings emphasized the Four Noble Truths, which acknowledge the existence of suffering, identify its causes, propose its cessation, and provide a path, known as the Eightfold Path, to achieve liberation.

The Spread of Buddhism

Following the Buddha's death, his teachings were initially transmitted orally by his disciples. Over time, these teachings were organized into collections known as sutras, which formed the foundation of Buddhist scriptures. As Buddhism spread throughout ancient India, it also encountered various regional and cultural influences, leading to the emergence of different Buddhist schools and traditions.

During the reign of Emperor Ashoka in the 3rd century BCE, Buddhism was patronized and actively propagated across the Indian subcontinent and beyond. Buddhist missionaries embarked on journeys to neighboring countries, spreading the teachings and establishing monastic communities.

Buddhism in East Asia

Buddhism found its way to East Asia, where it encountered unique cultural and philosophical contexts. In China, Buddhism underwent further development and integration with existing spiritual and philosophical systems, such as Confucianism and Daoism. This amalgamation led to the formation of distinct Chinese Buddhist schools, including Pure Land, Chan (Zen), and Tiantai.

The Emergence of Nichiren Buddhism

Nichiren Buddhism, named after the 13th-century Japanese monk Nichiren, traces its roots to the Lotus Sutra, a significant Mahayana Buddhist scripture. Nichiren's teachings emphasized the Lotus Sutra as the ultimate expression of the Buddha's enlightenment, presenting it as the quintessential teaching for the present age.

Nichiren's teachings sought to address the social and political issues of his time, promoting peace, justice, and the welfare of all beings. He believed that by reciting the mantra "Nam-myoho-renge-kyo" and embracing the Lotus Sutra's principles, individuals could unlock their highest potential and transform society.

Nichiren Buddhism in the Modern Age

Nichiren Buddhism's appeal lies in its relevance to the modern age. It addresses the challenges and complexities of contemporary life, offering practical tools for personal growth, social engagement, and spiritual transformation. Its core principles, such as the concept of interconnectedness and the power of inner transformation, resonate with individuals seeking meaning, purpose, and harmony in a rapidly changing world.

Nichiren Buddhism promotes the practice of chanting Nam-myoho-renge-kyo, which is believed to awaken one's inherent Buddhahood and tap into the limitless potential within. Through this practice, individuals cultivate wisdom, compassion, and the ability to effect positive change in their lives and communities.

Furthermore, Nichiren Buddhism emphasizes the importance of faith in one's own inherent Buddha nature, asserting that every individual possesses the potential for enlightenment. This empowering belief resonates with those who seek a spiritual path that acknowledges their innate goodness and capacity for growth.

Another aspect that sets Nichiren Buddhism apart is its inclusivity. It embraces people from all walks of life, irrespective of their social status, gender, or background. Nichiren himself encouraged the active participation of laypeople in the practice, breaking down the traditional hierarchy between clergy and laity.

Nichiren Buddhism also places great emphasis on social engagement and the pursuit of peace. Nichiren believed that the teachings of the Lotus Sutra had the power to transform society by fostering compassion, respect, and understanding among individuals. This perspective aligns with the modern world's yearning for social justice, harmony, and global cooperation.

In addition, Nichiren Buddhism's focus on the present moment resonates with individuals navigating the challenges of the contemporary world. By embracing the here and now, practitioners cultivate mindfulness, resilience, and a deep appreciation for the richness of everyday experiences.

Moreover, Nichiren Buddhism emphasizes the importance of personal study and understanding of the Buddhist teachings. It encourages individuals to delve into the sutras, engage in dialogue, and seek wisdom from various sources. This approach fosters intellectual growth, critical thinking, and a well-rounded understanding of Buddhist principles.

Nichiren Buddhism has flourished in various parts of the world, with organizations and communities dedicated to its practice and propagation. Its teachings have resonated with individuals seeking a dynamic and relevant spiritual path that addresses the complexities of the modern age.

Buddhism's rich history spans over two millennia and has left an indelible impact on the spiritual, cultural, and philosophical landscape of the world. Within the tapestry of Buddhist traditions, Nichiren Buddhism stands out as a vibrant and practical path for the present age. Its emphasis on personal empowerment, social engagement, and the transformative power of the Lotus Sutra makes it particularly relevant to individuals seeking a comprehensive and accessible spiritual practice. By embracing the principles of Nichiren Buddhism, one can embark on a journey of self-discovery, compassion, and positive change, ultimately contributing to a more harmonious and enlightened world.

As Nichiren Buddhism continues to spread, its global impact grows, reaching individuals from diverse backgrounds and cultures. The accessibility of its teachings, coupled with its adaptability to modern circumstances, has attracted people seeking spiritual fulfillment, inner peace, and a deeper understanding of themselves and the world around them.

In this age characterized by rapid advancements in technology, globalization, and interconnectedness, Nichiren Buddhism offers a path that integrates ancient wisdom with contemporary challenges. Its core principles of compassion, interdependence, and the belief in the inherent dignity and potential of every individual resonate with the universal aspirations for a more harmonious and compassionate world.

The practice of Nichiren Buddhism centers around the chanting of Nam-myoho-renge-kyo, which serves as a powerful tool for self-reflection, empowerment, and transformation. Through the repeated recitation of this mantra, practitioners tap into their inner wisdom, connect with the enlightened nature within themselves, and manifest positive change in their lives.

Nichiren Buddhism's focus on individual responsibility and agency aligns with the values of personal growth and self-empowerment that are prevalent in the modern world. It encourages individuals to take charge of their own happiness and well-being while also recognizing their interconnectedness with all beings and the environment.

Furthermore, the teachings of Nichiren Buddhism highlight the importance of dialogue, understanding, and respect among diverse cultures, religions, and belief systems. It encourages practitioners to engage in constructive and compassionate conversations, fostering a spirit of mutual learning and cooperation for the betterment of humanity.

In the face of complex global challenges such as environmental degradation, social inequality, and the erosion of ethical values, Nichiren Buddhism provides a comprehensive framework for addressing these issues at their root. By cultivating wisdom, compassion, and a deep sense of responsibility, practitioners are empowered to contribute positively to society and work towards the establishment of peace, justice, and sustainable living.

Nichiren Buddhism's relevance to the modern age lies in its ability to integrate the timeless wisdom of the Buddha's teachings with the evolving needs and aspirations of humanity. It offers a practical and accessible approach to spirituality that empowers individuals to navigate the complexities of life, find meaning and purpose, and make a positive impact on the world.

As more people discover the transformative potential of Nichiren Buddhism, its influence continues to expand, fostering a global community united by shared values and a commitment to personal growth and societal well-being. In this age of interconnectedness, Nichiren Buddhism serves as a beacon of hope, guiding individuals towards a more enlightened, compassionate, and harmonious future.

The history of Buddhism spans millennia, and its teachings have resonated with countless individuals across different cultures and epochs. Nichiren Buddhism, with its emphasis on the Lotus Sutra and its relevance to the present age, stands as a vibrant and transformative form of Buddhism. Its principles of empowerment, social engagement, and personal growth make it an ideal spiritual path for those seeking to navigate the complexities of the modern world while embodying the timeless principles of original Buddhism.

The Origins of Buddhism

BUDDHISM IS ONE OF the major religions in the world, with over 500 million followers worldwide. It is a religion that originated in ancient India and has spread throughout the world. The roots of Buddhism can be traced back to the teachings of Siddhartha Gautama, also known as the Buddha, who lived in the 5th century BCE.

Siddhartha Gautama was born into a wealthy family in Lumbini, in present-day Nepal. His father was a king, and Siddhartha was raised in luxury and comfort. However, at the age of 29, he became disillusioned with his privileged life and left his palace to seek spiritual enlightenment.

For six years, Siddhartha studied with various teachers and practiced meditation and asceticism. He eventually rejected these practices and began a new path, known as the Middle Way, which sought to balance spiritual practice with daily life.

Siddhartha achieved enlightenment under a bodhi tree in Bodh Gaya, India, at the age of 35. He became the Buddha, meaning "the awakened one," and spent the rest of his life teaching others his philosophy and way of life.

The Buddha's teachings centered on the Four Noble Truths, which state that suffering exists, that suffering is caused by desire and attachment, that it is possible to overcome suffering, and that the path to overcoming suffering is the Eightfold Path. The Eightfold Path consists of right understanding, right intention, right speech, right action, right livelihood, right effort, right mindfulness, and right concentration.

The Buddha's teachings were not immediately accepted, and he faced opposition from traditional religious leaders of the time. However, his message spread throughout India and eventually to other parts of Asia.

After the Buddha's death, his teachings were compiled into texts known as the Sutras. The Sutras were written in the Pali and Sanskrit languages and contain the Buddha's teachings on various subjects, such as morality, meditation, and wisdom.

Buddhism evolved over time, and different schools emerged as the religion spread to different regions. The two major schools of Buddhism are Theravada and Mahayana. Theravada, also known as the "Way of the Elders," is the oldest surviving school of Buddhism and is prevalent in Southeast Asia. Mahayana, meaning "the Great Vehicle," emerged in India in the 1st century BCE and is prevalent in China, Korea, and Japan.

Buddhism has had a significant impact on the world and has influenced many areas of life, including art, literature, and philosophy. Its emphasis on compassion, mindfulness, and wisdom has made it an appealing religion for many people, and it continues to attract new followers today.

In conclusion, Buddhism originated in ancient India, with the teachings of Siddhartha Gautama, the Buddha. His message of the Four Noble Truths and the Eightfold Path spread throughout Asia and has had a significant impact on the world. Today, Buddhism continues to evolve and adapt to new cultures and societies, while retaining its core principles of compassion, mindfulness, and wisdom.

The Life and Teachings of Shakyamuni Buddha (also known as Gautama Buddha and Siddhartha):

Shakyamuni Buddha, also known as Gautama Buddha or Siddhartha, was a spiritual teacher, philosopher, and religious leader who lived in what is now Nepal and India between the 4th and 6th century BCE. He is revered as the founder of the world religion of Buddhism and is recognized by most Buddhist schools as the Enlightened One who transcended Karma and escaped the cycle of birth and rebirth. He taught for around 45 years and built a large following, both monastic and lay, based on his insight into duḥkha, typically translated as "suffering," and the end of dukkha, the state called Nibbana or Nirvana.

Gautama was born into a wealthy family as a prince in present-day Nepal. His father, Suddhodana, was a Sakya king, and his mother, Maya, also came from a princely family. Seven days after his birth, his mother passed away, leaving him to the care of her sister and his stepmother Mahajapati, who was also a wife of Suddhodana.

The young Siddhartha was brought up in Kapilavastha, which was the capital of Sakya's kingdom. When he was born, several miracles occurred, according to legend, confirming the arrival of a great being into the world. His father and some prominent members of his court were aware that a divine child, destined to be a great person, was born amidst them. His parents named him Siddhartha, and they expected him to grow and become a successful and skillful king.

However, as he grew older, Siddhartha was moved by the suffering he saw in the world. He was particularly affected by the sight of an old man, a sick man, a dead man, and a wandering ascetic. These experiences led him to renounce his life as a prince and seek the truth about existence and the nature of suffering.

Siddhartha left his palace and began a quest for enlightenment. He studied with various spiritual teachers but eventually realized that their teachings did not offer a solution to the problem of suffering. He then turned to ascetic practices, fasting, and self-mortification, but these extreme practices did not provide him with the answers he was seeking.

One day, as he sat in deep meditation under a bodhi tree in Bodh Gaya, India, he had a profound realization and became the Buddha, the "Enlightened One." He had discovered the Four Noble Truths, which state that suffering is an inherent part of life, that the cause of suffering is craving, that suffering can be overcome, and that the path to the end of suffering is the Noble Eightfold Path.

For the rest of his life, the Buddha traveled throughout India, teaching the Dharma to all who would listen. He taught that the path to enlightenment involves cultivating wisdom, ethical conduct, and mental discipline. His teachings emphasized compassion, loving-kindness, and the importance of mindfulness in all aspects of life.

The Buddha's teachings have had a profound impact on the world. Today, Buddhism is one of the major religions, with millions of followers worldwide. The life and teachings of the Buddha continue to inspire people to seek truth, cultivate wisdom and compassion, and find peace and happiness in their lives.

The Life of Buddha: Exploring his Early Years:

Buddha, which means "one who is awakened" or "the enlightened one," is recognized as a historical figure by scholars, but there is still debate over the specific events and dates of his life. According to the most widely known story of his life, after exploring various teachings for many years, Siddhartha Gautama, also known as Buddha, spent a night in deep meditation beneath a tree. During this meditation, he achieved full awareness, and all the answers he had been seeking became clear, leading to his enlightenment.

Buddha was born into a wealthy family in present-day Nepal. After experiencing a great deal of suffering in the world, he decided to renounce his princely ways and worldly life. He traveled to Rajagriha, the capital of the famous Magadha Kingdom, where he met with King Bimbisara, who unsuccessfully tried to persuade him to abandon his decision. However, Buddha remained steadfast in his resolve and promised to return to Magadha to preach his gospel to the people after attaining enlightenment.

From there, Buddha went to meet a famous sage named Alara Kalama, who taught him the doctrine of Atman and the existence of Brahman. However, Buddha grew disillusioned with his teachings and left to search for truth on his own. He traveled to a forest near Uruvela on the banks of the river Nairanjana, where he met five wandering monks who were also seeking liberation from the cycle of birth and death through austerities and self-denial. They accepted Buddha as their leader and master after seeing his sincerity and commitment to practicing austerities.

Buddha's journey to enlightenment and his teachings would go on to form the foundation of Buddhism, which emphasizes the importance of understanding and transcending suffering in order to attain spiritual liberation.

Siddhartha's Journey to Enlightenment:

As a prince, Siddhartha lived a sheltered life within the palace walls. However, his curiosity about the outside world led him to venture out with a charioteer. During this journey, he encountered the harsh realities of human frailty and suffering, such as an old man, a diseased man, and a decaying corpse. He also met an ascetic who had renounced the world to seek release from the fear of death and suffering. Overwhelmed by these sights, Siddhartha left his kingdom, wife, and son at the age of 29 to follow a spiritual path that aimed to relieve the universal suffering he had witnessed.

For the next six years, Siddhartha lived an ascetic life, subjecting himself to severe self-mortification and studying various religious teachings. However, he eventually realized that this path was not leading him to enlightenment and that he needed to strengthen his body to pursue his spiritual goals. He left the austere life behind and started begging for food in nearby villages to regain his strength.

During this period, a village girl named Sujata served him milk-rice, which ended his six-year period of severe fasting. However, the five monks who had been with him until then were not happy with this change and left him to go to Isipitana, a place in the suburbs of ancient Varanasi. Despite their departure, Siddhartha continued on his journey towards enlightenment, which ultimately led to his becoming the Buddha.

The Buddha, The Enlightened One:

After his companions deserted him, Gautama spent some time alone in the forest, contemplating his next course of action. His initial setback only strengthened his determination to seek enlightenment.

Siddhartha sat beneath the Bodhi tree, vowing not to rise until he attained the truths he sought. He meditated until sunrise the following day and remained there for several days, purifying his mind and reflecting on his entire life, including his past lives.

During this time, he had to confront an evil demon who challenged his right to become the Buddha. But Siddhartha did not waver, and when the demon claimed the enlightened state for himself, Siddhartha touched his hand to the ground and asked the Earth to bear witness to his enlightenment. The Earth responded, banishing the evil demon.

Finally, a vision of the universe began to take shape in Siddhartha's mind, and he saw the answer to the question of suffering that he had been seeking for so many years. In that moment of pure enlightenment, Siddhartha Gautama became the Buddha, the Enlightened One.

The Buddha's Teachings:

With his newfound knowledge, the Buddha was initially hesitant to teach, knowing that what he had realized could not be fully expressed in words. However, according to ancient texts, the king of gods, Brahma, persuaded him to teach, and so he rose from his place under the Bodhi tree and set out to share his insights with others.

After traveling about 100 miles, he encountered the five ascetics who had left him before he achieved enlightenment. Siddhartha urged them to follow a path of balance, known as the Middle Way, which rejected both extreme asceticism and excessive sensuality. He then gave his first sermon, "Setting in Motion the Wheel of the Dharma," in which he explained the Four Noble Truths and the Eightfold Path, which would become the foundation of Buddhism.

The ascetics became the Buddha's first disciples, forming the core of the Sangha, or community of monks. Women were also welcomed into the Sangha, and all social, racial, and gender distinctions were disregarded, with only the goal of reaching enlightenment through the elimination of suffering and spiritual emptiness being important.

For the rest of his life, the Buddha traveled and preached the Dharma, hoping to guide others along the path of enlightenment.

Death:

Buddha passed away around the age of 80. Before he died, he urged his disciples to not follow any leader but to "be their own light." At the age of 79, he declared forty-one conditions for the welfare of the Order, mainly focusing on how monks should behave and pursue their spiritual paths. He delivered this message to Rajagriha and Nalanda.

Buddhist iconography often depicts the Buddha with a serene or smiling expression, lying on his right side with his head resting on his right hand. The dates of Buddha's life are traditionally given as 566-486 BC, and the exact nature of his death remains uncertain. However, some sources suggest that he may have died from an illness caused by eating tainted pork, which led to a disease called pig-bel, a necrotizing enteritis caused by the toxins of a Clostridium perfringens infection.

The Buddha's teachings have had a significant impact on world history, influencing not only other religions but also literature and philosophy, both in India and throughout the world. He remains one of the most influential figures in human history.

The World of Nichiren Buddhism

NICHIREN BUDDHISM IS A branch of Buddhism that was founded in the 13th century by the Japanese monk Nichiren Daishonin. This form of Buddhism is based on the belief that all people possess the Buddha nature, and that by chanting Nam-myoho-renge-kyo, one can unlock the potential to reveal that nature and achieve enlightenment.

Nichiren Daishonin believed that the chanting of Nam-myoho-renge-kyo was the most powerful and effective way to achieve enlightenment. He saw the potential for a world in which all people could live in harmony, free from suffering and conflict. This was not just for individuals, but for society as a whole.

The evolution of Nichiren Buddhism can be traced back to the original teachings of Buddha, who lived in India over 2,500 years ago. Buddha's teachings were transmitted orally for many centuries before being written down in various scriptures. Over time, Buddhism spread throughout Asia and developed into various schools and sects, each with its own unique teachings and practices.

In the early 13th century, Nichiren Daishonin emerged as a Buddhist reformer in Japan. He believed that the true essence of Buddhism was contained in the Lotus Sutra, one of the most important Mahayana Buddhist scriptures. Nichiren Daishonin saw the Lotus Sutra as a teaching that could be practiced by all people, regardless of their social status or level of education.

Nichiren Daishonin's teachings were revolutionary in that they placed great emphasis on the power of the individual to achieve enlightenment. He believed that every person had the potential to become a Buddha and that this could be achieved through the chanting of Nam-myoho-renge-kyo.

Over time, Nichiren Buddhism has evolved into several different sects, each with its own unique teachings and practices. These include the Soka Gakkai International (SGI), Nichiren Shoshu, and Nichiren Shu, among others.

SGI is one of the largest and most well-known Nichiren Buddhist organizations in the world. It was founded in 1930 by Tsunesaburo Makiguchi, a Japanese educator who believed in the transformative power of Nichiren Buddhism. SGI's main focus is on the promotion of peace, culture, and education, and it has millions of members worldwide.

Some of the other sects of Nichiren Buddhism include:

Nichiren Shu: Founded in Japan in the 13th century, Nichiren Shu is one of the oldest and largest sects of Nichiren Buddhism. It emphasizes the Lotus Sutra as the ultimate teaching of the Buddha and the importance of chanting the mantra "Nam-myoho-renge-kyo".

Nichiren Shoshu: Founded in the 20th century, Nichiren Shoshu is a smaller sect of Nichiren Buddhism that places great emphasis on the role of the priesthood in the practice of Buddhism. It also emphasizes the importance of the Gohonzon, a mandala that represents the enlightened life of the Buddha.

Rissho Kosei-kai: Founded in Japan in 1938, Rissho Kosei-kai emphasizes the Lotus Sutra as the ultimate teaching of the Buddha and the importance of social engagement and compassion in the practice of Buddhism.

Reiyukai: Founded in Japan in 1920, Reiyukai emphasizes the importance of gratitude, compassion, and self-reflection in the practice of Buddhism.

As for which sect is the best for a beginner to join, it ultimately depends on the individual's personal preferences and goals. It's recommended that beginners explore the different sects and their teachings, attend meetings and events, and talk to members before making a decision on which sect to join. Ultimately, the most important factor is finding a community and practice that resonates with you and supports your spiritual growth.

Nichiren Buddhism is a form of Buddhism that emphasizes the power of the individual to achieve enlightenment through the chanting of Nam-myoho-renge-kyo. The practice has evolved into several different sects, each with its own unique teachings and practices. These sects are practiced worldwide and have millions of followers who are dedicated to promoting peace, culture, and education.

The Life of Nichiren Daishonin

SECTION 1: EARLY LIFE and Spiritual Awakening (1222-1253)

In the year 1222, on the sixteenth day of the second month, in the coastal village of Kominato, Japan, a child named Zennichimaro was born. Little did anyone know at the time that this child would grow up to become Nichiren Daishonin, one of the most influential figures in Japanese Buddhism.

Zennichimaro belonged to a humble fisherman's family and led a simple life in a time of great political and social upheaval. As a young boy, he showed remarkable intelligence and an insatiable curiosity about life's mysteries. His thirst for knowledge led him to study various religious teachings, seeking the ultimate truth that could bring enlightenment and peace to the world.

In his early twenties, Zennichimaro, now known as Nichiren, became a disciple of the Tendai school of Buddhism. He dedicated himself to intense monastic training, immersing himself in scripture and philosophical debates. However, despite his efforts, he found himself increasingly disillusioned with the state of Buddhism in Japan. He saw corruption, the misuse of power, and the watering down of the true teachings.

It was during this time that Nichiren had a profound spiritual awakening. In 1253, at the age of 32, he experienced a vision while in meditation on Mount Hiei. He realized that the Lotus Sutra held the ultimate truth and the key to enlightenment. From that moment on, Nichiren committed himself to the propagation of the Lotus Sutra as the sole teaching that could bring salvation to all humanity.

Section 2: The Persecutions and Exiles (1253-1274)

Nichiren's uncompromising belief in the supremacy of the Lotus Sutra and his criticism of other Buddhist schools and the government's policies caused considerable controversy. He faced opposition from both religious authorities and political figures, leading to a series of persecutions and attempts on his life.

In 1260, Nichiren narrowly escaped death when a group of assassins attacked him at his hermitage in Matsubagayatsu. Undeterred by these threats, he continued to propagate his teachings fearlessly, emphasizing the urgency of embracing the Lotus Sutra in the face of social and political chaos.

The authorities, feeling threatened by Nichiren's growing influence, banished him to the remote Izu Peninsula in 1261. During his exile, he faced numerous hardships, including poverty, isolation, and natural disasters. However, these challenges only deepened his resolve, and he continued to write letters and treatises, urging his followers to persevere in their faith.

After enduring several years of exile, Nichiren was pardoned in 1263 and returned to Kamakura, the political center of Japan at the time. His presence sparked both admiration and hostility, as his teachings attracted a dedicated following but also drew the ire of influential religious and political figures.

Section 3: Final Years and Legacy (1274-1282)

In the later years of his life, Nichiren faced further persecution and exile due to his outspoken criticisms of the government and religious establishments. Despite these challenges, he never wavered in his mission to spread the teachings of the Lotus Sutra.

During this period, Nichiren focused on writing significant treatises, including his most renowned work, the "Rissho Ankoku Ron" ("On Establishing the Correct Teaching for the Peace of the Land"). In this treatise, he warned of the imminent threats facing Japan and stressed the necessity of embracing the Lotus Sutra to ensure peace and prosperity.

In 1281, Japan faced a severe military threat when the Mongol fleets led by Kublai Khan attempted to invade the country. Nichiren saw this as a manifestation of the consequences of deviating from the correct teaching of the Lotus Sutra. He fervently urged the government to embrace the teachings and seek divine protection through faith.

Despite his warnings, Nichiren's pleas fell on deaf ears, and the Mongols launched two failed invasions in 1274 and 1281, known as the Mongol Invasions of Japan. These military defeats further fueled animosity towards Nichiren, as his critics accused him of bringing misfortune upon the nation.

In his final years, Nichiren faced severe persecution, including an attempt on his life in 1279. However, his unwavering faith and determination to propagate the Lotus Sutra remained unshaken. He continued to write letters and engage in rigorous debate with his opponents, striving to awaken them to the truth of the Lotus Sutra.

Nichiren passed away on October 13, 1282, at the age of 61. His legacy as a fearless advocate of the Lotus Sutra and his unwavering commitment to the enlightenment of all humanity continues to inspire millions to this day.

Section 4: The Timeline of Nichiren Daishonin's Life

- 1222: Nichiren is born as Zennichimaro in Kominato, Japan.
- 1239: Nichiren becomes a disciple of the Tendai school of Buddhism.
- 1253: Nichiren experiences a spiritual awakening and dedicates himself to the propagation of the Lotus Sutra.
- 1260: Assassination attempt on Nichiren's life at Matsubagayatsu.
- 1261-1263: Nichiren is exiled to the Izu Peninsula.
- 1263: Nichiren is pardoned and returns to Kamakura.
- 1274: First Mongol invasion of Japan.
- 1279: Attempted assassination on Nichiren's life.
- 1281: Second Mongol invasion of Japan.
- 1282: Nichiren passes away on October 13 at the age of 61.

Nichiren Daishonin's teachings continue to resonate with people seeking enlightenment and peace in their lives. His emphasis on the power of faith, the universality of the Lotus Sutra, and the need for social and spiritual transformation serve as an enduring legacy.

Nichiren Daishonin's life was one of immense dedication and unwavering commitment to the propagation of the Lotus Sutra. From his humble beginnings in a fishing village to becoming a towering figure in Japanese Buddhism, Nichiren fearlessly challenged the religious and political establishments of his time.

Through persecution, exile, and hardships, he never compromised his belief in the transformative power of the Lotus Sutra. His teachings continue to inspire millions, emphasizing the importance of faith, compassion, and the pursuit of peace and enlightenment in an ever-changing world. Nichiren Daishonin's legacy lives on as a beacon of hope and guidance for all those seeking spiritual awakening and the betterment of society.

Section 5: The Impact of Nichiren Daishonin's Teachings

Nichiren Daishonin's teachings have had a profound and lasting impact on Japanese society and the world at large. His emphasis on the Lotus Sutra as the ultimate teaching for attaining enlightenment and his call for social transformation continue to resonate with followers of Nichiren Buddhism.

One of the key aspects of Nichiren's teachings is the concept of "Nam-myoho-renge-kyo," which represents the essence of the Lotus Sutra. This mantra encapsulates the belief in the inherent Buddha nature within all individuals and the potential for enlightenment in this lifetime. Chanting "Nam-myoho-renge-kyo" is seen as a practice to tap into one's inner wisdom and to overcome life's challenges.

Nichiren's teachings also emphasized the idea of social engagement and the responsibility of practitioners to contribute to the betterment of society. He encouraged his followers to actively participate in social and political affairs, advocating for justice, compassion, and the establishment of a harmonious society based on the principles of the Lotus Sutra.

Through his prolific writings, Nichiren addressed not only spiritual matters but also social and political issues of his time. His treatise "Rissho Ankoku Ron" called for the cessation of warfare and the establishment of a just and peaceful society. This work laid the foundation for the idea of "human revolution," the belief that individual transformation leads to societal transformation.

Nichiren's teachings have continued to evolve and spread beyond Japan, reaching followers around the world. The establishment of the Soka Gakkai International (SGI) in the twentieth century expanded the global reach of Nichiren Buddhism, promoting peace, education, cultural exchange, and social justice based on the principles of humanistic Buddhism.

Today, millions of people practice Nichiren Buddhism and find inspiration in Nichiren Daishonin's teachings. The focus on inner transformation, the pursuit of social justice, and the power of faith and chanting "Nam-myoho-renge-kyo" as a means to tap into the enlightened nature within are core tenets of the faith.

The life of Nichiren Daishonin, from his birth to his legacy, exemplifies a profound spiritual journey and a dedicated pursuit of truth and enlightenment. His unwavering commitment to the Lotus Sutra, his courage in the face of persecution, and his teachings on faith, social engagement, and humanistic values continue to inspire and guide individuals in their quest for personal growth, societal change, and the realization of lasting peace. Nichiren Daishonin's teachings remain a testament to the transformative power of Buddhism and the potential for positive change within each individual and the world.

Introduction to Nichiren Buddhism

NICHIREN BUDDHISM IS A profound and transformative spiritual path that traces its origins back to the teachings of the 13th-century Japanese Buddhist priest Nichiren Daishonin. Rooted in the Lotus Sutra, Nichiren Buddhism emphasizes the power of faith, chanting Nam-myoho-renge-kyo, and the pursuit of enlightenment in this present lifetime. This chapter aims to provide a comprehensive overview of Nichiren Buddhism, exploring its key principles, practices, and the profound impact it can have on the lives of its practitioners.

Nichiren Daishonin's Teachings: A Foundation for Nichiren Buddhism

Nichiren Daishonin dedicated his life to studying and practicing Buddhism, ultimately discovering the essence of the Lotus Sutra as the ultimate teaching for attaining enlightenment. He firmly believed that the Lotus Sutra contained the highest truth and the means to achieve true happiness for all people.

In his writings, Nichiren Daishonin expressed the importance of absolute faith in the Lotus Sutra. He wrote, "You must be firmly resolved never to discard your faith for as long as you live, no matter what may happen" (The True Object of Worship). This unwavering faith is the cornerstone of Nichiren Buddhism and is cultivated through the practice of chanting Nam-myoho-renge-kyo.

The Mystic Law: Nam-myoho-renge-kyo

At the heart of Nichiren Buddhism is the practice of chanting Nam-myoho-renge-kyo, which encompasses the entirety of the Lotus Sutra. This powerful mantra represents the underlying rhythm and life force of the universe. Nichiren Daishonin referred to it as the "Daimoku," meaning the title of the Lotus Sutra.

Through the consistent recitation of Nam-myoho-renge-kyo, practitioners tap into their inherent Buddha nature and connect with the boundless wisdom, compassion, and life force within themselves. This practice allows individuals to transform their lives and manifest their greatest potential.

Nichiren Daishonin beautifully encapsulated the transformative power of chanting when he wrote, "If you wish to free yourself from the sufferings of birth and death, you have endured since time without beginning and to attain without fail unsurpassed enlightenment in this lifetime, you must perceive the mystic truth that is originally inherent in all living beings" (Letter to Niike).

The Oneness of Self and Environment: The Principle of Three Thousand Realms in a Single Moment of Life

Nichiren Buddhism teaches the profound concept of the "Three Thousand Realms in a Single Moment of Life." This principle elucidates the interdependence and inseparability of one's inner life and external circumstances.

According to Nichiren Daishonin, all phenomena in the universe arise from the same life force and are interconnected. He states, "A person's character is not only revealed by his or her physical appearance but through the words and behavior that flow from the inner depths of that person's life" (The Three Kinds of Treasure).

By realizing the profound connection between our inner life and the world around us, we gain the power to transform our circumstances. Rather than feeling helpless victims of external events, we are encouraged to take responsibility for our own happiness and actively contribute to the betterment of society.

The Attainment of Buddhahood: Everyone Possesses the Buddha Nature

Nichiren Buddhism firmly asserts that every individual possesses the potential for Buddhahood. This concept, known as "Ichinen Sanzen," teaches that within a single individual, there exists the capacity to manifest the three thousand realms and attain enlightenment.

Nichiren Daishonin wrote, "The moment we chant Nam-myoho-renge-kyo with deep faith in the Gohonzon, the Buddha nature within us is summoned and begins to shine brightly. It is like awakening the dormant Buddha within ourselves, unlocking our inherent wisdom, compassion, and courage.

Nichiren Daishonin emphasized that Buddhahood is not something reserved for a select few or attained in some distant future. Rather, it is a state that can be realized in the present moment. He wrote, "The Lotus Sutra is the teaching that enables all people to attain Buddhahood, no matter how ignorant or lowly they may be" (The Opening of the Eyes).

By embracing the belief in our own Buddha nature and engaging in the practice of chanting Nam-myoho-renge-kyo, we can tap into our limitless potential and navigate the challenges of life with resilience, wisdom, and compassion.

Engaging with the Gohonzon: The Object of Devotion in Nichiren Buddhism

The Gohonzon is a sacred object of devotion in Nichiren Buddhism. It is a calligraphic mandala inscribed by Nichiren Daishonin, representing the life state of Buddhahood within ourselves. The Gohonzon serves as a focal point for our practice and a mirror to reflect our true nature.

Nichiren Daishonin wrote, "The Gohonzon is the object of devotion in the entire world, in the present as well as in the future" (Reply to Kyo'o). By chanting Nam-myoho-renge-kyo while facing the Gohonzon, we establish a profound connection with the Buddha nature within us and align ourselves with the universal life force.

The Role of the Mentor-Disciple Relationship

Nichiren Buddhism places great importance on the mentor-disciple relationship as a source of guidance and support on the path to enlightenment. Nichiren Daishonin emphasized the significance of finding a mentor who embodies the teachings and can inspire and guide others towards Buddhahood.

He wrote, "It is difficult to have faith in the Lotus Sutra without a good teacher, and it is difficult to understand the Lotus Sutra without a good teacher" (The True Aspect of All Phenomena). The mentor-disciple relationship provides the necessary guidance, encouragement, and insights to deepen one's faith and practice.

Nichiren Buddhism offers a profound and transformative path to realizing our inherent Buddhahood and attaining happiness in this lifetime. Through the teachings of Nichiren Daishonin, we learn the power of unwavering faith, the practice of chanting Nam-myoho-renge-kyo, and the interconnectedness of our inner life and external circumstances.

By embracing the Gohonzon as the object of devotion and cultivating a mentor-disciple relationship, we have the tools to navigate the challenges of life, tap into our limitless potential, and contribute to the betterment of society.

In the words of Nichiren Daishonin, "Winter always turns to spring. Never from ancient times has anyone heard or seen of winter turning back to autumn" (The Opening of the Eyes). Nichiren Buddhism teaches us that no matter our circumstances, we have the power to transform our lives and manifest our Buddhahood.

With a firm resolve, deep faith, and the practice of chanting Nam-myoho-renge-kyo, we can embark on a journey of self-discovery, enlightenment, and ultimate happiness. Nichiren Buddhism offers a path of hope, empowerment, and the realization of our highest potential.

What is Nichiren Buddhism

NICHIREN BUDDHISM, A BRANCH of Mahayana Buddhism, originated in 13th century Japan and has since become a global movement with millions of adherents. The school is named after Nichiren, a Japanese Buddhist priest whose teachings continue to play a central role in the institution.

Nichiren believed, like many of his peers, that the Lotus Sutra embodied all other Buddhist teachings. However, unlike his contemporaries, he contended that the Japanese title of the sutra, Nam-myoho-renge-kyo, contained all the dharma. He also believed that anyone could achieve Buddhahood by chanting the name of the scripture. Nichiren Buddhists practice chanting this scripture, called the Daimoku, along with other recitations and prayers, during the Gongyo ritual, which they perform twice daily.

The phrase "Nam-myoho-renge-kyo" is a transliteration of the Chinese characters for the Lotus Sutra's title. It can be translated as "I devote myself to the Lotus Sutra of the Wonderful Law." The mantra is chanted by Nichiren Buddhists as a means of activating their Buddha nature and realizing their full potential for enlightenment.

Nichiren Buddhism places great emphasis on the power of the individual to transform their own life and the world around them. It teaches that all beings possess the potential for enlightenment and that through the practice of chanting "Nam-myoho-renge-kyo" and studying the teachings of Nichiren Daishonin, one can unlock this potential and transform their life in a positive direction.

Nichiren Buddhism emerged during the Kamakura Period (1185-1333) when Japan was rife with natural disasters, civil war, and wealth disparities. Japanese Buddhists believed that the Latter Day of the Law, a period of moral and intellectual decline prophesied in the sutras, had arrived. This belief led to the emergence of new schools such as Zen, Pure Land, and Nichiren. Nichiren took a middle path by emphasizing individual change through religious faith, whereas Pure Land advocated a faith in other-power approach, and Zen stressed self-power meditation practice. Faith in action became the central theme of Nichiren's spiritual and political activism.

Nichiren's practices, such as the Daimoku chant, embody a spirit of egalitarianism that holds that enlightenment and the dharma are available to all, regardless of their background. Social activism and engagement have become essential components of Nichiren Buddhism for many practitioners today. After Nichiren's death, his followers grappled with codifying his teachings, leading to the founding of 37 different schools of Nichiren Buddhism.

Nichiren Buddhism has its roots in the Lotus Sutra, one of the most important Mahayana sutras that was composed in India around the 1st century BCE. The Lotus Sutra is considered to be the highest teaching of the Buddha, and it teaches that all beings possess the Buddha nature, the potential for enlightenment, and that all beings can attain Buddhahood.

Nichiren Daishonin, who lived in Japan in the 13th century, was a monk who became disillusioned with the state of Buddhism in his country. He believed that the Buddhist teachings had become corrupted and that the true teachings of the Buddha had been lost. He studied various Buddhist texts, including the Lotus Sutra, and eventually came to the conclusion that the mantra "Nam-myoho-renge-kyo" was the essence of the Lotus Sutra and the key to attaining Buddhahood.

In addition to chanting, Nichiren Buddhism also emphasizes the importance of studying Buddhist texts and participating in activities that promote the well-being of society. The practice of Nichiren Buddhism is centered around the Gohonzon, a scroll that contains the characters for "Nam-myoho-renge-kyo" and other symbols that represent the Buddha's teachings. The Gohonzon is regarded as a representation of the Buddha's life and serves as a focal point for meditation and chanting.

Nichiren Buddhism has been spread throughout the world through the efforts of the Soka Gakkai International, an organization that promotes peace, culture, and education based on the principles of Nichiren Buddhism. Today, Nichiren Buddhism has followers in many countries and continues to grow in popularity as a modern form of Buddhism that emphasizes the power of the individual to transform their own life and the world around them through the practice of chanting and the study of Buddhist teachings.

What is Myoho-Renge-Kyo

IN BRIEF, MYO OF *myoho* means "wonderful" or "mystic," and *ho* means "law," "principle," "teaching" or "phenomena." Together, *myoho* is translated as "Wonderful Law" or "Mystic Law." Nichiren Daishonin says: "*Myo* stands for the Dharma nature or enlightenment, while *ho* represents darkness or ignorance. Together, *myoho* expresses the idea that ignorance and the Dharma nature are a single entity". *Myoho*, then, expresses both the enlightened nature of a Buddha and the deluded nature of an ordinary person, and the fact that they are essentially one.

While most Buddhist schools see a vast difference between a Buddha and an ordinary person, Nichiren aimed to erase any idea of a separation between the two. For instance, in "The Heritage of the Ultimate Law of Life," he writes: "Shakyamuni Buddha who attained enlightenment countless kalpas ago, the Lotus Sutra that leads all people to Buddhahood, and we ordinary human beings are not different or separate from one another. To chant Myoho-renge-kyo with this realization is to inherit the ultimate Law of life and death."

He also writes, "*Myo* represents death, and *ho*, life", And in "On Attaining Buddhahood in This Lifetime," he writes, "*Myo* is the name given to the mystic nature of life, and *ho*, to its manifestations", Hence, *myoho* is also the essence of life itself that is manifest while one is alive and continues in a latent state in death.

Renge, literally "lotus flower," also has a profound meaning in Nichiren Buddhism. Because the lotus produces both flowers and seeds at the same time, it illustrates the principle of the "simultaneity of cause and effect." In other words, flower and seed, cause and effect, Nichiren says, are a "single entity".

Here, "cause" refers to the efforts or practice one carries out to become a Buddha, and "effect" to the actual attainment of Buddhahood. The simultaneity of cause-and-effect means that the very moment we chant Nam-myoho-renge-kyo intending to improve our lives, the life condition of Buddhahood, imbued with courage, compassion and wisdom, emerges within us and guides our actions.

The last character, *kyo*, Nichiren describes as the "words and voices of all living beings", *Kyo*, meaning "sutra" or "teaching," shows the teaching the Buddha expounded with his voice. Nichiren explains, "The voice carries out the work of the Buddha, and this is called *kyo*, or sutra", This means that our voices when chanting or speaking to others about Nam-myoho- renge-kyo resonate with and stimulate the Buddha nature within us, within others and in our environment.

There are many other perspectives from which Nichiren explains the meaning and significance of Nam-myoho-renge-kyo. Most important, though, is to remember that it signifies dedicating our lives to the Mystic Law. Acting based upon that Law, we work for the happiness of ourselves and others.

Nichiren says that, while Nam-myoho-renge-kyo was known by Buddhist teachers in the past, they did not teach it to others or spread it widely. He writes: "Now, however, we have entered the Latter Day of the Law, and the Daimoku [Nam-myoho-renge-kyo] that I, Nichiren, chant differs from that of earlier ages. This Nam-myoho-renge-kyo encompasses both practice for oneself and the teaching of others".

Myoho-Renge-Kyo is a concept that represents the Mystic Law and the teachings of the Lotus Sutra in Nichiren Buddhism. Adding "Nam" expresses a devotion to these teachings and a sincere desire to connect with the Mystic Law. By chanting Nam-myoho-renge-kyo, one can transform their karma and achieve enlightenment, which Nichiren believed was accessible to anyone.

Nam-myoho-renge-kyo

Nam-myoho-renge-kyo is a phrase that is central to Nichiren Buddhism, a branch of Buddhism that originated in Japan. It is a mantra that is chanted by followers of this school of thought, and is believed to contain within it the essence of the Buddhist teachings.

At its most basic level, Nam-myoho-renge-kyo can be broken down into three parts: "nam," "myoho," and "renge-kyo." "Nam" is a Sanskrit word that means "devotion" or "dedication." "Myoho" is a Japanese word that means "Mystic Law," and refers to the ultimate truth or reality that underlies all phenomena. "Renge-kyo" is another Japanese term that means "Lotus Sutra," which is a key Buddhist text.

Taken together, Nam-myoho-renge-kyo can be understood to mean "I devote myself to the Mystic Law of the Lotus Sutra." When chanted, this phrase is believed to activate the life force or Buddha-nature that resides within each person, and help them to tap into their full potential for happiness, wisdom, and compassion.

For followers of Nichiren Buddhism, chanting Nam-myoho-renge-kyo is seen as a form of meditation that helps to purify the mind and create positive energy. It is also believed to be a powerful tool for creating positive change in the world, by aligning one's intentions with the ultimate truth of the universe.

In addition to its spiritual significance, Nam-myoho-renge-kyo is also seen as a practical tool for dealing with the challenges of daily life. By chanting this phrase, one can overcome obstacles, cultivate inner strength, and tap into a sense of peace and calm that can help them navigate even the most difficult situations.

Overall, Nam-myoho-renge-kyo is a powerful phrase that has deep spiritual significance for followers of Nichiren Buddhism. It is seen as a tool for cultivating inner strength, connecting with the ultimate truth of the universe, and creating positive change in the world.

The Title of the Lotus Sutra

When friends or acquaintances express their curiosity about Nichiren Buddhism, they often ask about the meaning of Nam-myoho-renge-kyo. This is a profound and important question, and a brief or cursory answer cannot fully capture its essence. To gain a better understanding of this concept, it is helpful to consider Nichiren Daishonin's teachings.

According to Nichiren, "There is no true happiness for human beings other than chanting Nam-myoho-renge-kyo". He explains that while life is naturally filled with joy and suffering, there exists a deeper and more enduring sense of joy that surpasses the temporary cycles of happiness and suffering that everyone experiences. This is known as the "boundless joy of the Law".

Nichiren believed that chanting Nam-myoho-renge-kyo is the key to achieving a profound and genuine happiness that is deeply ingrained within oneself. It is a way to connect with the "Law" that permeates all existence and to tap into the wellspring of joy that lies within. By chanting this phrase, one can establish a sense of inner peace and happiness that is not contingent upon external circumstances.

Nichiren Buddhism teaches that Nam-myoho-renge-kyo is a powerful mantra that can help individuals cultivate an enduring sense of joy and happiness that transcends the ups and downs of life.

Nichiren Daishonin's writings and recorded teachings provide a detailed and multi-faceted explanation of the significance of Nam-myoho-renge-kyo. At its essence, this phrase represents the title of the Lotus Sutra, which is considered to be Shakyamuni Buddha's highest teaching.

The Lotus Sutra's original Sanskrit title is Saddharma-pundarika-sutra. In the 4th century, the renowned Buddhist scholar and translator Kumarajiva fully comprehended the meaning of the title and translated it into Chinese as Miao-fa-lien-hua-ching. In Japanese, these Chinese characters are pronounced as Myoho-renge-kyo.

To Nichiren, this phrase represented much more than just the title of a Buddhist text. Rather, it was the principle, or Law, that lay at the very heart and core of the Lotus Sutra's teachings. Nichiren added the word "nam" to Myoho-renge-kyo, making it Nam-myoho-renge-kyo, and declared the chanting of this phrase

THE TITLE OF THE LOTUS SUTRA   51

to be the practice of aligning one's life with this Law, which he identified as the fundamental law of life itself.

In summary, the title of the Lotus Sutra is Myoho-renge-kyo, which represents the principle or Law that lies at the very heart of the sutra's teachings. Nichiren Daishonin added the word "nam" and set forth the chanting of Nam-myoho-renge-kyo as the practice of attuning one's life with this Law, which he identified as the fundamental law of life.

Nam-myoho-renge-kyo is a profound and universal principle that is difficult to explain in just a few words. However, Nichiren Daishonin provided extensive commentary on the meaning of this phrase, and through his teachings, we can gain a deeper understanding of its significance.

According to Nichiren, the Sanskrit word namas, which is the root of the word "Nam" in Nam-myoho-renge-kyo, means "to dedicate one's life." This dedication, he explains, is to the principle of eternal and unchanging truth. By dedicating our lives to this principle, our wisdom becomes based on the understanding of this truth, enabling us to respond effectively to any changing circumstance.

Living our lives based on Myoho-renge-kyo means that we are in harmony with the Mystic Law, the ultimate truth or law of life. This allows us to deal wisely with any situation, creating the most valuable outcome.

Nichiren emphasizes that the teaching of Nam-myoho-renge-kyo is not limited to any one language or culture. The Sanskrit word "nam" represents the cultures and languages of the West, while the Chinese words "myoho," "renge," and "kyo" represent those of the East. As a merging of the languages of East and West, Nam-myoho-renge-kyo represents the voices of all humanity, a universal teaching.

Nichiren himself practiced this principle exactly as taught in the Lotus Sutra, encountering harsh persecutions as predicted by the sutra. By fully realizing a state of oneness with the essential law or truth of life, Myoho-renge-kyo, he "read" the Lotus Sutra with his entire life.

In his writing, Nichiren states that "The Buddha's will is the Lotus Sutra, but the soul of Nichiren is nothing other than Nam-myoho-renge-kyo." This phrase signifies the significance of Nam-myoho-renge-kyo to Nichiren, as he believed that it was the core of the Lotus Sutra's teaching.

Nichiren's practice and teachings of Nam-myoho-renge-kyo for the happiness of all people have earned him respect as the true Buddha of the Latter Day of the Law.

The Power of Chanting Nam Myoho Renge Kyo

According to Nichiren Daishonin, when we chant Nam-myoho-renge-kyo, we summon forth and manifest the Buddha nature inherent within us, as we revere Myoho-renge-kyo as the object of devotion. This concept of Buddha nature means that the potential for enlightenment exists within all people. Just as a caged bird's singing can summon and gather birds flying in the sky, the chanting of the Mystic Law can summon our Buddha nature, which will inevitably emerge.

In addition to summoning our Buddha nature, chanting Nam-myoho-renge-kyo can also call upon the protection of the Buddha nature of Brahma and Shakra and the rejoicing of Buddhas and bodhisattvas.

This letter, believed to have been written by Nichiren Daishonin in March of the third year of Kenji in 1277, was addressed to a woman named lay nun Myoho, who lived in Okamiya in Suruga Province (present-day Numazu city at Shizuoka Prefecture). Although little is known about lay nun Myoho, she maintained steadfast faith throughout her life, despite the loss of her husband and elder brother.

In this writing, Nichiren Daishonin establishes that the Lotus Sutra is the foremost among various schools of Buddhism, not necessarily because of its 28 chapters, but rather because of the hidden and profound meaning of Nam-myoho-renge-kyo, which should be understood as the essence of the Lotus Sutra. The letter takes the form of a question-and-answer dialogue.

The Daishonin emphasized that in the Latter Day of the Law, Nam-myoho-renge-kyo, which represents the heart and core of the Lotus Sutra, is the Law that can benefit all people. He also noted that regardless of whether people believe in the Law or criticize it, we should teach others about it. Furthermore, Daishonin explained the significance of Daimoku (the chanting of Nam-myoho-renge-kyo), stating that when we chant Daimoku, we can summon forth the Buddha nature within our lives. In this Gosho passage, Nichiren Daishonin clearly articulated the importance of the Gohonzon and Daimoku.

According to Nichiren Daishonin's teachings, the Gohonzon represents the object of devotion, which is the Buddha nature (Myoho-renge-kyo) inherent in our lives. By chanting

Nam-myoho-renge-kyo, we can manifest this Buddha nature and become one with the Buddha.

Buddhism teaches that each of us has the potential to become a Buddha, regardless of our circumstances. However, to manifest this state of enlightenment, we need to develop firm faith in this truth through our Buddhist practice. The Gohonzon serves as a mirror that reflects the object of devotion within us, which is our Buddha nature. Thus, the Gohonzon provides the environment through which we can bring out our Buddhahood. Chanting Nam-myoho-renge-kyo is the key to unlocking this potential within us. By cultivating faith in the Gohonzon, which is the manifestation of the Buddha's life or Nam-myoho-renge-kyo, and by practicing for the benefit of oneself and others, we can reveal the wonderful life-state of Buddhahood.

The practice of chanting Nam-myoho-renge-kyo to the Gohonzon reveals the Buddha nature within us, just as birds in the sky and caged birds call out to one another and strive to gather together. The Daishonin further explained that we can also reveal the Buddha nature of Brahma and Shakra, as well as the Buddha nature of all Buddhas and bodhisattvas, who will function to protect us. Through the practice of the Mystic Law, we can bring forth the Buddha nature from our environment and those around us, creating a response known as the oneness of life and its environment. This principle states that our environment possesses the ten worlds, and the state our environment manifests depends on the life condition of our lives.

SGI President Ikeda has emphasized the stupendous power of Daimoku and the essential rhythm it pervades in all life. By chanting resonant Daimoku and striving towards the goal of kosen-rufu, a person can experience limitless expansion and boundless growth in their strength and ability. The Mystic Law is the fundamental Law of the universe, and chanting Nam-myoho-renge-kyo is the essential practice that allows us to manifest our Buddha nature and achieve our fullest potential.

The power we have to transform our lives for the better through the practice of chanting Nam-myoho-renge-kyo is truly remarkable. By continuing to chant Daimoku with conviction and determination, we can achieve victories and overcome any obstacle that stands in our way. Let us never forget the immense potential that lies within us and continue to tap into it through our Buddhist practice.

The Practice of Prayer in Nichiren Buddhism

NICHIREN BUDDHISM PLACES PRAYER at the center of its practice. The followers of Nichiren often speak of offering earnest prayers, praying from the bottom of their hearts and having their prayers answered. But what exactly does prayer mean in Nichiren Buddhism, and how does it relate to the traditional understanding of prayer?

According to the Webster's Third International Dictionary, prayer is a solemn and humble approach to Divinity in word or thought, usually involving beseeching, petition, confession, praise, or thanksgiving. While the Buddhist understanding of prayer shares some similarities with this definition, there are also some key differences.

The practice of prayer is a universal human activity, and it has been present in various forms throughout history. As humans became aware of their relative powerlessness in the face of natural forces and their own mortality, they began expressing intense feelings of petition, praise, or thanksgiving. However, in

Nichiren Buddhism, prayer takes on a specific physical form. Practitioners recite portions of the Lotus Sutra and chant the phrase "Nam-myoho-renge-kyo," which represents the mystic law that is present in all life.

The chanting of "Nam-myoho-renge-kyo" is an audible expression of prayer, which sets it apart from other forms of prayer that may be more inwardly focused. In Nichiren Buddhism, prayer is seen as a way to make manifest inner qualities, bringing them out into the world. The focus is not on petitioning or beseeching a higher power for something, but on manifesting one's own inner potential through the act of prayer.

Prayer in Nichiren Buddhism is not a one-time event or a sporadic practice. It is a daily ritual that is meant to be incorporated into one's life in a meaningful way. By regularly chanting and reciting portions of the Lotus Sutra, practitioners hope to deepen their understanding of the teachings and achieve greater spiritual growth.

In conclusion, the practice of prayer is an essential part of Nichiren Buddhism. While it shares some similarities with traditional forms of prayer, it also has unique characteristics that set it apart. Through the physical act of chanting and reciting, practitioners aim to manifest their inner potential and deepen their understanding of the teachings.

Nichiren Buddhism centers on prayer directed to the Gohonzon, a mandala that symbolizes the ideal state of Buddhahood. Rather than an idol or god to be supplicated or appeased, the Gohonzon serves as a catalyst for inner change and reflection. Nichiren encourages followers to focus their prayers on real-life issues and stresses the inseparability of earthly desires and enlightenment. Burning the "firewood" of our desires through prayer can bring forth the flame of renewed energy and inner wisdom, transforming intense desires and sufferings into compassion and wisdom.

Prayer is the means by which we can bring forth our Buddha nature, a fundamental, compassionate life force inherent in the cosmos possessed equally by all people. Aligning our individual lives with the rhythm of the living cosmos unleashes untapped sources of self-knowledge, wisdom, vitality, and perseverance. The inner changes that occur are reflected in our external circumstances, and the experience of having our prayers "answered" is the manifest result of this process.

Daisaku Ikeda posits that the ultimate form of prayer is a vow to contribute to the happiness of others and the development of human society. This vow and pledge to action profoundly attune our lives to the larger life of the universe and bring forth our highest, noble selves. As Nichiren states, mastery of Buddhist teachings will not relieve us of mortal sufferings unless we perceive the nature of our own life. Therefore, prayer involves self-reflection, sometimes involving a painful confrontation with our own destructive tendencies.

Nichiren Buddhism views prayer as a transformative process that aligns our individual lives with the rhythm of the cosmos, unleashing untapped sources of self-knowledge, wisdom, vitality, and perseverance. By making specific, concrete, and focused prayers, we can transform intense desires and sufferings into compassion and wisdom. The ultimate form of prayer is a vow to contribute to the happiness of others and the development of human society, attuning our lives to the larger universe and bringing forth our highest selves.

The Limitless Potential of Nam-myoho-renge-kyo

IN NICHIREN BUDDHISM, ACTION is considered the most important aspect of one's practice. Simply chanting Nam-myoho-renge-kyo is not enough; it is through applying our Buddhist practice to our daily challenges and taking action that we can truly manifest the genuine power of our faith. This is evident in the changes we see in our character, the benefits we receive, and the victories we achieve in life.

Nichiren Daishonin, the founder of this Buddhist school, emphasized the importance of faith in one's heart when chanting Nam-myoho-renge-kyo. This means having a firm conviction in our own potential and that of others, and being determined to bring about our own happiness and the happiness of those around us, as Nichiren taught. When we chant with this kind of conviction, we will begin to see apparent proof of the power of the Mystic Law in our lives.

As SGI President Ikeda explains, chanting Nam-myoho-renge-kyo is a path to absolute victory. Nichiren Buddhism enables us to develop a serene life state of inner abundance, characterized by the noble virtues of eternity, happiness, true self, and purity. Those who embrace faith in Nam-myoho-renge-kyo possess far greater wealth than those who have the most staggering fortunes or the most luxurious mansions. This is because Nam-myoho-renge-kyo is the life and fundamental law of the universe, and when we chant it, we have nothing to fear or worry about. The words of Nichiren Daishonin are never false, and the purpose of our faith and practice is to achieve happiness and victory in our lives. This is the reality of the Buddhism of Nichiren Daishonin, the one and eternal Buddha of the Latter Day of the Law.

The practice of Nichiren Buddhism requires action, faith, and determination to manifest the genuine power of chanting Nam-myoho-renge-kyo. By developing these qualities and applying them to our daily lives, we can achieve the ultimate goal of absolute happiness and victory.

The Language of Gongyo and Daimoku

THE LOTUS SUTRA IS regarded as a sutra that was preached directly from the Buddha's own mind. Since the Buddha's mind is exceptional, those who read this sutra, even if they do not comprehend its meaning, will gain immense benefits. This is comparable to an infant drinking its mother's milk without comprehending its composition. Similarly, when we chant Daimoku and recite the Gongyo liturgy, we benefit from them regardless of whether we understand their meaning.

Of course, it is better to understand the meaning as it strengthens our confidence in the Mystic Law. However, if we do not put our understanding into practice, it is ultimately pointless. The profound meaning of the Mystic Law cannot be fully grasped through theoretical means alone.

Each species in the animal kingdom has its own unique means of communication or "language." We humans cannot understand them, but birds understand the language of other birds, and dogs understand the language of other dogs. Similarly, when we chant Daimoku and recite the sutra during Gongyo, our voices are communicated to the Gohonzon and understood in the realm of Buddhas and Bodhisattvas. In a way, we are speaking the language of Buddhas and Bodhisattvas. Even if we do not understand the literal meaning of what we are saying, our voices during Gongyo and chanting Daimoku to the Gohonzon reach all Buddhas, Bodhisattvas, and Buddhist gods throughout time and space. The protective functions within life and the universe are activated towards fulfilling our prayers, even though we cannot see them.

Unlocking the Power of Chanting

CHANTING NAM-MYOHO-RENGE-KYO IS A practice that has the potential to bring transformative benefits to our lives. However, it is natural to wonder what we should think about when we chant. The good news is that there are no hard and fast rules. Here are some suggestions that may help you make the most of your chanting experience.

First and foremost, when beginning each chanting session, it is advisable to concentrate on establishing a precise and clear rhythm while listening to the sound of your Daimoku. As you continue, you will find that any problems, desires or preoccupations that you may have will naturally come to mind as prayers. Allow yourself to be bathed in your own intuitive buddha wisdom.

Gradually, this process will lead you to make decisions in your daily life based on this wisdom, which is an expression of your true self. You will begin to orientate your life towards the happy future you realize could be yours. You may find yourself re-inspired with courage and confidence to keep battling when things look bleak, or suddenly see a solution to what seemed like a hopeless situation. Sometimes, you may simply keep fatigue at bay to finish an urgent task. In short, chanting Nam-myoho-renge-kyo to the Gohonzon is designed to help you with any problem or circumstance, no matter how insignificant it may seem.

As your chanting session comes to a close, take the time to listen to your voice chanting during the last few moments of your Daimoku. Scan your body and feel joy rising within you. Ideally, continue to chant until you feel this joy welling up from deep within your life.

Remember, the power of chanting comes not from the words themselves, but from the focus and intention that we put into our practice. Through this simple yet profound practice, we can unlock the power of our true self and connect with the boundless wisdom and compassion of the universe.

Why Aren't My Prayers Getting Answered?

MANY FOLLOWERS OF NICHIREN Buddhism may have wondered why their prayers are not being answered, despite seeing others receive wonderful benefits from the practice. It can be frustrating to feel like you're doing everything right but not seeing the results you desire. However, it's important to remember that rectifying your attitude towards your practice can bring benefits your way.

One common example is when we experience a minor accident or mishap. While it's natural to feel grateful for being protected by the Gohonzon, we should also take such occurrences as a warning to strengthen our faith even more. Nichiren Daishonin teaches that a slight misfortune can often be a precursor to a catastrophe, so it's essential to take the Gohonzon's warning seriously and reawaken our faith.

It's also important to remember that not every illness or accident necessarily means that something is wrong with our faith. However, such situations can be an opportunity to re-examine our practice and further strengthen our faith. A woman once received guidance regarding her husband's sickness. After a chest X-ray showed a concerning shadow, her husband began practicing more sincerely, reflecting on and changing his attitude towards practice. When he had another chest X-ray taken later, there was no shadow at all, much to the doctor's surprise.

This story shows how an illness or mishap can serve as a wake-up call to reexamine and improve our faith. Nichiren Daishonin wrote in the Gosho that such situations can be a merciful consideration of the Buddha, and we should view them as an opportunity to grow in faith. By correcting our attitudes and resolving anew to develop our faith, we can eventually solve our problems and turn them into an impetus for our growth.

it's important to keep our "eyes of faith" wide open and use every situation, whether positive or negative, as an opportunity to strengthen our practice and deepen our connection with the Gohonzon. By doing so, we can eventually see the benefits we seek and experience the power of Nam-myoho-renge-kyo in our lives.

Finding Fulfillment Within

NICHIREN DAISHONIN PROCLAIMED, "IF you wish to free yourself from the sufferings of birth and death you have endured throughout eternity and attain supreme enlightenment in this lifetime, you must awaken to the mystic truth which has always been within your life. This truth is Myoho-renge-kyo. Chanting Myoho-renge-kyo will, therefore, enable you to grasp the mystic truth within you."

In this statement, Daishonin addresses the fundamental problem of human existence and shows the way to its solution. He suggests that the natural desire of human beings is to escape suffering and seek happiness. He explains that we can overcome our sufferings by awakening to the truth that has always been present within our life. According to Daishonin, the gem of the Buddha nature (Myoho-renge-kyo) is already within every individual. By discovering it, we can enjoy supreme enlightenment right here in this mundane world.

However, merely understanding intellectually that our own life is the entity of the Mystic Law is not enough. Daishonin emphasizes the importance of developing deep faith in our own Buddha nature. He warns that even though we may chant and believe in Myoho-renge-kyo, if we believe that the Law is outside of ourselves, we are not embracing the Mystic Law, but some inferior teaching.

To seek both the causes and solutions to our problems in the environment is an example of thinking that the Law is outside oneself. This means that we rely on external circumstances or other people to handle our happiness. It might also mean that we measure our self-worth solely based on our bank balance, job title, or other external factors. Such external conditions are temporary and fleeting, and seeking them for happiness will only bring suffering.

Daishonin's teachings emphasize that we all possess the potential for enlightenment and happiness within us. We need to have faith in ourselves, awaken to the truth within us, and not seek happiness in external circumstances or other people.

Profound Realization of 'Myo' and 'Ho'

The concept of "Myo" in Buddhism represents the mysterious nature of life that exists from moment to moment. It is a reality that cannot be comprehended by the mind or expressed through words. When we look into our own minds, we cannot perceive any color or form that can prove its existence. However, since our thoughts are constantly changing, we cannot say that the mind does not exist either.

Life is a mystic entity that goes beyond the traditional dichotomy of existence and nonexistence. It transcends the limitations of language and concepts. Life exhibits the qualities of both existence and nonexistence, yet it is neither of them. This elusive reality is the ultimate reality, the mystic entity of the Middle Way.

The term "Myo" refers to the mystic nature of life, while "ho" represents its manifestations. When we chant "Myoho-renge-kyo," we are acknowledging and embracing the mysterious nature of life and its infinite manifestations.

Through this concept, we can recognize the wonder of the universe and the interconnectedness of all things. It helps us to understand the importance of living in the present moment, as life is constantly changing and evolving.

In essence, the concept of "Myo" represents the mystic nature of life that goes beyond our understanding, while "ho" represents its manifold manifestations that we can perceive. Together, they form the basis of the Mystic Law and the ultimate reality that we seek to understand and embrace through the practice of Buddhism.

The lotus flower, or "Renge" in Buddhism, holds a special significance as a symbol of the Mystic Law. It represents the potential for enlightenment that lies within all beings, just as the lotus flower grows from the muddy depths to bloom in beauty and purity.

By recognizing that our life in the present moment is characterized by the mysterious nature of "Myo," we also come to understand that our life at other moments is an expression of the Mystic Law. This profound realization is the essence of the Mystic Sutra or "kyo."

Through the chanting of "Myoho-renge-kyo," we can tap into the inherent wisdom and compassion of the universe and reveal our true nature as Buddhas. The lotus flower, with its ability to rise above the muddy water and blossom into a thing of beauty, serves as a powerful metaphor for our own spiritual growth and transformation.

In essence, the lotus flower represents the wonder of the Mystic Law and the potential for enlightenment that exists within all beings. By embracing this symbol and recognizing the true nature of our existence, we can unlock the power of the universe within ourselves and manifest our inherent Buddha nature.

In Nichiren Buddhism, Daimoku is regarded as the fundamental rhythm of the universe and the most revered of voices. It is a chanting practice that involves repeating the phrase "Nam-myoho-renge-kyo" to connect with the Mystic Law of life and summon forth the Buddha nature of all living beings.

Nichiren Daishonin, the founder of Nichiren Buddhism, emphasized the power of Daimoku, stating that with just that single sound, we can manifest the Buddha nature within us and in all other living beings. This blessing is immeasurable and boundless.

Through Daimoku, we can transcend the limitations of our ignorance and attain enlightenment. We are like the eggs of ignorance, pitiful and helpless, but with the nurturing warmth of the mother bird, which is akin to the chanting of Nam-myoho-renge-kyo, we are free to soar into the sky of the true aspect of all phenomena and the reality of all things.

Chanting Daimoku isn't about being loud or seeking attention. It's about cultivating the dominant voice of compassion that seeks to bring all beings to enlightenment. Our Daimoku resounds with many voices. The most basic voice is our earnest chanting of Daimoku. But we also hear the warm voice of encouragement, the vibrant voice of courage, the heartfelt voice of joy, the earnest voice of pledge and commitment, and the clear voice of wisdom. These voices are the source of an infinite wellspring of benefit.

In summary, Daimoku is a powerful practice that enables us to connect with our Buddha nature and the Mystic Law of life. It is through the chanting of Nam-myoho-renge-kyo that we can break free from the limitations of our ignorance and attain enlightenment. The power of our Daimoku lies not in the loudness of our voice, but in the dominant voice of compassion that seeks to bring all beings to enlightenment.

The Transformative Power of Faith and Prayer

In the practice of Buddhism, faith and prayer are essential components that enable individuals to tap into the universal macrocosm and manifest their Buddha nature. The power of faith is fundamental to the Lotus Sutra, as it determines the level of enlightenment one can attain. While accepting the teachings of the sutra may be easy, continuing with unwavering faith in the face of challenges can be difficult. However, it is only through persistent faith that Buddhahood can be realized.

Those who uphold the Lotus Sutra must be prepared to face difficulties, but by summoning forth the great power of faith, and chanting Nam-myoho-renge-kyo with a prayer for steadfast and correct faith, one can inherit the ultimate Law of life and death and manifest it in their life. The ultimate goal is to realize that earthly desires are enlightenment, and that the sufferings of birth and death are nirvana. However, such realizations are impossible without the heritage of faith.

Just as a single arrow shot by a great archer will unerringly hit the mark, a strong and deep prayer offered with unwavering concentration of mind can move the entire universe. Faith enables the microcosm of the self to sense the universal macrocosm, and it is inextinguishable hope. The basis of this practice is prayer, which transforms hope into confidence.

To offer prayers is to engage in a dialogue, an exchange with the universe. Prayer is not feeble consolation, but rather a powerful and unyielding conviction that embraces the universe with our lives. Through prayer, individuals can connect with the universal macrocosm and manifest their inherent Buddha nature. Doubt, anxiety, and regret can hinder this process, but by opening and directing one's heart toward something great, faith can overcome these obstacles.

The transformative power of faith and prayer is an integral aspect of Buddhist practice. By maintaining unwavering faith, individuals can inherit the ultimate Law of life and death and realize their inherent Buddha nature. Through prayer, individuals can engage in a dialogue with the universe and manifest their deepest desires. It is through persistent faith and prayer that the transformative potential of Buddhism can be realized.

Chanting Can Benefit Our Entire Family

NICHIREN BUDDHISM IS A practice that not only brings benefits to ourselves but also to our loved ones. In fact, the benefits we receive from our practice can extend beyond our immediate family to countless living beings, as Nichiren Daishonin wrote in the Gosho. The analogy of bringing water from the ocean illustrates how the benefits of our practice can be shared among our family members.

The fundamental principle of Nichiren Buddhism is the oneness of the person and their environment. This means that our inner state of life is reflected in our external circumstances, and vice versa. By chanting Nam-myoho-renge-kyo, we are tapping into the infinite potential of the universe and awakening our Buddha nature. As a result, we become a positive force in the world, and our surroundings are positively affected by it.

When we chant for our own happiness, we are also chanting for the happiness of those around us. Our practice has the power to influence the life condition of others, up to a certain point.

This means that by improving our own life condition, we can also improve the life condition of our loved ones.

Furthermore, our practice can also inspire others to seek the same benefits. When we demonstrate the positive changes in our lives that result from our practice, we become a shining example for others to follow. Our family members may become curious about our practice and decide to try it for themselves.

In conclusion, the power of Nichiren Buddhism extends beyond our individual selves to benefit those around us. By chanting Nam-myoho-renge-kyo, we can positively influence the life condition of our loved ones and inspire them to seek the same benefits. The oneness of the person and their environment is a reality, and our practice has the potential to transform both ourselves and our surroundings.

The Complexity of Changing Someone Else's Karma

NICHIREN DAISHONIN EMPHASIZED THE importance of studying and practicing the Lotus Sutra, a central text in Mahayana Buddhism. In one of his letters, he writes to a disciple, "Admirable Nichiro, because you have read the entire Lotus Sutra with both the physical and spiritual aspects of your life, you will also be able to save your father and mother, your six kinds of relatives, and all living beings."

To understand the concept of karma, it is essential to recognize that it refers to the potential energies residing in the inner realm of life that manifest themselves as various results in the future. The Sanskrit word karma originally meant action, thoughts, words, and deeds. According to this concept, every action, both good and evil, leaves a latent influence on one's life. When activated by an external stimulus, the karma produces a corresponding effect. Therefore, one's actions in the past have shaped their reality at present, and their actions in the present determine their future.

It is natural to want to ease the suffering of a friend or relative experiencing illness, relationship problems, or some other difficulty. However, we must recognize that our desire to change someone else's karma may stem from our own subjective standpoint, influenced by our own karma. It is essential to check the motives underlying our desire to intervene in someone else's life. Are they based on our own fears or our own karma to suffer that we need to change? Moreover, what we see on the surface of a person's life may be just the tip of an iceberg. It is not our place to make a judgment based on such limited knowledge of the complexity of that person's life.

To address complex problems, it is crucial to look long-term, and the adage, "It is better to give a starving person a fishing-rod rather than just a fish," illustrates this point. Similarly, by sharing Nichiren Daishonin's Buddhism, we can provide people with both the fishing rod and the fish. This practice equips them with the tools to change their karma, enabling them to create a positive future for themselves and others.

Transforming Misfortune into Great Good Fortune

MISFORTUNES AND CHALLENGES CAN often seem insurmountable, leaving us feeling hopeless and powerless. However, according to the principles of the Mystic Law, the key to overcoming such difficulties lies in our own beliefs and faith. No matter how great the misfortune may appear, it is essential to fully believe in the power of the Mystic Law to transform any situation into a source of happiness and growth.

It is not enough to simply hope for the best or doubt the effectiveness of the Gohonzon. Rather, we must wholeheartedly embrace the teachings of the Daishonin and have faith in the power of the Mystic Law to turn even the most serious problems into opportunities for good fortune. When faced with a challenge, it is our belief in this principle that determines whether we will ultimately achieve victory or defeat.

Indeed, there is no problem that cannot be transformed into a springboard for happiness, and no poison that cannot be turned into medicine. Even if one fails in business or experiences other setbacks, maintaining faith in the Mystic Law is crucial for recovery and continued success. However, it is important to be mindful of the tendency to let failures in one area of life affect our faith in other areas.

By emphasizing the power of the Mystic Law and encouraging ourselves and others to maintain faith in the face of adversity, we can transform seemingly impossible situations into sources of growth and good fortune.

In the face of adversity, it's easy to feel defeated and believe that victory is impossible. However, it's essential to remember the power of the Gohonzon, a manifestation of the Mystic Law. It has the ability to transform what seems impossible into something achievable. Those who give up without even trying are missing out on the potential of the Mystic Law's power. It is only when one truly believes in its power and practices accordingly that success can be achieved.

The strategy of the Lotus Sutra is to put faith in the Gohonzon first and then make every effort upon that basis. By doing so, one can bring the impossible within reach. With dedicated practice, good fortune will naturally follow. Nichiren Daishonin's Buddhism is a teaching for accumulating inexhaustible good fortune, a state of enduring happiness that surpasses wealth, education, and status.

Even those who seem to have everything can be miserable if their lives are not in harmony with the fundamental Law of life. Practicing to the Gohonzon means having already received the ultimate good fortune of encountering the Mystic Law. As one continues to practice, they will accumulate more good fortune, leading to greater happiness and fulfillment in life. Therefore, it's crucial to have faith in the Mystic Law's power and make every effort to practice accordingly.

Changing Problems into Springboards for Growth

THE PURPOSE OF FAITH is to attain happiness, and Buddhism teaches us that faith is the means by which we can transform every obstacle we face into a stepping stone for our personal growth. This is the principle of turning poison into medicine. By this means, we can confidently assert that the troubles we have faced were ultimately necessary for our present happiness. While some people might claim that they are carefree, this is never really the case. Everyone has their own share of concerns, whether they are aware of them or not. For instance, even a drunkard who claims to have no troubles will likely have a wife and children who worry about him, despite his own blissful ignorance.

As human beings, we all have our own desires and hopes. We may wish for our children to perform well in school, for our spouse to receive a raise, or for our partner to be more kind to us. These desires can bring great joy when they are fulfilled, but can also lead to worry and anxiety when they remain unmet. However, we must recognize that each of these concerns has a root cause that is the result of our past karma manifesting itself in the present.

Buddhism enables us to resolve our problems by addressing their underlying causes. Through our faith, we can gain the power to have our desires fulfilled. While some members may understand this guidance quickly, others may find it more challenging to comprehend, even when they hear the same guidance repeatedly. The difference between these two groups of individuals lies in their reliance on Daimoku, or chanting Nam-myoho-renge-kyo to the Gohonzon. Those who earnestly chant and rely on the Gohonzon to overcome their difficulties are more likely to grasp the guidance they receive.

In contrast, those who try to solve their problems using methods other than the strategy of the Lotus Sutra often struggle to understand the guidance they are given. We can liken this to a teacher who gives a lecture to all students for the same length of time on the same subject, yet some score highly on a test while others do not. In such cases, the difference in results lies not with the teacher, but with the students.

When it comes to resolving problems of karma, it is unlikely that anyone can obtain the same benefits without chanting Daimoku. While some people might claim to have done so, in reality, this is very rare. The causal law of life tells us that our troubles with our family members, spouses, and others are often the result of our bad karma. At discussion meetings, I am often asked for guidance on how to deal with troublesome children, for instance. While the problems of different individuals may vary slightly, they all stem from the same basic principles, and thus require the same kind of guidance.

I encourage everyone to become good listeners so that they can apply the guidance they receive to a variety of situations. Through faith, we can overcome any obstacle and attain true happiness.

The Significance of Faith in Every Situation

When life presents us with setbacks and mishaps, it's natural to feel frustrated and upset. However, in the practice of faith, we can choose to see these challenges as opportunities for growth and reflection. According to this philosophy, when something negative happens to us, it could be a warning from the Gohonzon, the object of devotion in Nichiren Buddhism, urging us to take a closer look at our attitude toward faith.

It's essential not to ignore or dismiss these warnings because doing so could lead to more significant problems down the road. Complaining and dwelling on our misfortunes will only increase our suffering and cause us to doubt our faith. On the other hand, if we choose to view these experiences as a strict warning from the Gohonzon, we can take a step back and examine our relationship with our practice. This reflection allows us to express gratitude for the Gohonzon's protection and identify areas where we need to improve our sincerity and determination.

THE SIGNIFICANCE OF FAITH IN EVERY SITUATION

When we begin to shift our perspective in this way, we can start to see even minor incidents as valuable and significant to our faith. By recognizing the importance of every experience, we can transform what might have been a cause for unhappiness into a cause for joy. This approach is how we learn to change poison into medicine and turn our challenges into opportunities for growth.

It's worth noting that this approach to faith emphasizes the intangible benefits of practice over the tangible ones. While there's nothing wrong with pursuing material and physical success, true Buddhism teaches that these things have nothing to do with absolute happiness. Absolute happiness comes from within and is rooted in our connection to the Gohonzon. Thus, when we experience both good and bad times, we can turn to the Gohonzon for guidance, express gratitude for our blessings, and pray for the strength to overcome our challenges.

When we encounter setbacks in life, we have a choice in how we respond. We can either complain and become further entrenched in our suffering or view it as an opportunity to reflect and grow our faith. By doing the latter, we learn to see the value and significance of every experience, even the minor ones, and transform our hardships into causes for happiness. Remember, in the practice of faith, we can always depend on the Gohonzon for guidance and support.

In Buddhism, the concept of turning poison into medicine refers to transforming a negative experience into a positive one. This idea is central to the practice of Nichiren Buddhism, which emphasizes the importance of faith and determination in overcoming obstacles and achieving happiness.

Visible benefits, such as material wealth or physical comfort, are not as significant as the intangible benefits of faith. While these benefits may bring relative happiness, they do not necessarily lead to absolute happiness, which is the ultimate goal of Nichiren Buddhism. Therefore, it is important not to become swayed by superficial things and to focus on the essential elements of one's faith.

The concept of conspicuous and inconspicuous benefits can be understood in terms of relative and absolute happiness. While material and physical improvements bring relative happiness, they are only temporary and do not lead to absolute happiness. In contrast, the intangible benefits of faith, such as inner peace, wisdom, and compassion, bring about absolute happiness.

It is essential to understand the difference between relative and absolute happiness to avoid losing confidence in one's faith when visible benefits do not materialize. Practitioners must remain dedicated to their practice, even when facing challenges and setbacks. Through consistent chanting and prayer to the Gohonzon, one can transform negative experiences into positive ones and achieve absolute happiness.

The Gohonzon, a scroll containing Chinese and Sanskrit characters, is the object of devotion in Nichiren Buddhism. It is believed to represent the enlightenment and wisdom of the Buddha and is considered the source of all benefit and protection. Practitioners can rely on the Gohonzon to provide guidance and support in their spiritual journey.

In summary, the practice of Nichiren Buddhism emphasizes the importance of faith and determination in overcoming obstacles and achieving absolute happiness. Visible benefits are temporary and do not lead to absolute happiness. It is crucial to maintain a positive attitude toward faith and to focus on the intangible benefits that bring about absolute happiness. By chanting and praying to the Gohonzon, practitioners can transform negative experiences into positive ones and rely on it for guidance and support.

The Power of Words: The Essence of the Lotus Sutra in Nam-myoho-renge-kyo

THE HEART OF THE Lotus Sutra lies in its title, or the Daimoku, of Nam-myoho-renge-kyo. Chanting this phrase in the morning and evening is equivalent to correctly reading the entire Lotus Sutra. In Buddhism, words hold great power. They have the ability to elicit emotions such as happiness, sadness, anger, and love, and language has a profound effect on our lives.

Nichiren Daishonin, "They say that if you so much as hear the words 'pickled plum,' your mouth will water. Even in everyday life, there are such wonders, so how much greater are the wonders of the Lotus Sutra?"

Myoho-renge-kyo is the title and essence of the Lotus Sutra, which is considered to be the highest of Shakyamuni's teachings. The title was originally translated from Sanskrit into ancient Chinese characters, and Nichiren Daishonin added the Sanskrit word "Nam," which means "devotion," in front of the characters.

Therefore, Nam-myoho-renge-kyo means devotion to the ultimate Law of the universe.

The characters themselves hold profound principles of life, and when taken together, they express how everything in the cosmos works in one harmonious relationship. It is said that everything has its essential point, and the Daimoku of Nam-myoho-renge-kyo is the essential point of the Lotus Sutra. By chanting it, one can tap into the power of the universe and align oneself with the rhythm of life.

Communication is essential in any field, but it is particularly important in the realm of science and mathematics, where the use of formulas and language can be incomprehensible to those not trained in those disciplines. Scientists and mathematicians, however, are able to convey even the most difficult concepts to one another with precision and accuracy by using these expressions.

Similarly, Daisaku Ikeda explains that when we chant Nam-myoho-renge-kyo, even if we do not fully understand its profound meaning, we can tap into the condition of Buddhahood. Through our chanting, our voices penetrate the cosmos and reach the life condition of Buddhahood, permeating our lives and unlocking the palace of Buddhahood - the supreme life condition of eternity, happiness, true self, and purity. It is like music that reaches and filters into people's hearts, calling forth a sympathetic response from them.

While it may seem unbelievable at first, Nam-myoho-renge-kyo is the essence of everyone's life, and chanting this phrase can have countless positive effects on us, from the very core of our being. The degree to which we can benefit from chanting Nam-myoho-renge-kyo depends entirely on our own sincere efforts in practice, not on any inherent power in the phrase itself, which is limitless.

The natural law of life is present in everything, but only by chanting Nam-myoho-renge-kyo and taking action in our daily lives can we activate it and enable it to work for our happiness and the happiness of others. Buddhism teaches the principle of the "four powers": the power of the Buddha, the power of the Law, the power of faith, and the power of practice. The first two are embodied in the Gohonzon, but they are only activated by the powers of faith and practice of the person who chants to it.

In other words, the power of our faith and practice determines the extent to which the power of the Gohonzon can manifest in our lives. By chanting Nam-myoho-renge-kyo with sincerity and taking action in our daily lives, we can tap into the infinite potential within us and transform our lives in immeasurable ways.

How 'Nam-Myoho-Renge-Kyo' Differs from Chanting Other Words?

WORDS HOLD TREMENDOUS POWER. They have the ability to elicit a range of emotions, from happiness to sadness, anger to love. Language influences our lives in profound ways that we may not even realize. Nichiren Daishonin once said, "They say that... if you so much as hear the words 'pickled plum,' your mouth will begin to water. Even in everyday life there are such wonders, so how much greater are the wonders of the Lotus Sutra."

The Lotus Sutra is the highest teaching of Shakyamuni, and Myoho-renge-kyo is its title and essence. Originally translated from Sanskrit into ancient Chinese characters, Nichiren Daishonin added the word "nam" to the title, meaning "devotion" in Sanskrit. Thus, Nam-myoho-renge-kyo signifies devotion to the ultimate Law of the universe.

Each of the characters in this phrase holds profound principles of life. Taken together, they express how everything in the cosmos works in one harmonious relationship. While it may seem difficult to believe or understand, chanting this phrase can have a profound effect on our lives.

Chanting Nam-myoho-renge-kyo enables us to tap into the power of the universe and align ourselves with the rhythm of life. It is like music that reaches and filters into people's hearts, calling forth a sympathetic response from them. Daisaku Ikeda explains that through our chanting, our voices penetrate the cosmos and reach the life condition of Buddhahood. This unlocks the palace of Buddhahood - the supreme life condition of eternity, happiness, true self, and purity - permeating our lives and transforming us from within.

Chanting Nam-myoho-renge-kyo with sincerity and taking action in our daily lives activates the natural law of life, enabling it to work for our happiness and the happiness of others. The principles of the "four powers" in Buddhism - the power of the Buddha, the power of the Law, the power of faith, and the power of practice - are embodied in the Gohonzon, but they can only be activated by the powers of faith and practice of the person who chants to it.

Thus, the power of our faith and practice determines the extent to which the power of the Gohonzon can manifest in our lives. By chanting Nam-myoho-renge-kyo and taking action in our daily lives, we can tap into the infinite potential within us and transform our lives in immeasurable ways. So, although it may seem unbelievable at first, chanting Nam-myoho-renge-kyo can have countless positive effects on us, from the very core of our being.

Language and words hold incredible power, influencing our emotions and actions in ways that we may not even realize. Nichiren Daishonin, a Buddhist monk and scholar, once stated that even everyday words have the ability to elicit a response, as simple as hearing the words "pickled plum" and feeling one's mouth water. He goes on to suggest that if everyday words can have such an effect, imagine the wonders that can come from chanting the Lotus Sutra.

The title and essence of the Lotus Sutra is Myoho-renge-kyo, which represents the highest teachings of Shakyamuni, as translated from Sanskrit into ancient Chinese characters. Nichiren Daishonin added the Sanskrit word "nam" to the front of the characters to indicate devotion to the ultimate Law of the universe. The characters themselves hold profound principles of life, together expressing the harmonious relationship between everything in the cosmos.

While this may be difficult to comprehend, the act of chanting Nam-myoho-renge-kyo can have a profound effect on one's life. Daisaku Ikeda explains that even if we do not fully understand the meaning behind the phrase, chanting it can tap into the condition of Buddhahood. The sound of our voice permeates the universe, reaching the life condition of Buddhahood and all the Buddhas. Through this, we can unlock the palace of Buddhahood, which is the supreme life condition of eternity, happiness, true self, and purity.

This process is similar to music, which can reach and touch the hearts of people without explanation, calling forth a sympathetic response. The key is to remember that anyone can tap into the state of Buddhahood by chanting Nam-myoho-renge-kyo. It influences all other states in our life and guides our actions, even in the midst of day-to-day struggles and problems. While it may be difficult to believe at first, Nam-myoho-renge-kyo is the essence of everyone's life, and chanting it can have countless positive effects from the core of our being.

The power of chanting Nam-myoho-renge-kyo is limitless, but its effectiveness in benefiting our lives depends entirely on the sincerity and effort we put into our practice. This is because the natural Law of life is present in everything, but it can only be activated by chanting Nam-myoho-renge-kyo and taking action in our daily lives. The principle of the "four powers" in Buddhism emphasizes the power of the Buddha, the Law, faith, and practice. While the first two are embodied in the Gohonzon, they are only activated by the powers of faith and practice of the individual who chants to it.

The power of our faith and practice is what determines the extent to which the power of the Gohonzon can manifest in our lives. Josei Toda, the second president of the Soka Gakkai, stressed the importance of understanding this point. He observed that some new members are preoccupied solely with getting benefits, without paying attention to strengthening their own powers of faith and practice.

The statement "Knock and it shall be opened unto you" serves as an excellent illustration of the four powers. If we exert our powers of faith and practice to a factor of 100, the powers of the Buddha and the Law will also be manifested to the power of 100. Likewise, if we exert our powers of faith and practice to a factor of 10,000, the powers of the Buddha and the Law will manifest to the power of 10,000. Therefore, we should dedicate ourselves to faith and practice without reservation and fix this principle in our minds.

In conclusion, the power of chanting Nam-myoho-renge-kyo is immense, but it can only be fully realized through our own efforts and dedication to faith and practice. By doing so, we activate the natural Law of life, tap into our own state of Buddhahood, and enable it to work for the happiness of ourselves and others.

The Use of Bells in Nichiren Buddhism's Gongyo Practice

IN NICHIREN BUDDHISM, THE practice of ringing bells before Gongyo prayers is a traditional ritual that holds significant importance. Gongyo is a fundamental practice in Nichiren Buddhism, which includes the recitation of specific portions of the Lotus Sutra and the chanting of the mantra "Nam-Myoho-Renge-Kyo."

Bells have been used in many cultures for centuries, and they serve several purposes, such as calling people to prayer, marking important events, and announcing the beginning or end of a ceremony. In Nichiren Buddhism, the sound of the bell serves as a reminder to practitioners to focus their minds and enter into a state of mindfulness before starting the Gongyo prayers.

The bell is rung three times before the start of Gongyo to signify the beginning of the ceremony. This symbolizes the three treasures in Buddhism, which are the Buddha, the Dharma, and the Sangha. The Buddha represents the ultimate truth, the Dharma represents the teachings of the Buddha, and the Sangha represents the community of followers of the Buddha. By ringing the bell three times, practitioners are reminded of the importance of these three elements in their practice and are encouraged to approach the ceremony with reverence and respect.

Furthermore, the sound of the bell is said to have a purifying effect on the environment, and it is believed to repel negative energies and spirits. This is why, in many Buddhist temples, bells are rung during ceremonies or when entering or leaving the temple. In Nichiren Buddhism, the bell is rung to create a peaceful and harmonious atmosphere that facilitates the practice of Gongyo and helps practitioners to focus their minds on the recitation of the Lotus Sutra and the chanting of "Nam-Myoho-Renge-Kyo."

Another reason for ringing the bell is to signify the beginning and end of each section of the Gongyo ceremony. The Gongyo ceremony is divided into two halves: the first half includes the recitation of the first section of the Lotus Sutra, while the second half includes the recitation of the second section of the Lotus Sutra and the chanting of "Nam-Myoho-Renge-Kyo." The bell is rung twice at the end of the first half and three times at the end of the second half to indicate the completion of each section of the ceremony.

The ringing of bells before Gongyo prayers is an essential ritual in Nichiren Buddhism. It serves as a reminder to practitioners to focus their minds and approach the ceremony with reverence and respect, creates a peaceful and harmonious atmosphere that facilitates the practice of Gongyo, and signifies the beginning and end of each section of the ceremony. By participating in this ritual, practitioners are reminded of the importance of mindfulness and concentration in their practice and are encouraged to deepen their understanding of the Lotus Sutra and the teachings of Nichiren Buddhism.

The Prime Point of Faith: Daimoku First

WHEN A DIFFICULTY ARISES, don't assume a casual attitude, thinking, "Because I've been chanting Daimoku, the problem will somehow solve itself," Instead, take the matter seriously, pray to the Gohonzon to change poison into medicine, and courageously challenge your problem. Your earnest prayer will bring forth abundant wisdom and vigorous energy from within, which inturn will enable you to find a way out of your situation, no matter how adverse it may be.

No matter what situation may confront you, don't allow yourself to become completely caught up in means and methods, but put into practice the teaching in the Gosho which states, "Employ the strategy of the Lotus Sutra before any other." Establish an attitude of "Daimoku first under all circumstances." Then, based on your Daimoku, you can work out the best method. This is the prime point of faith. A posture cantered on the Gohonzon. Human beings are inclined to seek comfort and shun difficulties. Remember, however, that one can only train and improve himself through struggle and effort. Be a person of unswerving faith who chants persistently, no matter what may occur.

When something good happens, regard it as a benefit from the Gohonzon and chant Daimoku in heartfelt appreciation. When something bad happens, recognize that the only way to change it fundamentally is through faith in the Gohonzon, and chant Daimoku in earnest. If you maintain pure faith in this way for five years, ten years, twenty years and so on, upholding the attitude of "the Gohonzon first" and "Daimoku first," your life will naturally follow a course along which all your desires will be fulfilled. We are told that if we recognize devilish functions for what they are, we will not be defeated by them. To give an analogy, when you realize that what you thought was a ghost is actually a withered tree swaying in the wind, then you will not be frightened by it any longer.

Shakyamuni was harassed by Devadatta, and Nichiren Daishonin was persecuted by Hei no Saemon. They were not "devils," however. Regardless of the age, the devilish nature always lurks within life, trying to make believers abandon their faith, to foment ill feelings between them and disrupt their unity. Only our strong faith enables us to detect such "devils." Consider everything which impedes our faith to be the working of these devilish tendencies. Pray to the Gohonzon with the inflexible resolution to conquer these devilish influences and change poison into medicine. Then no problem will remain unsolved.

The Gosho states, "Were it not for these [devils], there would be no way of knowing that this is the true teaching." Devil in Buddhism means the negativity inherent in life which acts to impede our practice by causing us various problems. The trouble is that we cannot see our devilish nature itself. It doesn't announce, "I am the devil," when it emerges. That is why it is necessary to pray to the Gohonzon so that we can recognize and defeat it. When you resolve to struggle in earnest for the cause of Kosen-rufu, obstacles and devils will arise to prevent you from doing so. Most times, you must battle the devil within before going out to struggle elsewhere. Bear this in mind so that you will always be able to make a fresh start in your faith.

The Gosho states, "many evil forces are vanquished by a single great truth."! No matter how fierce the workings of one's devilish nature may be, they are no match for the Gohonzon. This clearly explains why we must pray to the Gohonzon. In giving guidance in faith, we must be careful not to be blinded by the surface problem alone and get caught up in looking for techniques to solve it. The Gosho teaches, "Buddhism is like the body and society is like the shadow. When the body is crooked, so is the shadow." Faith is the body, and the problem is the shadow. It is therefore important to urge those who seek guidance to correct their attitude in faith before anything. In giving guidance, you may learn something about a member which he or she does not want to be made public.

Never be so careless as to divulge it to others. By making such thoughtless disclosures, you betray the confidence placed in you and create distrust. Keep confidential matters strictly to yourself. It is only common sense that we respect other people's privacy.

Some members enjoy the high spirits generated by the atmosphere of meetings, but are weak when it comes to maintaining their personal practice. No matter how well one may understand the depth and greatness of Buddhism, if he fails to practice, his faith remains at the theoretical level. Always remember the teaching that faith is expressed through practice. Some people say that they will undertake nothing until they have developed sufficient capability to do so. As long as they adhere to this notion, they won't be able to achieve anything. Take a person who has never swum in his life. As long as he refuses to jump into the water, saying that he will do so when he has learned how to swim, he can never master the art.

One learns how to swim by actually plunging into the water and desperately trying to float, aided by someone with abundant experience. Then, after repeated practice, he becomes an excellent swimmer. The willingness to engage in activities does not emerge automatically, simply because your leaders urge you. It wells forth when you face a problem and resolve to tackle it with all your might. To illustrate, suppose you see a child fall into a pond. What will you do? It is only natural that you promptly dive into the water and save him. Certainly no sane adult would stand by idly without helping, thinking, "It's too chilly, I might catch cold." The same is true with faith. When you recognize faith as essential to your happiness, you will not hesitate to practice.

First, fervently chant to the Gohonzon. Then you will realize how important it is to engage in activities, and you will find an irrepressible desire to do so welling forth. Sometimes you may be too busy with your work to attend meetings as you would like to, but don't feel ashamed of yourself or give up activities entirely. Certainly you must have a few days off during the month, which you can spend doing activities. And even if you cannot attend a meeting, you can learn what happened there from those who took part. The question is not whether you have time, but whether you are truly willing. Some members say, "I have no ability to convert other people." They should understand that this is precisely why they must pray to the Gohonzon—to develop that ability.

If all the people to whom we introduce true Buddhism took faith instantly, Kosen-rufu would be achieved without effort. In actuality, however, our movement is a long and arduous task. That is because it is difficult for many people to understand Buddhism. This is quite to be expected, however. Think of those parents who, estranged from their children, their own flesh and blood, cannot communicate with them, or of a husband and wife who were married while in the passion of love but who now find a gulf widening between them. If people so closely connected find it hard to communicate, it is only natural that we should have a hard time trying to make other people, who are not even related to us, understand Buddhism.

Even if the person you are trying to convince will not swallow the practice, do not complain. Complaining means you are being defeated by your environment. The more difficult the task, the more Daimoku you must chant.

Then you can achieve the greater result. The most valuable element of a discussion meeting is the contributions of the participants. It requires enormous courage to speak up before an audience. We must therefore appreciate their courage and treasure their remarks. The words uttered by one person often inspire all the others, motivating them to strive even further for their own happiness. Contributing to kosen-rufu means more than just engaging in Shakubuku or carrying out other activities. You yourself must become a valuable asset to kosen-rufu.

In other words, strive to become indispensable in your chapter, your place of work, and your family. Perhaps you have heard the story known as "The Poor Woman's Lamp." A poor woman cut off her hair to buy oil for a lamp as an offering to the Buddha. Though she could afford only a small amount, her lamp continued to burn throughout the night, while all the lamps donated by wealthy people went out in the strong winds coming down from Mount Sumeru. Some of you may be too busy to do activities. Others may be in financial straits.

However, no matter what your situation, it is vital that you resolve to find even a little time to struggle for kosen-rufu in order to repay your debt of gratitude to the Gohonzon. Therein lies the cause for accumulating good fortune. No matter what your struggle, you need a strong life force in order to win. When your life force is strong, you can turn even the worst of problems into fuel for your own development. Think of wheat seedlings: the more often they are trodden under, the stouter they grow. Become individuals who are flexible yet strong.

The Gosho teaches that although the Buddha nature exists within the life of each individual, it cannot be perceived, much less revealed, unless one encounters a good influence. Without the proper influence, the seed of Buddhahood in one's life cannot sprout, let alone bear blossoms and fruit. You must take a long-range view of life. If you lose sight of faith because of trifling matters or because you are swayed by the words and actions of people around you, you are hurting no one but yourself.

Maintain your faith throughout life so that in the end you will look back and feel the utmost joy and satisfaction. That is the greatest benefit one can get from his practice of faith. Some members say that their circumstances do not allow them to practice. They are like seeds which hate the dirt. Without the influence of earth and fertilizer, seeds cannot sprout and grow. In order to make our seed of Buddhahood sprout, we must use the environment unfavorable to our practice, in other words, our problems as a springboard for our own growth.

The Role of Faith and Effort in Achieving Happiness

HAPPINESS AND LONGEVITY ARE two of the most sought-after goals in life. People make tremendous efforts to achieve these objectives through work, marriage, and child-rearing. However, not everyone who exerts themselves in these areas succeeds in finding happiness and longevity. This raises the question of whether effort alone can enable one to achieve these goals.

The answer is that effort is important, but it is not the only requisite for attaining happiness and longevity. Despite one's best efforts, there are no guarantees of success, as evidenced by people who incur heavy debts despite working hard or those who cannot find happiness in their marriages despite their efforts. Parents may do everything they can to raise their children to be excellent adults, but not all children live up to their parents' expectations. Thus, it is clear that effort alone is not sufficient to guarantee happiness and longevity.

People generally want to live as long as possible, and to do so, they watch their diet and take care of their health. However, taking care of one's health is not a guarantee of a long and healthy life. In the early days of their organization, some members stopped taking part in activities altogether, arguing that they had to work and that the Gohonzon did not feed them. However, as Mr. Josei Toda pointed out, even if one eats properly and takes care of their health, it does not guarantee a long life. There are undeniably some areas beyond the reach of human power, and accidents can occur despite taking great caution.

This is precisely why prayer is so important in achieving happiness and longevity. It is not enough to rely solely on one's efforts and caution. There are some things that are beyond our control, and we need to turn to a higher power for help. By maintaining a pure and strong faith, we can pray sincerely to the Gohonzon for guidance and support in our endeavors. This faith should not be self-centered or casual, but rather should reflect on our past experiences and be a determination for the future. Through prayer and faith, we can find the strength and courage to overcome the challenges that life presents and attain true happiness and longevity.

Human beings have a universal desire to be happy, and this quest for happiness drives them to invest their time and energy into various activities such as work, study, and personal relationships. While these pursuits are essential for leading a fulfilling life, they do not guarantee happiness. For instance, despite working hard and putting in their best efforts, some people end up incurring heavy debts or facing professional failures. Similarly, not all married couples find happiness in their relationships, and parents may not see their children meet their expectations despite their best efforts. Hence, it is clear that effort alone cannot lead to happiness and fulfillment.

Food is essential for human survival, but it does not ensure longevity or good health. As Mr. Josei Toda used to say, just eating three square meals a day does not guarantee a long life. Similarly, despite exercising caution, we may still be vulnerable to accidents or illnesses. While taking care of our physical health and safety is crucial for leading a happy life, it is not enough.

There are some aspects of life that are beyond human control and cannot be avoided by our efforts alone. These factors could be financial or health-related, or they could be external circumstances such as natural disasters or accidents. In such situations, we may feel helpless and powerless. It is at these times that we must turn to our faith and spirituality.

Sincere prayer and faith can provide us with the strength and resilience to face life's challenges. This is why chanting and other activities of faith are essential in maintaining a strong and pure faith that can help us navigate life's ups and downs. A self-centered and casual faith that lacks reflection on the past and determination for the future will not suffice. It is a pure and robust faith that we must strive to maintain every day.

While effort and hard work are essential for leading a happy and fulfilling life, they are not the only prerequisites. We must also take care of our physical health, be mindful of our safety, and have a strong and sincere faith to face life's challenges.

The desire for a long and healthy life is a universal goal for most people, and many take steps to maintain their health and longevity. However, despite our best efforts, we cannot guarantee that we will live a long life free from illness. Even with a healthy diet and regular exercise, unexpected accidents or illnesses can still occur.

It is essential to recognize that there are areas of life that are beyond human control. Despite our efforts to avoid them, we cannot prevent certain situations from happening. For this reason, it is important to have a strong faith and to pray sincerely to the Gohonzon for guidance and protection. Chanting and maintaining a pure and strong faith from day to day, reflecting on the past and having determination for the future, is crucial in maintaining a sense of stability and peace.

In conclusion, while good health practices and effort are important for happiness and longevity, they are not the only contributing factors. Life is unpredictable, and we must recognize that some situations are beyond our control. Through our faith and prayer, we can find comfort and guidance, even in difficult times. Therefore, we should strive to maintain a pure and strong faith that sustains us in all aspects of our lives.

A Powerful Tool for Achieving Your Deepest Desires

THE POWER OF FAITH is an essential component of many spiritual and religious traditions. In the words of Nichiren Daishonin, "To accept is easy; to continue is difficult. But Buddhahood lies in continuing faith." This quote emphasizes the importance of unwavering faith and determination, especially in the face of difficulties.

For those who follow the sutra, it is essential to be prepared for challenges and obstacles that may arise. It is necessary to summon forth the great power of faith and to chant Nam-myoho-renge-kyo with the intention of having steadfast and correct faith, especially at the moment of death. Inheriting the ultimate Law of life and death requires no other way but through this practice. It is through this inheritance that one can manifest the ultimate Law in their own life.

The realization that earthly desires are enlightenment and that the sufferings of birth and death are nirvana is essential to truly understanding the power of faith. It is only through this heritage of faith that one can fully embrace the Lotus Sutra. Without this heritage, the act of embracing the Sutra would be fruitless.

One of the most powerful aspects of faith is the ability to sense the universal macrocosm through the microcosm of the self. Faith is a source of hope that is inextinguishable, and prayer is the foundation of this practice. Through prayer, hope turns into confidence, and the act of praying becomes a dialogue with the universe. It is through this dialogue that we embrace the universe with our lives and direct our hearts towards something greater.

Prayer is not just a feeble attempt at consolation; it is a powerful conviction that requires unwavering faith. It is the foundation of the practice of faith and the source of its power. Only through prayer and steadfast faith can we hope to inherit the ultimate Law of life and death and manifest it in our lives.

The power of prayer is a remarkable force that can move the entire universe, just like a single arrow shot by a great archer unerringly hits the mark. When a prayer is offered with unwavering ichinen, or concentration of mind, it can resonate across the three thousand realms that exist within a single moment of life. In this way, prayer becomes a conduit for the manifestation of our deepest desires.

However, prayer requires more than just a concentrated mind. We must also be free from doubt, anxiety, and regret and direct our hearts towards something great. This something great could be the attainment of Buddhahood or the realization of our most cherished aspirations. In any case, prayer requires faith, the power that enables the microcosm of the self to sense the universal macrocosm. Faith is the unshakeable belief in the power of prayer and in the inherent goodness of all beings.

Prayer is the basis of our practice, and it transforms hope into confidence. Through prayer, we engage in a dialogue with the universe, and we become one with it. Our lives become intertwined with the universe, and we experience the power of the interconnectedness of all things. Prayer is not just a feeble consolation; it is a powerful conviction that can transform our lives and the lives of those around us.

Prayer is a powerful tool that can help us achieve our deepest desires and connect us with the universe. With faith and a concentrated mind, we can move the universe and achieve our goals. By embracing the power of prayer, we can transform our lives and the world around us.

Transforming Our Attitude in Faith for Positive Change

I HAVE BEEN TO various parts of the world. No matter which country I visit, the people express the same wish: "I want to be happy." This is a desire common to people all over the globe. However, when it comes to Buddhism, the religion which can fulfill that desire, many of them complain that not enough study material is translated, or that it is difficult to grasp.

I always reply to them: "The only language I speak is Japanese. I don't know how to say 'sugar' in German or French, but I've discovered that sugar in any country is sweet. I didn't have to learn how to say it in this language or that in order to discover its sweetness. Whether you understand the language, it is an indisputable fact that sugar is sweet wherever you go. Translation is, of course, essential and greater effort is now being made in that direction. However, Nichiren Daishonin's Buddhism is a universal teaching. Whatever language you happen to speak, the Gohonzon will give you benefits, no matter in which country you live." I once went to a certain country on a guidance tour. There a woman member came to me to seek advice.

She did not seem to have practiced her faith earnestly. She had secretly saved up a part of the household allowance, but her husband had discovered it, and a bitter quarrel had ensued. A headstrong woman, she had not spoken to her husband, done the laundry or prepared meals for an entire year. In the meantime, she began to chant a million Daimoku, single-mindedly praying for a divorce. I met her the day after she had completed her goal of a million Daimoku.

"I have heard that in this religion no prayer will go unanswered," she said. "So why hasn't mine been answered?" I told her that prayers which will make one happy are fulfilled, but that those which would make one unhappy are not. What would happen if all wishes, both well and ill intended, were answered? I asked her, "You say you have chanted a million Daimoku for a divorce, but how many Daimoku have you chanted for your husband to take faith?" She replied that she had chanted none. "Is it because you have a bad husband that you are suffering?" I asked her, "No, it isn't. It's because you have the karma to suffer on account of your husband.

You say you have a bad husband, but you don't seem to realize that you haven't exactly been a good wife to him, either." Then I told her about the Ikegami brothers who lived in Nichiren Daishonin's day. Their father strongly opposed their faith. In that respect, he was certainly a bad father. But why did the brothers have to undergo such fierce opposition? According to the Gosho, it was in order that they could change their destiny. Their father's opposition was, in this sense, a great help to them. People complain about their parents or spouses, but they themselves are the ones who are miserable. Buddhism views everything from the standpoint of the individual himself.

If you are unhappy, it is because you yourself made some cause for that unhappiness, whether in this lifetime or a previous one. However, when people are complaining about others, they aren't considering that they themselves may have created some bad karma in the past. That's why they don't even think of apologizing to the Gohonzon for that, but merely go on resenting their spouses or parents. Finally, I said to her, "Apologize to the Gohonzon for your past conduct, and pray for your husband to take faith in true Buddhism." On the following morning, the woman came to the airport in a hired car to see me off. "Thank you very much for your guidance last night," she said. "When I went home, kneeled before the Gohonzon and chanted Daimoku, I started crying and couldn't stop."

"You have been a selfish wife and an inconsiderate mother," I said to her. "If you practice your faith earnestly, you will not only become a good wife and a wonderful mother, you will also grow into an indispensable asset for the movement of kosen-rufu. When you go home, apologize to your children, too." She looked embarrassed. "I have to apologize to my children, too?" she asked. She repeated the question two more times. I told her that any parent would apologize to his child if he stepped on its foot by mistake. Certainly, no parent would refuse to do so simply because it was his own child.

The woman said that she found it difficult to apologize to her children. So I said to her, "If you chant Daimoku to the Gohonzon and look at yourself, you will find yourself saying 'I'm sorry' to them quite naturally." She promised me she would strive for her human revolution so that she could report her positive growth to me. After I returned to Japan, I received a letter from her. She said that as soon as she came home from the airport, she prepared a meal and set it on the table, but her husband would not even touch it. Apparently she had not yet said "I'm sorry" to him.

How could any husband accept a meal without an apology from a wife who had not spoken to him for an entire a year She had not yet apologized to her children, she wrote, but when she told them all of what I had said to her, their attitude toward her changed a hundred and eighty degrees! The letter was filled with her determination to make a fresh start in faith. This example shows how important it is to pray sincerely to the Gohonzon so that we can discern our destiny from a correct perspective, with the awareness that our own reformation is the key to solving all problems.

The Unwavering Faith of Nichiren Daishonin

Nichiren Daishonin wrote a letter in 1272 while he was in exile on Sado Island. The letter was addressed to Sairen-bo, a disciple of Nichiren and a former priest of the Tendai school who was also living in exile on the island. The letter is believed to be a response to questions raised by Sairen-bo about the power of prayer in Buddhism.

Nichiren's letter contains a powerful statement that has since become famous among his followers: "Though one might point at the earth and miss it, though one might bind up the sky, though the tides might cease to ebb and flow and the sun rises in the west, it could never come about that the prayers of the practitioner of the Lotus Sutra would go unanswered." This statement uses various analogies to emphasize the unwavering faith that Nichiren had in the power of prayer.

The letter was written shortly after the Tsukahara Debate, during which Nichiren displayed a dignified personality that deeply impressed Sairen-bo. Sairen-bo was soon converted to Nichiren's teachings, and his questions about the efficacy of prayer were likely motivated by a desire to deepen his understanding of the practice.

Overall, Nichiren's statement in the letter highlights the importance of having faith in the power of prayer and the Lotus Sutra. It has since become a guiding principle for many of his followers, who strive to maintain a strong sense of faith and conviction in their Buddhist practice.

Nichiren Daishonin once proclaimed with conviction that it is impossible to miss the earth when one points to it, nor is it possible for anyone to bind up the sky. Furthermore, it is utterly impossible for the tides to cease ebb and flow, nor is it possible for the sun to rise from the west. Despite all of these impossible events, the Daishonin firmly believed that the prayers of the practitioner of the Lotus Sutra would never go unanswered, and he roared with the courage and conviction of a lion.

But what is the reason for this unshakable faith in the power of prayer? SGI President Ikeda offers an explanation, describing prayer as the courageous struggle to banish cowardice and engrave the conviction of a better future deep within one's life. Prayer is a tool to destroy fear, banish sorrow, ignite hope, and challenge ourselves to fit our lives into the motion of the universe. By never giving up and believing in ourselves, we can align our lives with the rhythm of the magnificent cosmic life and direct our existence towards happiness.

President Ikeda also warns against despising oneself, as it is equivalent to going against Buddhism and degrading the Buddhahood within one's own life. Instead, we should strive to believe in ourselves, never looking down upon ourselves, and always challenging ourselves to grow and become better.

Ultimately, earnest and strong prayers can strengthen us and bring us closer to our goals. With the power of prayer, we can align our lives with the universe and overcome any obstacle in our path towards happiness and fulfillment.

Prayer is the Key

PRAYER IS A FUNDAMENTAL practice in Nichiren Buddhism that holds great significance in the pursuit of enlightenment and the transformation of our lives. This chapter delves into the profound nature of prayer, drawing insights from the writings of Nichiren Daishonin and Dr. Daisaku Ikeda, two influential figures in Nichiren Buddhism.

Nichiren Daishonin's Teachings on Prayer

Nichiren Daishonin emphasized the power of prayer as a means to tap into our inherent Buddha nature and attain enlightenment. He wrote, "If you wish to free yourself from the sufferings of birth and death, you have endured since time without beginning and to attain without fail unsurpassed enlightenment in this lifetime, you must perceive the mystic truth that is originally inherent in all living beings" (Letter to Niike).

Prayer is not merely a request for external intervention; it is an expression of our faith and a declaration of our determination to overcome challenges. Nichiren Daishonin believed that through prayer, we activate the boundless wisdom, compassion, and courage that reside within us.

Dr. Daisaku Ikeda's Insights on Prayer

Dr. Daisaku Ikeda, a contemporary Buddhist leader and proponent of Nichiren Buddhism, expands upon the significance of prayer in his writings. He explains that prayer is a transformative dialogue with our own lives and the universe. In his book "The Wisdom of the Lotus Sutra," he states, "Prayer is the process of establishing a profound connection with the deepest part of our being, the Buddha nature, which is also the eternal, unchanging, and universal nature of life itself."

Through prayer, we align our hearts and minds with the rhythm of the universe, drawing forth the life force that sustains all existence. Dr. Ikeda teaches that prayer is a powerful tool for actualizing our potential and creating positive change in our lives.

The Nature of Prayer in Nichiren Buddhism

In Nichiren Buddhism, prayer is not limited to asking for external blessings or material desires. It encompasses a deep dialogue with our inner selves, an affirmation of our Buddhahood, and a commitment to foster positive transformation. Nichiren Daishonin wrote, "Prayer arises from faith and through faith, it is answered" (The Opening of the Eyes).

Prayer is an expression of our faith in the limitless potential within us and the power of the Mystic Law. It is a dynamic force that propels us towards realizing our highest aspirations and unlocking the wisdom needed to overcome obstacles. Through prayer, we cultivate the strength to persevere and navigate the complexities of life.

The Attitude of Prayer

Nichiren Daishonin stressed the importance of approaching prayer with a determined spirit. He wrote, "Pray with a sincere and determined mind, and the gods and Buddhas will protect you; chant Nam-myoho-renge-kyo with the spirit of many in body but one in mind, and you will be capable of broadening your way in general" (Reply to Kyo'o).

Prayer should be accompanied by a spirit of earnestness, deep reflection, and unwavering resolve. It is an active engagement with the universe and a commitment to transforming ourselves and society.

The Power of Collective Prayer

In addition to individual prayer, collective prayer holds immense power in Nichiren Buddhism. Dr. Ikeda explains, "When people gather together in prayer, their power of prayer increases exponentially, generating an even greater force for change."

Collective prayer amplifies the shared determination and positive energies of a community, creating a powerful force that can impact individuals, communities, and even the wider world.

Prayer is a key practice in Nichiren Buddhism, serving as a means to connect with our inherent Buddha nature and unlock our highest potential. It is a dynamic dialogue with our lives and the universe, embodying our faith, determination, and aspiration for positive change.

Through prayer, as taught by Nichiren Daishonin and elucidated by Dr. Daisaku Ikeda, we awaken the boundless wisdom, compassion, and courage within us. It is not a passive plea for external intervention, but an active engagement with our own lives, tapping into the wellspring of our Buddha nature.

Prayer is a transformative process that transcends individual desires and extends to the betterment of society. It is a declaration of our commitment to manifesting our Buddhahood and contributing to the welfare of others.

In the words of Nichiren Daishonin, "Pray with a sincere and determined mind, and the gods and Buddhas will protect you; chant Nam-myoho-renge-kyo with the spirit of many in body but one in mind, and you will be capable of broadening your way in general" (Reply to Kyo'o). This guidance encourages us to approach prayer with sincerity, determination, and a spirit of unity.

Collective prayer further amplifies the power of individual prayers. When individuals come together in shared intention and purpose, their collective prayer generates an exponential force for positive change. Through collective prayer, communities can foster harmony, resilience, and transformation on a larger scale.

Dr. Daisaku Ikeda emphasizes the interconnected nature of prayer, stating, "In the innermost depths of our being, we are connected to all things in the universe." Prayer enables us to tap into this interconnectedness and align ourselves with the rhythm of the universe. It is a reminder that our lives are not isolated but intricately woven into the fabric of existence.

Prayer in Nichiren Buddhism is not confined to a specific time or place. It can be practiced in various forms, such as reciting daimoku (Nam-myoho-renge-kyo) or engaging in silent contemplation. The essence of prayer lies in the sincerity, depth, and unwavering spirit with which it is carried out.

Ultimately, prayer is the key that unlocks our latent potential and enables us to navigate the challenges of life with wisdom, resilience, and compassion. It is through prayer that we manifest our Buddhahood and contribute to the realization of peace and happiness in our lives and the world.

In the words of Dr. Daisaku Ikeda, "Prayer is the voice of the human spirit speaking to the divine spirit. It is an act of drawing forth the limitless wisdom, courage, and strength within us."

Let us embrace prayer as a transformative practice, recognizing its power to unlock our inherent Buddha nature, connect us with the universe, and create positive change. Prayer is the key that opens the doors to our highest potential and paves the way for a brighter and more harmonious world.

Ms. Kumi Noguchi (vice chapter Women Division leader) living in Toyama City used to be a healthy and vibrant teenager who even took part in a gymnastic competition during her secondary school days.

After her graduation in 1958, Ms. Noguchi becomes a primary school teacher but one month later, she was diagnosed to have contracted an incurable disease—Rheumatoid Arthritis (RA), a chronic, inflammatory autoimmune disorder that causes the immune system to attack the joints. It is a disabling and painful inflammatory condition, which can lead to a substantial loss of mobility due to pain and joint destruction. She was constantly overwhelmed by the fear of dying, and the intense physical pain that attacked her entire body.

In November 1965, Ms. Noguchi was introduced to Nichiren Buddhism by her aunt. Six months after taking up faith, Ms. Noguchi could sit on the floor with her legs folded and could even ride a bicycle. As she savored the wondrous beneficial power of the Mystic

Law, she renewed her determination to overcome her illness fully. She prayed single-mindedly and exerted herself in propagation activities. In spring 1969, when seven of her friends joyfully received their Gohonzon, the excruciating rheumatic pain that had plagued her for the past seven years stopped abruptly.

However, that did not mark the end of her suffering. Her life continued to be mercilessly attacked by her "storms of karma". Her RA relapsed and her condition deteriorated so much she was bedridden at home. The only thing that she could move in her body were her eyeballs. In June 1970, her doctor told her, "Your bones have become so fragile that it is impossible to operate on them. Consider yourself lucky that you have been able to work till recently. I'm sorry, but you have to spend the rest of your life quietly in bed."

Over the following one year and three months where she spent her days in the hospital, Ms. Noguchi continued to chant Daimoku on her hospital bed with an unwavering resolve, "I'm going to transform this karma no matter what, through my prayers to the Gohonzon I will make the impossible possible!"

After her discharge, she continued to be attacked by various illnesses, including severe side effects from her medication, acute hepatitis (liver inflammation), gastric ulcer and the throes of death. Amidst such circumstances, she continued chanting Daimoku single-mindedly every moment of her life, unless she was having her meals.

When she completed her first million times of Daimoku in October 1971 (since she began keeping count from May 1971), she could work, something that was deemed impossible by medical science. From that day onwards, she continued to work for the next 30 years until her retirement in 2003.

Filled with profound gratitude for the good health she now enjoys, she continues to exert herself in kosen-rufu activities for the happiness of others.

No matter who we are, as long as we are human, during moments of life's great adversities such as death or illness, it is only natural that we are overwhelmed by negative tendencies in our lives such as fear, cowardice, lament, insecurity, doubt, anger or resentment. During such moments, it is most critical that we continue offering sincere prayers to the Gohonzon with persevering faith. By tenaciously offering prayers without giving up till the end, we will surely be able to surmount all obstacles, no matter how harsh they may be, by summoning forth immense courage, wisdom and life force from the depths of our lives.

President Ikeda said in his guidance, "Prayer is the key to opening the multiple doors to innate human potential." With these words deeply engraved in our lives, let us achieve great victories in our lives and in the kosen-rufu movement.

The Eternity of Life

IN HIS PROFOUND WISDOM, Daisaku Ikeda teaches us that having a clear understanding of death can empower us to live without fear and with strength, purpose, and joy. Buddhism perceives the universe as a vast living entity, where cycles of individual life and death continuously repeat themselves. Death, therefore, plays a crucial role in the life process, allowing for renewal and new beginnings.

Throughout its history, Buddhism has placed great importance on facing the reality of death head-on. Death, along with illness and aging, is recognized as one of the fundamental sufferings that all individuals must endure.

Despite this focus on death, Buddhism is not pessimistic in its outlook on life. Ignoring or avoiding the inevitability of death only leads to a superficial existence. Instead, acknowledging and accepting the nature of death can liberate us from fear and allow us to live with strength, purpose, and joy. Through a clear understanding of death's nature, we can fully embrace life and all of its experiences.

The universe, according to Buddhism, is a vast living entity characterized by cycles of life and death that repeat endlessly. Our bodies, which consist of approximately 60 trillion cells, undergo these cycles daily as cells die and are replaced through metabolic processes. Death is therefore an essential aspect of the life process, facilitating renewal and new growth. Upon death, our lives return to the vast ocean of existence, similar to how a wave crests and then subsides back into the wholeness of the sea. Through death, the physical elements of our bodies and the fundamental life force that sustains our being are recycled throughout the universe.

In an ideal situation, death can be experienced as a period of rest, similar to a rejuvenating sleep that follows a day's exertions and efforts.

Buddhism holds that there is continuity that persists through cycles of life and death, implying that our lives are, in a sense, eternal. As Nichiren wrote, "When we examine the nature of life with perfect enlightenment, we find that there is no beginning marking birth and, therefore, no end signifying death."

In the 5th century C.E., Vasubandhu, a great Indian philosopher, developed the "Nine-Consciousness Teaching," which provides a detailed understanding of the eternal functioning of life. According to this system, the first five layers of consciousness correspond to the senses of perception, and the sixth layer corresponds to waking consciousness, including the ability to interpret the information supplied by the senses and the capacity for rational judgment.

The seventh layer of consciousness, or mano-consciousness, corresponds to the subconscious, where our profound sense of self-resides, as described in modern psychology. Below this is the eighth layer, or Alaya-consciousness, which contains the potential energy, both positive and negative, created by our thoughts, words, and deeds. This potential energy, referred to as karma or profound life-tendency, is not fixed and unchangeable, as some might assume.

Our karmic energy, described as the "raging current" of the Alaya-consciousness, interacts with the other layers of consciousness. At this deepest level, human beings exert influence upon one another, on their surroundings, and on all life. It is also at this level that the continuity of life over cycles of birth and death is maintained. When we die, the potential energy representing the "karmic balance sheet" of all our actions - creative and destructive, selfish and altruistic - continues to flow forward in the Alaya-consciousness. This karma shapes the circumstances in which the potential energy of our lives becomes manifest again, through birth, as a new individual life.

At the deepest level of consciousness lies the continuity of life over cycles of birth and death. When we die, the potential energy of all our actions continues to flow forward in the alaya-consciousness, shaping the circumstances in which our lives become manifest again as a new individual life.

In addition to the eight layers of consciousness described in the Nine-Consciousness Teaching, there is also the ninth level, which is the source of cosmic life that supports even the functioning of the alaya-consciousness. Through Buddhist practice, one can stimulate and awaken this fundamentally pure Amala-consciousness or wisdom, which has the power to transform even deeply established negative energy.

As the questions of life and death shape our views on everything, a new understanding of their nature can open new horizons for humankind and unleash previously untapped stores of wisdom and compassion.

The Eight Winds

The concept of "Worthy persons" refers to individuals who are not influenced by the eight winds: prosperity, decline, disgrace, honor, praise, censure, suffering, and pleasure. Such individuals are not carried away by prosperity or grieved by decline. According to Nichiren Daishonin's letter "The Eight Winds," the heavenly gods protect those who remain steadfast in the face of the eight winds. However, harboring an unreasonable grudge against one's lord will not provide protection, regardless of how many prayers are offered.

In 1277, Nichiren Daishonin wrote "The Eight Winds" to Shijo Kingo, a follower who was upset with his lord's decision to move him and his family to a distant province. The letter encouraged Kingo to maintain unwavering faith and let go of any unreasonable grudges to receive a satisfactory outcome.

When we begin practicing Buddhism, many of us seek something that will fundamentally improve our lives, not just provide temporary relief from stress. However, we may mistakenly believe that practicing Buddhism will eradicate all problems and ensure good times without impediment. In reality, problems seldom disappear, and good times do not always manifest as expected.

According to the dictionary definition, the eight winds are conditions that prevent individuals from advancing towards enlightenment. People are often influenced by their attachment to the "four favorites" (prosperity, honor, praise, and pleasure) or their aversion to the "four dislikes" (decline, disgrace, censure, and suffering).

The Eight Winds are an unavoidable part of our lives, confronting us daily with their various conditions. However, we can learn to navigate them and not let them steer us off course.

It is natural for humans to seek prosperity and pleasure, while avoiding decline and pain. These desires are understandable since prosperity often means more possessions and comfort, while pain and decline are unpleasant. However, if we focus solely on these pursuits, we may lose sight of true happiness. True happiness is not just having an abundance of pleasure and the absence of pain. Instead, it is the ability to remain confident and optimistic in the face of daily challenges.

Josei Toda, the Second Soka Gakkai President, wrote about the nature of absolute happiness. It is a state where one feels immense worth and satisfaction, regardless of their situation. To be alive is a joy, even when faced with anger-provoking situations. Once we attain such a state of mind, we experience boundless joy in life.

When I moved to Los Angeles, I had aspirations of becoming an actor, but I was only able to secure minor work that barely paid enough to get by. I remember landing a national commercial where I had to eat hamburgers. On the day of the shoot, I was treated like a star with my own trailer and all the perks that come with it. I went home feeling accomplished, only to find an eviction notice on my door that same evening. The wind of pleasure had me in the morning, but the wind of decline hit me hard that evening. In that moment, all I could do was continue chanting Nam-myoho-renge-kyo and carry on with my work.

Thankfully, the commercial turned out to be successful, and I received a bit of income just in time to avoid being evicted. This experience taught me a valuable lesson: change can happen in a heartbeat, and we need to keep our heads straight in order to persevere.

So, how do we increase our chances of finding happiness and success? By always grounding ourselves in our faith and pushing forward through each obstacle.

In one of his letters to Shijo Kingo, the Daishonin wrote, "Muster your faith and pray to this Gohonzon. Then what is there that cannot be achieved?" This means that we can accomplish anything we set our minds to by relying on our practice and determination.

No matter how much we have achieved or what obstacles we face, another challenge may be right around the corner. The key is to persist in our practice, knowing that it is the means to our progress and ultimate success. As SGI President Ikeda once stated, "Taking faith in the Daishonin's Buddhism does not mean that all difficulties will disappear. Being alive means that we will have problems of one kind or another. But no matter what happens, it is important that we remain firm in our hearts."

Our persistence, even in the face of defeat, strengthens us and assures us of victory. The goal of Buddhism is not to avoid problems, but to develop a state of life where problems cannot define or defeat us. By becoming stronger and more resilient, we can weather any storm, no matter how hard the eight winds may blow.

Changing Your Destiny

THE GOSHO TEACHES US that if we try to treat someone's illness without understanding its root cause, we may end up making the person sicker than before. Therefore, it is essential not to offer superficial advice to our fellow members, but rather to help them identify and address the fundamental cause of their problems. Otherwise, we may inadvertently worsen their situation.

For instance, if a thief chants Daimoku to the Gohonzon with stolen goods in their possession, they cannot erase their wrongdoing through chanting alone. They must return the stolen items to their rightful owner and make reparations for their actions. This is a familiar example used to illustrate the principle of erasing negative karma. To eradicate our past slanders, we must chant to the Gohonzon diligently and make significant efforts for the sake of kosen-rufu.

When we face mishaps or challenges, we should not blame the Gohonzon for our misfortune. If we are the only ones experiencing a particular problem, then we realize that the cause lies within ourselves. Even if a thief embraces faith, they still have to take responsibility for the crimes they committed previously. Similarly, we must bear the effects of our past negative causes before we began chanting. However, by practicing to the Gohonzon, we can eradicate this bad karma more lightly than we would otherwise.

We must be mindful of the fundamental causes of our problems, make sincere efforts to chant to the Gohonzon, and take responsibility for our actions to change our destiny. As Nichiren Daishonin wrote in the Gosho, "Rely on the Law and not upon persons. Rely on the meaning of the teaching, not on the words of others."

Just like a well-bred seed needs to be covered with earth to sprout, we human beings need difficulties and obstacles to grow and develop our Buddha nature. However, when faced with hardships, we often lose courage and try to avoid them or complain. It is precisely at such times that we must examine our faith, make a new determination, and chant earnestly. In this way, we can not only overcome the problem but also further develop ourselves.

Looking back, we realize that our present happiness owes to our past hardships, just as a seed owes its growth to the dirt. Therefore, we should not put off our practice until we have spare time, but make it a priority even in our busy lives. Our foremost aim should be our own human revolution, which we achieve through consistent and sincere practice.

As leaders, we need to be honest with our members and show them that we are also struggling with our bad karma, trying to overcome it with all our might. We don't need to try to look perfect, as it would only slow down our progress. Instead, we should let our members see that we are challenging ourselves and setting an example for them to follow.

We must embrace difficulties and obstacles as opportunities for growth and development, and make our practice a priority even when we are busy. By doing so, we can change any poison into medicine and achieve our human revolution.

Living True Buddhism

Nichiren Buddhism places great emphasis on the three types of actions, namely thoughts, words, and deeds, as a fundamental part of Buddhist practice. The Daishonin is the only person who fully embodied the three types of actions by reading the Lotus Sutra in deed, word, and mind. For us, carrying out the three types of actions means actively engaging in good deeds, speaking kind words, and thinking positively. It is a critical aspect of our practice.

Memorizing passages from the Gosho and repeatedly reading them may give us a sense of having read them in deed. However, we must ensure that we have understood them both in word and mind and have put them into practice in our daily lives. Simply understanding a principle is meaningless if we do not apply it in practice.

As the second president of the organization, Josei Toda once said, understanding a theory is one thing, but putting it into practice is another. Knowing that sugar is sweet does not make a cake sweet if it has no sugar. Similarly, understanding that life is eternal does not make it a part of our lives. We need to actively apply these teachings in our daily lives to make them a part of who we are.

In most cases, we may believe that we have read a passage in deed, when in reality, we have only done so in word and mind. We must review well-known passages from the Gosho and reflect on whether we are reading them in deed. For example, "When the skies are clear, the ground is illuminated. Similarly, when one knows the Lotus Sutra, he understands the meaning of all worldly affairs." By reflecting on and applying these teachings in our daily lives, we can make meaningful progress in our practice of Nichiren Buddhism.

Buddhism is often compared to the body, while society is likened to its shadow. The two are intertwined, and if the body is crooked, so is the shadow. This analogy is easy to comprehend, and it's something that we often explain to others when giving guidance. However, the question is whether we are truly living these teachings ourselves. We tend to forget to straighten the body of our faith and instead focus solely on unbending the shadow. As the Gosho states, "one should become the master of his mind rather than let his mind master him," but many of us still find ourselves being controlled by our earthly desires.

SGI President Daisaku Ikeda has emphasized the need to change our ways of thinking, saying that we must move beyond our limited perspective of the world and instead observe it from the standpoint of the sun. With the second phase of kosen-rufu underway, it's important that we each consider our individual missions and what we need to do to accomplish them. We must ask ourselves if we are truly following President Ikeda's advice.

In the Gosho, "Curing Karmic Disease," it is stated that there are six causes for illness, with the most deeply rooted being the effects of evil karma. Yet when we fall ill, we tend to focus only on the immediate cause and seek medical cures without considering the underlying reasons. It's important to understand the causes of our suffering and to address them accordingly.

As we progress in our practice and deepen our understanding, we will encounter the three obstacles and four devils, which will try to interfere with our progress. These devils will not announce themselves as such but instead will lodge themselves in the weak spots of our faith. To overcome them, we must not be swayed and must summon the courage and wisdom to face them head-on. It is only then that we can truly live the teachings of Buddhism and bring about a better society.

The Seed of Buddhahood

IT IS NATURAL THAT even we who have faith should encounter various problems in the course of our lives. With the power of faith, however, we can solve all those troubles. One day we will look back and think, "Because of that problem, I could grow, and a new road in life opened up for me." Buddhism calls this the benefit of "changing poison into medicine. I once heard a young medical student relate to his experience. Before he began practicing Buddhism, his mother had been bedridden with rheumatism. His father was a physician, but he could not cure his wife's disease. On top of it, the couple would engage in endless quarrels. How the youth resented the gloomy and depressing atmosphere of his family! This motivated him to take faith in Nichiren Buddhism.

One after another, the other members of his family followed suit. As a result, his mother recovered from her illness and his family became a bright and harmonious one. The family was well-off. Had the father and mother been devoted to each other, and had the mother been healthy, the family would most likely not have taken faith in true Buddhism. It was because his parents fought like cats and dogs, and because his mother was ill, that the youth sought the Gohonzon and established his faith. Now, hearing this, some of you may decide, "Okay, we'll start quarreling with each other from today. That way, our children will develop." But this is missing the point. Everyone has their own worries.

I once heard an old woman remark, "I have the worst karma in the world." "How do you know it's the worst?" I asked. "I don't know," she replied. "I never thought about it." I asked her if she knew how deep her neighbor's karma was. She said she didn't. In adversity, everyone thinks that he or she is the unhappiest person on earth. However, it is true that the deeper the mud, the larger the lotus flowers which bloom in it. Similarly, if one decides, "Okay, because this mud is so deep, I'm going to chant more Daimoku than other people," then he can change poison into medicine.

I make it a rule to tell people to pray to the Gohonzon before they brood over their problems or complain. Some of you may be worried about your marriage partners not doing Gongyo. But, no matter how many times you may complain, it will not make them embrace the Gohonzon. The Gosho teaches benefits come from chanting Daimoku. Nowhere does it say that you can get benefits by complaining, even if you do so a million times. Fundamentally, everyone wants to be happy.

The key to attaining happiness lies in whether we can overcome the negative influences of our environment or whether we will be defeated by them. We must build up a powerful life force in order to win. Think of the wheat. The harder it is trodden under, the stouter the seedling that grows. This very process assures a rich harvest. The same holds true for human development. No matter how well-bred a seed may be, as long as it is placed on a table it will not sprout, much fewer bear fruit. Only when it is buried in earth can it sprout!

Each of us has the seed of happiness—in other words, the seed of Buddhahood—within. It is covered with the "earth" of various problems, which motivate us to chant Daimoku to the Gohonzon. Then the seed will sprout, Thus the "earth" serves as a good influence. Some of you may be worried because of your mates, children, or parents. But so long as you merely complain about them, you cannot solve your problem. Instead, resolve to turn your anxiety into an impetus for changing your karma, into a springboard for attaining enlightenment—in other words, into a good influence.

Then muster your power of faith and practice, and chant and chant until you have solved your problem. Only your faith in the Gohonzon can enable you to do this. Without the Gohonzon, it is impossible to transform your problem into a good influence for changing your karma.

Essentials of Individual Guidance

THE GUIDANCE WE PROVIDE should prioritize matters of faith, rather than focusing solely on means and methods that are unrelated to faith. It is crucial that we also prioritize the protection of members' privacy when seeking guidance. As members place their trust in us, they may reveal sensitive information that they would not share with others. It is imperative that we maintain their trust and confidence by keeping any secrets shared with us confidential, without exception. It is worth noting that Mr. Toda was particularly strict about this aspect of our work.

The Gosho, "Letter to Misawa," states, "With the appearance of this teaching, all the teachings advocated by the scholars and teachers of Buddhism during the Former and Middle Days of the Law will be like stars after sunrise or an awkward apprentice beside a skilled craftsman." When Mr. Toda gave guidance to those who clung to a low state of life, he did not deny their attachment. Instead, he tried to make them realize for themselves that their condition of life was low by indicating a higher one. For example, suppose your baby is playing with a broken toy.

You worry it may injure him, and tell him to throw it away, yet he clings to it even more tightly than before. Instead, if you buy him a new, finer plaything, he will discard the old one without being told. The same principle applies to individual guidance, Mr. Toda used to say. He did not tell members to rid themselves of their desires; he led them to awaken, of their own accord, to a higher level of faith so that they could transform such desires into causes for enlightenment.

Another thing we should remember when giving individual guidance is that we must discern whether the recipient is truly seeking advice or merely complaining. If he is simply complaining and we cannot perceive it, our guidance may do him more harm than good. Mr. Toda was very sharp at recognizing the difference.

Sometimes he would severely reprimand someone, saying, "It is your tendency to complain, which causes all your unhappiness." He would remind that person of the need to strengthen his life force, which was now so weak that he was being defeated by his environment and could do nothing other than complain.

Suppose a woman comes to you and says, "My husband comes home drunk every night and goes to bed without doing Gongyo. Please give him guidance." You take her remark at face value and comply. The husband is enraged that she divulged his weakness to a third party.

Your guidance, far from helping, has instead provoked a domestic quarrel. In such a case, Mr. Toda would say, "It is your destiny to have a hard time because of your husband. That, in terms of your life, is the reason he drinks and you go through hardships. You are the one who is suffering, aren't you? Instead of complaining about him, try to change your own destiny, which is the underlying cause of your unhappiness. Pray to the Gohonzon that he will begin to practice earnestly as soon as possible."

You should pray that he will embrace the Gohonzon, not that he will stop drinking, It won't do you any good just to blame him and his liquor, The Buddhist way to look at it is that your own faith has so far not been strong enough to enable you to change your destiny. Hence his drinking and your hardships. Realize that the only way to improve the situation fundamentally is to pray that he will begin practicing. It is also important for you to chant lots of Daimoku in apology because you have been blaming everything on him without assuming responsibility for your own karma.

The Great Blessing of the Gohonzon

WE NEED TO ENSURE that our individual guidance focuses solely on matters of faith. The purpose of providing guidance to individual members is to encourage them from the standpoint of faith and help them resolve to practice with renewed determination. If we neglect matters of faith and only provide them with means and methods in a secular sense, then it is no longer considered guidance in faith.

For instance, if a member becomes ill and seeks guidance from their leader, we should not advise them on whether or not to undergo surgery. Such decisions are best left to the patient and their physician. Similarly, when members face other troubles in their daily lives, we must understand that they have tried every means available to solve them, and teaching them methods alone will not suffice.

The Gosho does not provide specific instructions on how to cure illness or overcome poverty. Instead, it reminds us that the fundamental cause of all our sufferings lies within our own destiny and teaches us to strengthen our faith to change our destiny for the better. For instance, if a parent is troubled over their child's illness and prays fervently for their recovery, they must realize that it is their destiny to face difficulties because of their child's illness. Whenever parents with ailing children came to Mr. Toda, he would remind them of their karma and say, "You have the karma to experience difficulties because of your child. That's why they have fallen ill."

We must safeguard the privacy of members seeking guidance. They confide in us because they trust us, and we must keep any such secret to ourselves and under no circumstances divulge it. Mr. Toda was very strict about this.

We must recognize that the only way to change our destiny is by changing ourselves," as Nichiren Daishonin taught. This principle applies not only to our own lives but to those of our loved ones. Whether it's a family member or ourselves who is ill, we must transform the situation into an opportunity to strengthen our faith and change our destiny for the better. The Daishonin's teaching that "those who are ill can attain Buddhahood" is a reminder that illness can awaken a great seeking spirit within us.

It's not until we face adversity, like illness or other problems, that we become aware of our past negative causes and bad karma. When we do fall ill, we should remind ourselves that this is an opportunity to awaken our faith and change our destiny. We must use our determination to face the challenge head-on and find ourselves in a higher state of life.

This principle is not limited to illness but is applicable to all troubles we face in life. Through individual guidance, we aim to convince each suffering member of this principle and encourage them to solve their problems based on faith. As we do so, we can transform our suffering into a path towards greater enlightenment and happiness.

The concept of "Buddhist apology" (sange in Japanese) is often discussed in relation to changing karma and eradicating slander. It is important to understand that this term does not reflect a casual attitude. It is not enough to simply regret past actions and ask the Gohonzon for forgiveness. We must naturally pay the karmic debt we have accumulated since the distant past. However, due to our faith, we may experience the retribution of our negative karma less severely.

Nichiren Daishonin teaches that some people may appear to have repented, but they have not done so deeply enough. A "profound apology" involves maintaining strong faith. When faced with difficulties, it is easy to forget about profound apology and instead blame others for our hardships. However, it is a fact of life that things do not always go as we want them to. Holding grudges against others will not lead to any positive outcomes. Instead, we should have a positive attitude and see these people as good influences that will strengthen our faith.

The purpose of individual guidance is to help the recipient understand the importance of taking an active posture towards life and strive for their human revolution based on the Mystic Law. The Lotus Sutra Reveals the Buddha's Enlightenment, a Gosho, explains the great blessing of the Gohonzon. The sutra states, "The Lotus Sutra is the Buddha's teaching, the embodiment of his wisdom. If you profoundly believe in even a single character or 'dot' of it, you will become a Buddha without changing your present form. This is just as white paper, when dipped in ink, becomes black, or as black lacquer, when mixed with white pigment, turns white."

In summary, the concept of "Buddhist apology" should not be taken lightly. We should strive for a profound apology by maintaining strong faith and taking an active posture towards life. It is important to see difficulties and hardships as opportunities to strengthen our faith rather than blame others. The Lotus Sutra teaches that even a single character or dot of the Buddha's teachings can lead us to become Buddhas.

Helping Others with Individual Guidance

When providing individual guidance, one may assume that there are countless factors to consider, but in reality, there are relatively few. The crucial element is ensuring that the person giving guidance comprehends the purpose of such guidance. In Japanese, "guidance" is translated as shi, which means "to point to," and do, which means "to guide." The question is, what are you pointing to and where are you guiding someone? The answer is clear: you point to the purpose of faith and guide them to the Gohonzon, the basis of our faith.

Throughout my encounters with various members who are struggling with diverse issues and difficulties, I've noticed that they often forget about the boundless power of the Gohonzon when they are at their most vulnerable. They become so consumed by the events happening around them that their faith in the Gohonzon wanes. The first and most critical aspect of giving individual guidance is to remind them of this fact. In other words, you must urge them not to be swayed by external factors and to return to the Gohonzon, the foundation of their faith.

The human life is susceptible to influence. This vulnerability cannot be corrected by merely disciplining one's thoughts. Human existence is a mysterious entity that exhibits different conditions in response to external influences. Reading a tragedy brings tears to one's eyes, while a hilarious story can cause uncontrollable laughter. Therefore, encountering positive influences is crucial in life. What better influence exists than the Gohonzon, the source of the primary power to resolve any issue?

Why are people born in this world? Ultimately, they are born to be happy and fulfill their mission. Tree leaves emerge in spring, grow in summer, and fall to the ground in autumn. This is their natural life cycle. However, some leaves are eaten by worms, while others are not. Some leaves are blown away by the wind, while others remain on the branches. Similarly, while everyone strives to be happy in their own way, some fall ill, while others do not. Some experience disasters, while others remain safe and sound. There are various differences among human beings, and while some may attribute these differences to good or bad luck, Buddhism does not. According to Buddhism, such disparities result from karma created in previous existences.

People must suffer in this life because of the causes they have formed in the past. Everyone wants to be happy. When someone meets with failure or suffering, they may blame others or society.

Although external factors may be responsible for the cause, no problem can be entirely resolved unless one seeks the fundamental cause. Those who embrace the Gohonzon are no exception. It is essential to make members understand that the causes of everything they experience lie within them. However, realizing this is insufficient. They must endeavor to turn poison into medicine. By sincerely praying to the Gohonzon to improve their destiny, they can transform their negative karma into the cause of happiness. This is why our Buddhism is called the Mystic Law, and you must bear this in mind when providing individual guidance.

The Role of Leaders

Let's reflect on the role of a district chief in Nichiren Buddhism. As previously mentioned, positions within the organization are associated with increasing levels of responsibility. As a district chief, you are entrusted with a greater responsibility than a group chief or a chapter chief. However, being promoted to this position does not mean that you have attained greatness, nor does it imply that the vice district chief, who was previously your senior, is now your subordinate. Such thinking can impede your ability to effectively carry out your responsibilities.

As a district chief, your primary duty is to teach each member in your district about the greatness of faith in the Gohonzon and lead them towards happiness. Your members are not your subordinates; instead, you should view them as peers. Nichiren Buddhism is not organized like a typical company, and it would be a mistake to consider yourself superior to your members or attempt to order them around. It's essential to recognize that each position in the organization corresponds to a specific scope of activity, and the greater the area, the heavier the responsibility.

When dealing with members who were previously your seniors, avoid feeling sorry for them, as this can create an undesirable effect. Instead, recognize their capabilities and help them make full use of their potential. In my opinion, being a district chief is not a remarkable feat. Your role is to provide guidance to each group chief based on the experience you gained while serving in that capacity. Use your experience to develop each group in your district into an excellent community of people.

In summary, being a district chief in Nichiren Buddhism requires a great deal of responsibility, but it does not imply that you have reached a superior status. Your primary responsibility is to teach and guide your members towards happiness, recognizing their potential and encouraging them to reach their full potential. Remember that each position comes with a corresponding scope of activity, and you should view your members as peers, not subordinates. Use your experience to develop your district into a vibrant and thriving community.

Let us consider what it means to be a district chief. As previously mentioned, positions in Nichiren Buddhism are a measure of responsibility. Each position, including the group chief, district chief, and chapter chief, has its own responsibility to discharge. Being promoted from group chief to district chief means that you must shoulder much more responsibility. However, becoming a district chief does not mean that you have become superior to others or that the vice district chief, who was your senior, is now your subordinate. If you think this way, you will face difficulties in carrying out your activities. As district chief, your responsibility is to teach each member in your district the greatness of faith in the Gohonzon and lead them to happiness. Your members are not your subordinates in any way. The organization of Nichiren Buddhism is fundamentally different from that of a company. Therefore, it is a grave mistake to think you are the most important person in your district or to attempt to boss your members around.

As district chief, your responsibility is to recognize the capabilities of your members and empower them to give their best performance. The larger the area, the greater and more significant the responsibility. Dealing with a member who was previously your senior requires a different approach. You should not pity them because you have risen above them. Instead, use your experience to guide them and enable them to perform to their full potential. To be a district chief is nothing extraordinary; it merely requires giving advice to each group chief based on your experience as a group chief. Your duty as district chief is to utilize your experience in developing each group in your district into a magnificent group of people.

It is a common misconception that your duty as district chief is to give orders and directions. This belief is similar to the idea that children should be obedient to their parents. However, children resist parental authority but welcome the advice of a kind and caring mother. Similarly, if you take a high-handed approach to your members, they will resist you. If you assume that your members should accept everything you say because you are the district chief, they will never be convinced. Guidance means to provide encouragement, as noted by the third president, Mr. Ikeda.

To be an outstanding district chief means to foster many exceptional group chiefs. This applies to all positions. An exceptional chapter chief is one who develops numerous outstanding district chiefs. A capable group chief is one who encourages every member in their group to deepen their faith, practice, and study. If the district chief is excellent but none of the group chiefs are, there must be something amiss. In summary, the district chief's responsibility is to develop each group chief into a remarkable leader and assist every member of their district in truly understanding Nichiren Daishonin's Buddhism.

However, theory is one thing, and practice is quite another. Nichiren Buddhism publications emphasize the importance of Gongyo repeatedly, and members should strictly observe Gongyo both morning and evening. However, in reality, some members find it challenging to perform Gongyo. This is why the responsibilities of the district chief and the group chief are vital and challenging to fulfill. If a schoolteacher imparts everything they have learned to their students without considering their different grades, they cannot expect excellent results. Similarly, it is inadvisable for the district chief to overwhelm their members, regardless of their different situations, with everything they have learned from their senior leaders or their own experience.

A district comprises many people who are in different circumstances, including those who have recently joined, those being influenced by their environment, those whose families oppose their faith, those too busy to take part in activities, and those who hold grudges against a leader. It can be challenging to deal with such a diverse group of members. However, it is essential to remember that as a district chief, your position demands that you take on this responsibility.

It is vital to recognize that every member in your district is essential and deserves your attention. Instead of feeling overwhelmed by difficult situations, use them as an opportunity to grow. By taking the time to understand each member's challenges and finding a solution together, you will show them that you care and encourage them to deepen their faith.

Treating every member with respect, kindness, and compassion is your mission as a district chief. This way, you can accumulate good fortune and grow both as a leader and a human being. Do not let any member's situation discourage you; instead, see it as an opportunity to further your own growth. I hope you will be convinced of this and proceed with your activities with confidence.

Treasuring Each Individual

We, as believers of the Gohonzon of the Three Great Secret Laws, strive to practice the three ways of faith, practice, and study. But why do we do this? On an individual level, our aim is to improve our destiny and attain enlightenment in this lifetime. On a collective level, we aim to propagate our faith to the best of our ability and accomplish kosen-rufu, the task entrusted to us by the original Buddha and Nichiren Daishonin. To achieve these goals, it is essential that we establish and maintain a correct attitude in faith by following the teachings of the Daishonin in the Gosho.

The Gosho is the very scripture that the original Buddha left for us on the Latter Day of the Law. Each sentence and phrase in it was written out of his infinite mercy. Hence, it is vital that we read and devote ourselves to applying it to our lives. By deeply engraving the passages of the Gosho in our minds, we can deepen our faith. Reading the Gosho fills us with courage, conviction, and hope, and drives us to strive harder in our practice.

It is essential to understand that the spread of the Mystic Law in a family or a community begins with a single person. The joy of faith demonstrated by a single person embracing the Gohonzon, the actual proof of their destiny's transformation and the revitalization of their life, sparks a desire for Buddhism in the people around them. Therefore, those of us who feel a sense of mission for kosen-rufu must value every member and engage in sincere dialogue and guidance to enable all members to evoke strong faith. We must renew our sense of gratitude every day for our good fortune to study the Gosho and share its wisdom with others.

"The True Entity of Life," states, "Only I, Nichiren, at first chanted Nam-myoho-renge-kyo, but then two, three and a hundred followed, chanting and teaching others. Likewise, propagation will unfold this way in the future. Doesn't this signify 'emerging from the earth'? At the time of kosen-rufu, the entire Japanese nation will chant Nam-myoho-renge-kyo, as surely as an arrow aimed at the earth cannot miss the target." Exactly as the above passage says, we now find ourselves moving in a broad current toward kosen-rufu, an achievement unprecedented in Buddhist history. This we owe entirely to the immeasurable mercy of the original Buddha.

Now is the time for each of us to establish correct faith in the Gohonzon, develop our wisdom and capability, and show to the world the actual proof of the Gohonzon's benefit. For this purpose, it is becoming more and more important to inspire individuals by continuing one-to-one guidance, teaching passages of the Gosho, and relating experiences.

Of all activities, the first president, Tsunesaburo Makiguchi, exerted his greatest energy on individual guidance. He gave considerate and detailed advice to whomever came to see him at his house in Mejiro, Tokyo. A discussion meeting of only a few people would consist mainly of Mr. Makiguchi giving guidance to individual participants. I remember one frosty night in winter. A woman who had come for his advice was about to leave, carrying her child on her back. Mr. Makiguchi rose, fetched several sheets of newspaper and inserted them between the child's back and the neneko (a short coat which covers both mother and child). "This will keep your baby warmer," he said.

Both the second president, Josei Toda, and the third president, Daisaku Ikeda, took the initiative in giving individual guidance with all their might. Steady, thorough guidance of individual members is the tradition of the Nichiren Buddhism, the activity to which the successive presidents have attached the greatest importance since the early days of the organization. Speeches we hear at large meetings tend to leave only a vague impression and easily slip from memory. What remains in our minds throughout our lives is the guidance we receive personally from our seniors, words of encouragement we hear at a meeting of only a few people, or quotations from the Gosho which seem to penetrate and dispel all our agonies.

Indeed, it is not too much to say that one-to-one guidance, filled with sincerity and confidence, has accumulated to form the solid foundation of the grand movement for kosen-rufu, which we see today.

The fundamental spirit of "treasuring each individual" is a guideline that the Daishonin taught through his own behavior, as stated in the Gosho. In "Letter from Sado," he emphasizes the importance of each individual by stating, "There is very little writing paper here in the province of Sado, and to write to you individually would take too long. However, if even one person cannot hear from me, it will cause resentment. Therefore, I want all sincere believers to meet and read this letter together for encouragement." Similarly, in "Reply to Toki," the Daishonin expresses his concern for an individual's well-being and states, "I am deeply concerned about your wife's sickness. I feel as if I had fallen ill. Therefore, I keep telling the Buddhist gods day and night to cure her."

All activities for kosen-rufu are performed as emissaries of the Gohonzon, and it is essential that we pray fervently to manifest even a fraction of the original Buddha's boundless mercy in carrying out these activities. However, treasuring each individual member should not be accomplished at the cost of the unity and harmony of the whole. It is crucial for all members of a family or organization to respect each other's position, trust each other, and form a life-to-life bond with one another so that each can give full play to their capabilities.

To build a harmonious family or organization, we need the unity of itai-doshin (many in body, one in mind) and firm solidarity, in which each member has a unique and indispensable role to play. Both individual guidance and the treasuring of each individual member assume their true significance when considered in the whole context.

One's Way of Living

THOSE PEOPLE WITH NO place to live in wish they owned their own homes. Those who are poor wish they had money. Those without offspring may wish they had children. They all think that once their wishes are fulfilled, they'll be happy. Happiness of this kind, however, is only relative. Happiness in the genuine sense of the word is absolute, a state of life in which you have sufficient life force to change any adverse circumstances whatsoever into causes for your own growth, Everyone wants to be happy, but in reality one meets troubles and hardships. Often, one blames other people or society for his difficulties. True, the immediate cause may lie in other people or society.

But why is one person suffering from a particular problem and not someone else? Until one realizes that the fundamental cause of his trouble lies within himself, there can be no correct solution. Suppose someone makes an outstanding achievement in his profession. He is widely acclaimed for it and wins international fame. But does this mean that he has become truly happy? Not necessarily. Some celebrated people feel unhappy, for precisely because of their fame they have less freedom of action than before or cannot devote themselves to their families as they might wish.

True happiness is not a matter of fame but of one's state of life. You can judge someone's happiness by his desires. Someone with a lofty goal is a cheerful person.

Suppose you are a lotus plant. At first, you may resent the filthy muck in which you find yourself. But later you will realize it was because of that muck that you could bud and bear beautiful blossoms.

Likewise, when you consider your adverse circumstances as good influences, you are on the road to your human revolution. As long as members of a family, an organization or a community each act out of egoistic motives, there will be gulfs between them. Only when one purifies his life to where he desires not only his own happiness but also others' will a "spiritual Silk Road" be created. Soka Gakkai International President Ikeda, in a speech at Moscow State University on May 27, 1975, declared that there is a pressing need for a spiritual Silk Road connecting the minds and hearts of the peoples of the world. I think we also need a spiritual Silk Road on a smaller scale-one which connects us to our families, to our organization, and to our community.

Some members seem to believe that one who has faith should never get sick, have accidents or be robbed. They therefore begin to doubt their faith when some of their fellow members meet misfortune.

They must realize that even those with faith are bound to encounter difficulties as long as they live in this world. Difficulties are like waves of the sea. Life is, as it were, a struggle against those waves. Will we be able to ride over them or will we be engulfed by them? This depends on the strength of our faith in the Gohonzon.

Buddhism teaches that both the past and the future are contained in the present moment. Each day, each moment, is precious, for our actions from moment to moment determine the course of our lives in that we are creating a new karma. Regard the present moment not only as the effect of the past but also as a cause for the future. A person can suffer for many reasons because of his or her children, parents, spouse, lack of money, sickness, bad human relations and so on. Considering the Buddhist law of causality, however, the cause for all such problems lies within that individual's own life, although they become manifest in relation to his circumstances.

No matter how much you may thank your parents verbally for their efforts in raising you, they won't be happy as long as you keep on bullying your brothers and sisters. They would rather see you taking good care of the younger children than hear mere words of gratitude. Similarly, no matter how much you may praise the Gohonzon, if you and your members do not get along harmoniously with one another, the Gohonzon, so to speak, will not be happy.

Some members say that because their spouses oppose their faith, they cannot fully devote themselves to activities, and there is constant discord in their homes. Instead of complaining, they should regard their mates as good influences and determine to strengthen their faith. A positive attitude of this kind will enable the seed of Buddhahood within their own lives to sprout. Suppose your spouse opposes your faith. You realize that he or she does so from lack of understanding. Earnestly pray to the Gohonzon that he or she will come to understand true Buddhism and take faith in it.

Then you will find sufficient wisdom welling up within you to know exactly what you should do beyond mere expedient means. It is also important for you to show actual proof of your human revolution—in other words, to show that you are definitely changing in a positive way because of your faith. Don't forget that it is your karma to be married to someone who does not understand your faith and practice. Also, remember that while it's okay to hate a person's acts of slander, you should not hate the person himself.

The Gosho teaches, "Buddhism is like the body and society is like the shadow. When the body is crooked, so is the shadow." In terms of our daily practice, this passage means that we should make faith the basis of everything. For example, our faith is the body, and all of our problems are the shadow. It is vital, therefore, that we devote ourselves night and day to our practice of faith in Nichiren Buddhism. As we straighten up the "body" of our faith, so to speak, all aspects of our lives will gradually change for the better.

As we advance along the correct path of faith, strengthening our life force, we are step by step approaching a state of life which is filled with benefit.

Understanding the True Benefits of Faith

WHEN ONE FINDS THEMSELVES in a state of stagnation in their practice of Buddhism, it is crucial to remind oneself of the ultimate reason why they are pursuing this faith. Without a clear understanding of this purpose, it can be challenging to approach any aspect of the practice with enthusiasm.

Consider the analogy of a timid person who mistakes a dead tree for a ghost in the dark of night, and becomes consumed by fear. It is the person's own fearfulness that clouds their ability to discern reality. They are both the victim and assailant of their own fear, and thus, cannot blame the tree. Similarly, some members may be swayed by their environment due to a lack of strong faith that can recognize devilish functions for what they are.

We should approach our immediate circumstances in the context of our fundamental purpose in life, just as we view the earth in relation to the universe, rather than the other way around. It is essential to always remember why we chose to have faith in the Gohonzon and what our mission is.

The true benefits of faith are not always immediately apparent. Just as a person gradually ages from a baby to an elderly individual, the benefits of faith also accumulate over time. Continuing to practice is essential in accumulating great good fortune, even if it may not be evident from a short-range viewpoint. If you feel that there is nothing you can do to change your stubborn spouse, for example, it is important to remember that pulling a rope in a tug of war will not budge if your opponent is stronger. Rather than fighting, it is important to pray to the Gohonzon for the strength to contribute to kosen-rufu.

Similarly, good medicine may taste terrible and cause momentary discomfort but ultimately cure an illness. This analogy illustrates the importance of accepting minor losses in order to achieve significant gains. One's life's fruitfulness depends on whether it is attended by small gains and great losses or small losses and great gains. By evaluating things with this yardstick, you can accurately assess any situation. It is common for some people to feel as though benefits are not coming their way. However, by continuing to practice and maintaining faith, the true benefits will gradually reveal themselves.

Relying solely on immediate perceptions to make judgments is unreliable. Our immediate perceptions are limited, and the human eye is only capable of seeing small benefits while remaining blind to the greater ones. Therefore, in faith, having a spirit of appreciation is crucial. For instance, suppose a member gets hit by a bicycle while going to work, but only sustains a scratch. When he returns home in the evening, he expresses deep gratitude to the Gohonzon.

On the other hand, if his day ends without any incident, he may complain, "What a dull day it's been!" without realizing that meeting no accident is fortunate in itself. When we maintain our gratitude to the Gohonzon, we can easily recognize the benefits that come our way, no matter how big or small they may seem.

A Mother's Journey from Blame to Apology: A Lesson in Parenting

THE OTHER DAY I heard of the experience of a women's division member whose son had run away from home over ten years ago. This had been her greatest anxiety. Two years ago the son returned to the same prefecture in which his mother lived, but he would not come to her house. What came instead were dunning notes from the loan sharks to whom he was indebted. Day in and day out she was filled with complaint and hatred for her son, constantly blaming him and thinking, Because of that child, I have to go through all this suffering.

One day, she attended a guidance meeting. Hearing a leader talk, she realized it was she herself who had the destiny to suffer on account of her child. There and then, she profoundly regretted having borne a grudge against her son. The Gosho states, "Even a minor offense will destine one to the evil paths if one does not repent of it. But even a great slander can be eradicated if one repents of it. Why did she have to suffer on account of her child? It was because of the negative causes she herself must have made in the past. Nevertheless, she had placed the entire blame on her son. True, he might have been the immediate cause of her hardship, but the fundamental cause lay in her own karma and she had thus far been powerless to change it. All this she now completely understood.

From that day, she changed her entire attitude in faith; She chanted and chanted, apologizing to the Gohonzon for the slanders she must have committed in her past existence and for the grudge she had harbored against her child, Soon her son, after an absence of more than a decade, returned to live with her again. Also, he took faith in Nichiren Buddhism. At a meeting in his district, he publicly 'apologized and said, "I am truly sorry for all the trouble I've caused over these many years." Tears filled his eyes as he pledged to strive and develop himself.

A child will change for the better when his parent corrects his or her attitude in faith. Take this deeply to heart, and you'll be able to change your bad karma. As long as you blame the other person, thinking, "If it weren't for him, I could be happy," then he never will change. Rather, gaze into your own life and destiny, and change your attitude first. Then, much to your surprise, a change will occur in the other person according to the principle of the inseparability of life and its environment.

Achieving a Work-Life-Buddhism Balance

WHEN SOME MEMBERS ARE told they must balance work and Nichiren Buddhism activities, they may misunderstand and think that it means not devoting themselves fully to either one. They believe that Buddhism advocates for a moderate approach, which is a wrong interpretation. Let me use the experience of a group chief as an example. He was a member of the young men's division and was appointed as a group chief in the men's division. Instead of reducing his activities, he increased his involvement even more vigorously. He also ran a small factory with about a dozen employees, but in a few months, he realized that his business was not doing well. Many people would have stopped their activities until the business was rehabilitated, but he went a step further.

He resolved to exert himself all-out to rebuild his business and not to neglect activities even a bit. He earnestly chanted Daimoku so that he could do both most satisfactorily. Firstly, he divided his firm into two sections: production and business functions, for which he had previously held himself entirely responsible. He appointed one employee as head of production while he himself took charge of business. He also adopted a system of computing pay according to productivity, so that each employee performed their job with increased gusto. These new arrangements proved to be a great success. Not only did the firm's business begin flourishing again, but the group chief found even more time than before for activities.

Note that he did not choose between work and activities. He resolved to carry out both successfully with an eye to the future, and only then did he see a fresh path open before him. To reconcile work and activities is not to perform both halfway, but to perform both to the fullest extent. For this purpose, consider carefully what you should do and chant earnestly. Then wisdom will inevitably well up within you, showing you a splendid way out of your difficulty.

Overcoming Grief: A Family's Journey to Kosen-rufu

I HAVE WITNESSED COUNTLESS members experience a renewal in their lives and demonstrate remarkable proof of their human revolution, all thanks to the powerful influence of the Gohonzon. Some of these members, who dedicated themselves wholeheartedly to the cause of true Buddhism, unfortunately passed away while on the path to kosen-rufu, leaving behind a sense of deep regret among their friends. However, what brings me the greatest joy and reassurance is the fact that their bereaved families have been able to bravely overcome their grief and continue to vigorously advance towards happiness.

I would like to share the story of one such family, consisting of two sisters and a brother who lost their parents some twenty years ago. Shortly before their mother's passing, she gathered her children together and, as her final words, imparted to them the importance of never abandoning their faith in the Gohonzon, no matter what challenges they may face in the future. Despite opposition from their relatives, the three siblings persevered and continued to uphold their faith, always supporting and cooperating with each other throughout the many hardships they faced.

Today, all three siblings are actively engaged in the movement of kosen-rufu. The eldest daughter is a mother of seven, the second daughter a mother of three, and the youngest son a father of two. Each of them has built a happy and harmonious family, and I can vividly picture the smiling face of their deceased mother, proud of her children's unwavering commitment to the Gohonzon.

The Gosho teaches us, "Because of the significant benefit accruing from the revered Maudgalyayana's belief in the Lotus Sutra, he not only became a Buddha himself but his parents also attained Buddhahood." Although this passage specifically mentions Maudgalyayana, its principle applies to each of us. If a child is determined to succeed his parents in the movement for kosen-rufu and exerts himself in faith, practice, and study, he will not only attain Buddhahood himself, but his ancestors and descendants will also receive blessings.

Such a child can lead anyone related to him to happiness. For a deceased member, nothing brings greater joy than knowing his child is carrying out his mission for kosen-rufu and showing actual proof of his own happiness. This is the most significant thing a child can do for his deceased parent.

Being a Representative of Nichiren Buddhism

DO YOU RECALL THE period when anti-Japanese sentiment erupted in Southeast Asia, and several Japanese firms were burned by angry mobs? During my subsequent visit to the area, I inquired about the businesses that suffered destruction and those that did not. I learned that it was not dependent on the nature of the industry.

Some firms were spared because, when the mob was ready to set them ablaze, the neighborhood residents held them back, stating, "The Japanese employed here have never harmed us." The firms that had always maintained cordial relations with the local populace and had earned their trust were unharmed. This principle applies not only to Japanese companies overseas but also to our daily lives. In our respective communities, each of us is a representative of the Nichiren Buddhism organization.

It will be impossible to promote Buddhism widely in society if we are disliked by our neighbors or frowned upon by people in our community due to our conduct. To contribute to kosen-rufu is not just about attracting new followers and participating in Nichiren Buddhism activities. The question is whether our existence itself is an asset to kosen-rufu.

We must be citizens with good common sense who are liked and trusted by individuals in our neighborhood, community, and workplace. Please exercise extreme caution in avoiding the disgrace of the Lotus Sutra through unreasonable words, actions, or insignificant incidents. Strive to become outstanding individuals, so everyone will remark, "He is genuinely respectable. Everything about him is refreshing."

Value your connections with others and expand circles of friendship and trust in your community. Be persuaded that kosen-rufu rests in your daily actions.

From Busy to Balanced: Buddhism into Your Daily Life

TO A WOMAN WHO says she is too busy to do activities, As individuals are unique, so are their destinies and circumstances. There are children who are sickly and require much care, and there are those who are healthy and easy to raise. Some husbands are understanding, and others are not. You say you are busy taking part in the affairs of your neighborhood association and practicing Japanese dance. Why are you doing all this? I'm sure it's because you want to contribute even a little to society and also to improve yourself. Therefore, you have no alternative but to pray to the Gohonzon so that each day you will divide your time most effectively between Nichiren Buddhism activities and other matters which concern you.

This not implies that you should always give priority to Nichiren Buddhism activities, second to your dance and third to the neighborhood association. Circumstances differ from day to day. You must decide each day what to do first and what to do second, third and so on in order to complete all of them effectively. Once at a daytime meeting, a stay-at-home parent sought my advice.

Her husband violently opposed her faith. Before leaving for the meeting, she had told him she was going to visit a friend. There was a chapter leaders' meeting scheduled for that evening, but she had not mentioned it to him out of fear of his reaction. She was a group women's chief. If she failed to appear, her chapter women's chief might be disappointed in her.

On the other hand, if she attended the meeting, she would be home much later than she had said. Her husband would find out that she had been to a meeting and fly into a rage. "What should I do?" she asked. "Should I take part in the meeting, or should I go home straight from here so my husband won't say anything? This is one of those questions which leaders find themselves at a loss to answer. I replied this way: What if I told you to go to the leaders' meeting because it is your duty as a group women's chief? Your body would be at the meeting, but your mind would not. All the while you would think, 'My husband is probably home by now. He'll be furious when I come back. What excuse can I give?'

On the other hand, what if I said, Since you didn't mention the scheduled meeting to your husband, go straight back, Your family is more important. Don't worry about the meeting'? Physically you would be at home, but mentally you would worry about not fulfilling your chapter responsibilities. Whichever the case, your body would be in one place while your mind would be in another. Nor can you solve the problem by staying halfway between your home and the meeting site. So, you see, I cannot answer your question one way or the other. "The important thing is for you to consider where your problem originates. It comes from your lack of courage from your failure to mention the meeting to your husband.

You only worry about immediate results without reflecting on your own weakness. You may say, 'I keep every activity a secret from my husband. If I told him, he would make my life unbearable.' But that's not the correct attitude to take. Suppose you have an important meeting to attend. If you mention it to your husband, He will be angry. So you slip out stealthily. Later, he finds out and becomes furious. Next time you leave even more furtively. When you return, he will be even more furious than before. This is a vicious circle. It only widens the gap between you and your husband. The trouble is that you try to avoid looking at your karma and instead just make up some story so that you can sneak out. You practice Buddhism so that you can change your karma.

Therefore, you should never try to avoid or gloss over the actual problems you face in life. Instead, bring forth your courage and attack your problems directly by chanting fervently to the Gohonzon so that you can change that karma. At times, you may think that, that is the long way around, but it is actually the shortest and fastest way to change your whole life steadily and surely, one step at a time.

First, understand that you yourself must enhance your character of faith to the point where your husband will respect your Buddhist practice and eventually embrace it himself. Then tell him honestly you have a meeting scheduled. If he gets violent about it, you need not go. But don't use this as an excuse to neglect your practice. Rather, call to your mind the Gohonzon and the teaching that no prayer will go unanswered. Fervently pray to the Gohonzon so that your husband also will take faith. At the same time, be sure to fulfill your responsibilities in the relationship.

Determine that you have no alternative but to chant Daimoku in order to change your destiny for the better. In this way, you can eventually win your husband's understanding. The same holds true for you. You see only superficial circumstances and cannot look at your own destiny. Remember that we practice our faith in order to bring about a fundamental change in our destiny. If you are to succeed, you must not try to evade the problem confronting you. Muster your courage, squarely grapple with your problem, and pray and pray to the Gohonzon until you solve it.

It may seem to take a long time, but this way you are slowly but steadily advancing toward your change of destiny. As long as you say you cannot engage in activities for this or that reason, you cannot make progress. You have a past-oriented attitude; You are always stressing the way things have been up till now and not the way they should be. Now you are too busy to do Nichiren Buddhism activities and handle all the other things you have to do.

It is precisely for this reason that you should devotedly chant Daimoku, praying that you will use your time most effectively and perform both Nichiren Buddhism activities and other necessary affairs perfectly. That is what our faith is for, isn't it? Sometimes members say, "My company is now in its busiest season. Stacks of bills are falling due. I've got to work till late every night.

I'll start activities as soon as I have some spare time." They are like someone with an injured leg who, when urged by consulting a doctor, replies, "I'll go see one when I'm able to walk again." Some people laugh when they hear this, but when it comes to their own affairs, they say, "I'll begin doing activities when I get out of my financial straits and have some time to spare." That's putting the cart before the horse. If someone doesn't have enough money and has no free time, it follows that he lacks both good fortune and sufficient vital life force.

It is exactly for this reason that individuals in this situation must devote themselves to the practice of faith. In your own ease, always consider how you can carry out both Nichiren Buddhism activities and other matters, and pray to the Gohonzon for the best solution. Then act wisely as each day and each situation demand.

How Problems Help us Grow

TO A LEADER WHO left the organization because of conflicts with other leaders. The only place that a lotus can bloom and grow thick, healthy roots is in the mud and slime of a lotus pond. If the lotus hated its dirty pond and snuck away to some school swimming pool, how could it ever bloom? What would happen to its roots? People may complain of all kinds of troubles in life, but it's only because of such difficulties that you can attain your human revolution. This is the principle of changing poison into medicine. If you clean the mud out of the pond and pave it with concrete, what'll happen to the lotus? It'll never bloom.

The pond represents our problem-filled world; the lotus is you and the mud is your problems the indispensable nourishment for your human revolution, your own growth. No matter how muddy or dirty its pond is, the lotus can still bloom beautifully.

Therefore, in order to attain your human revolution, stay in the pond and struggle to grow right in that mud. In other words, without all kinds of difficulties and problems in life, you can't really grow as a human being. The organization may do something you don't agree with, but that doesn't mean you have to get out. Your effort to overcome those difficulties makes you grow. But whatever you do to overcome them should be based on sincere Daimoku to the Gohonzon.

Otherwise, you will neither change your karma nor achieve any lasting success.

In order to change your karma, you have to bring forth strong vitality and establish an unshakable self amid this troubled, mundane world. With consistent efforts, you can bring the beautiful flower of your human revolution to bloom. You might still feel that your particular pond is so deep and dirty that you'll never be able to reach the surface. Maybe the seed of your human revolution is buried deeper than those of other people. However, the deeper and the dirtier the pond, the larger and the more beautiful the lotus flower when it blooms. Never run away again.

Instead, chant lots of Daimoku to the Gohonzon. Apologize to the Gohonzon for having tried to escape from the pond, and pledge to become an individual who can really contribute to kosen-rufu. Always remember the principle of the lotus flower.

Financial Problems as Opportunities

When providing individual guidance, a leader should not only focus on the immediate problem, but also strive to help the individual establish a correct attitude in their faith. In situations where two parties are involved, it is important to avoid taking sides and being swayed by the words of only one party. Providing guidance that favors one party could result in resentment from the other, making the problem even more complex.

As we strive for human revolution, we will inevitably encounter various challenges and problems. However, it is important to remember that a seed cannot sprout unless it is covered with dirt. In this analogy, the seed represents our internal cause, while the dirt represents the external cause. Just as a plant's seed requires dirt in order to sprout, each of us has the seed of Buddhahood implanted within us, which requires external challenges and difficulties in order to grow.

As leaders providing guidance, we must remember to approach problems with a balanced and unbiased perspective, and to help those we guide develop a correct attitude in their faith. We should encourage them to see problems as opportunities for growth and transformation, and to view external challenges as essential nourishment for their internal development. Through this approach, we can support others in realizing their potential and cultivating their own human revolution.

In Buddhism, the external cause that allows the seed of Buddhahood to sprout is called a "good friend" or a "good influence." This good influence may take many forms, such as disease, troubles with one's children, and sometimes financial problems.

Let's focus on financial problems for a moment. A rich person worries about the money they lend, while a poor person worries about the money they borrow. The important thing is whether these individuals can use their respective problems as a catalyst for their human revolution. When money troubles arise between members, it is important not to approach such problems solely from the standpoint of who is to blame, the lender or the borrower. Instead, it is crucial to provide proper guidance in faith so that they can reflect upon their attitude towards money.

For the lender, it may be necessary to remind them that lending money out of a lack of confidence is not true mercy, but rather "small mercy." Encourage them to have faith in the Gohonzon instead of relying on their wealth. For the borrower, it is important to encourage them to depend on their own efforts and the Gohonzon instead of relying on someone else's wallet.

Moreover, when faced with these problems within the organization, it is important to view them as opportunities to transform negative karma into positive. Avoid blaming members and instead provide considerate guidance in faith, which will help to strengthen their faith and foster growth. Chanting Daimoku earnestly can help to transform this poison into medicine.

In rare cases, financial problems may become so severe that it is necessary to remove a member from their position. However, it is crucial to remember that this is not a punitive measure. It is essential to provide compassionate guidance and encouragement to help the individual reflect on their faith, chant Daimoku earnestly, and eventually resume their position.

When providing guidance, it is important to remember to not only address the immediate problem but also devote heart and soul to helping the individual establish a correct attitude in faith. Be careful not to be swayed by one party's perspective in a dispute, as this could lead to resentment from the other party. Ultimately, through many experiences, both those who give guidance and those who receive it will strengthen their faith and make further growth.

The Gohonzon: The Only Reliable Support in Life

I ONCE HAD A conversation with a housewife seeking advice about her husband's undependable nature. She shared that he had closed down the small restaurant he had run for many years and had since failed in every job he took on. I explained to her that men are not born to be leaned upon by women. It's not wise to depend on someone who is not dependable themselves. At times, we can't even rely on ourselves, so how can we expect others to be reliable? Although your husband may not like hearing this, it's the reality. Let's consider a hypothetical situation where your husband is dependable. What if he falls ill, fails in his business, or worse, dies prematurely? You would have no one to rely on.

The only reliable support in life is the Gohonzon. Your husband is not someone to lean on, but someone to relate to with love. The same goes for children. You raise them out of love and not for any ulterior motive.

As people grow older, some of them may turn to their children for support. However, when they feel let down, they become resentful and complain about it. They may have raised their children with the expectation of receiving care in their old age, rather than out of genuine love. This is not the right attitude for parents to have. Instead, it is essential to chant to the Gohonzon and pray that your husband will become an invaluable asset to the movement for kosen-rufu and that your children will grow up to be fine adults. Keep chanting until your prayers are answered. These prayers will be conveyed to your husband and children, and their hearts will be enriched, causing them to protect you. This is the true meaning of love.

The same principle applies to personal relationships within the Nichiren Buddhism organization. The chapter women's chief should not rely on the chapter chief. When leaders and members of various divisions work together with the Gohonzon at the center of their activities, unity and harmony will arise naturally within their chapter. A man who dominates everyone at home makes his family miserable and hostile towards him. If he shows concern for them and fulfills his responsibilities, praying that they will all contribute to the movement for kosen-rufu, his wife and children will respect and love him. The same holds true for the leader of our organization.

A Story of Triumph Over Adversity

I'D LIKE TO SHARE with you a story about a young woman in a certain overseas country who was a member of the young women's division. When she was in junior high school, her father left the family, leaving her mother anguished. However, her mother found solace in Nichiren Buddhism, and the daughter, deeply moved by her mother's earnestness, started chanting Daimoku with her every day. Just three months later, the father returned home. Moreover, through his wife and daughter's sincere efforts to spread the Daishonin's Buddhism, he began practicing too. Fast forward ten years, and the daughter has become an excellent leader of the young women's division in her country, while her mother is active as a leader of the women's division.

I once had the opportunity to meet this young woman, and I said to her, "To you, your father was a good influence. You should not hold ill feelings towards him, but instead, be grateful to him. If he had not left, your mother would not have found faith in Buddhism, and neither would you. In that case, you could not possibly have achieved your current state of life." I continued, "Without the

Gohonzon, you might have blamed your father for making your mother unhappy and harbored hatred towards him for the rest of your life. However, faith in the Gohonzon can transform hate into gratitude and turn it into a catalyst for your personal growth. This is the greatness of the Gohonzon's power." She nodded in agreement, saying, "I completely understand now."

It is said that beautiful lotus flowers blossom in muddy swamps. Suppose you are one of those flowers. At first, you may find the mud repulsive, but upon reflection, you realize that it's because of that mud that you could grow and blossom. Then, you understand that you should not resent the mud. Similarly, if you regard all your circumstances, no matter how adverse, as positive influences and persist with pure and strong faith, you will never fail to find a way out of your troubles. Be firmly convinced of this and strive even more to deepen your faith.

The Correct Way to Practice Faith

When practicing faith, it's important not to fall into the trap of habitual behavior. We must renew our determination and approach each day with a fresh, positive mindset. You may encounter obstacles that make it difficult to participate in activities, such as work responsibilities, financial strain, household chores, or taking care of children. However, these challenges are opportunities to chant Daimoku more earnestly and apply your Buddha's wisdom to improve your circumstances.

Just as an employee cannot receive payment without showing up to work, our practice of faith requires active engagement. We cannot expect to gain a month's worth of benefit from thirty days of sporadic activity, nor can we gain three days' worth of benefit from only three days of practice. This idea is illustrated in the Gosho story of a woman who sold her hair and burned a small amount of oil as an offering to the Buddha. Despite the humble nature of her offering, it continued to burn throughout the night while the lavish lamps donated by the wealthy were extinguished by the wind.

No matter how busy or financially strapped we are, we must commit to finding even a small amount of time to fight for kosen-rufu and repay our gratitude to the Gohonzon. This effort is a significant cause for accumulating good fortune. Even if we have a demanding job or travel often for work, we can create the same value as a full week's worth of activities by chanting Daimoku and focusing on our Buddhist practice during the limited time available to us. Eventually, we will reach a state of life where we can devote as much time as we please to our activities.

Although all living things possess the Buddha nature, it requires a good influence to manifest itself. This influence may come in the form of a good teacher or external circumstances. In our everyday lives, we face various worries and troubles, such as relationship issues, health problems, financial difficulties, and more. However, by chanting Daimoku and engaging in Shakubuku, we can transform these challenges into a springboard for our human revolution. Instead of using obstacles as an excuse to avoid activities, we can view them as opportunities for growth and development. This is the correct way to practice faith.

Don't Wait for the Perfect Time

SOME MEMBERS MAY EXPRESS that they are too busy to participate in activities, believing that they will join when they have fewer work obligations. As leaders, we understand their situation, but simply sympathizing with them is not enough guidance. It's similar to someone with an injured leg refusing to see a doctor because they can't walk. We must encourage them to pray wholeheartedly, even in the face of financial or work-related pressure, and strive to participate in activities, no matter how infrequent.

I once met a jeweler whose wife was a dedicated member, but he himself wasn't participating in any activities. When I asked him about it, he said he had to work late every day. I reminded him that he had at least one day off each month and encouraged him to pray fervently that he could devote himself to activities on his day off. I advised him to live up to that determination and grow in faith. He eventually realized that his attitude toward faith was wrong and started participating in activities as much as his work permitted. Today, he is one of the top leaders in a ward in Tokyo.

As leaders, it's essential not to merely sympathize with our members' difficulties but to help them call forth their powers of faith and practice. By encouraging them to pray wholeheartedly and strive to participate in activities, even in the face of obstacles, we can guide them to grow in their faith. Remember this when giving guidance to your members.

The Warning Signs of Faith

SOME OF YOU MAY feel frustrated and wonder why other members are receiving wonderful benefits from the Gohonzon while your prayers go unanswered. But don't worry, if you rectify your attitude, benefits will come your way. Consider this: if you have an accident and escape with only a minor injury, you may be contented with the fact that your practice saved you from a disaster. However, such an attitude is too easygoing for true faith. While it is natural and proper to feel gratitude towards the Gohonzon for protection, sometimes minor mishaps can be warnings from the Gohonzon to strengthen your faith and be more careful.

A slight misfortune can often be a precursor to a catastrophe, so take the Gohonzon's warning seriously and reawaken your faith. Imagine a child lying in bed in the morning, ignoring his mother's repeated requests to get up. When she finally explodes in frustration, the child may wonder if he is being punished due to his bad karma. However, such questions can wait until after he gets up. Similarly, it is wise to use illness or accidents as opportunities to re-examine and improve your practice, and to further strengthen your faith. Not every setback means that something is wrong with your faith, but it's important to take advantage of these moments to enhance your practice.

Some time ago, a woman sought guidance from me about her husband's illness. She explained that during a chest X-ray, a shadow appeared, causing concern. At that time, her husband was not practicing Buddhism sincerely, but this warning prompted him to take his practice more seriously. He reflected on and changed his attitude towards faith. Sometime later, during another chest X-ray, there was no shadow at all, much to the doctor's surprise. When she first approached me, I advised her that he should apologize to the Gohonzon for his lack of sincerity and pledge to the Gohonzon to do his best to contribute to kosen-rufu.

The shadow in the X-ray served as an alarm clock, warning him when he was not sincere in his faith. But once he was awakened, it ceased to ring, and its existence became unnecessary. Nichiren Daishonin states in the Gosho that illness can be an opportunity to grow in faith. He adds, "Your husband's disease may well be the merciful consideration of the Buddha." A mishap can also serve as a warning, telling us that "There is something you need to understand. Strengthen your faith so you can find out what it is." It is essential to correct our attitudes wherever necessary and renew our commitment to developing our faith. As long as we keep our "eyes of faith" wide open, we will eventually be able to solve our problems, transforming them into impetus for growth.

Having faith does not give us an excuse to be careless or take things for granted. If you have been adopting an easy-going attitude, then it is time to change it. Be strict with yourself, live your life wisely, and receive significant benefits that can reduce your karmic retribution. One day, you will look back with gratitude and say, "That was undoubtedly an excruciating experience, but it is precisely because of that hardship that I became who I am today."

Inspiring Inactive Members to Return

HOW CAN YOU HANDLE those members or friends who have stopped practicing? The best approach is to continue to offer patient guidance, tailored to their individual situation. People are unlikely to be motivated to act simply based on your words. If words alone were sufficient, you could just record a senior leader's guidance on tape and have inactive members listen to it. In that case, there would be no need for so many leaders. But, of course, this would not be effective. Why? Because guidance is not just about the words used, but also about the sincerity, enthusiasm, and overall personality of the person offering guidance, as well as the content of what is being said. All of these elements express one's compassion. Keep giving guidance patiently until your compassion has a profound impact on the person's life. If you fail the first time, don't give up, try again.

If you still don't succeed, visit the member a third, fourth, and so on, with appropriate intervals in between. The frequency of your visits or the content of your conversations is not as important as the compassion and enthusiasm you demonstrate in your attempts to help the person awaken. The benefits you receive do not depend on whether the other person resumes their practice. Paying them frequent visits and speaking to them earnestly is, in itself, fulfilling the Buddha's work.

It's often said that the best way to give guidance is by leading through our own example of the human revolution. However, the truth is that we ourselves are still in the process of our own human revolution. If we had to be perfect before guiding others, we might never be able to do so. Think of this as being a parent to a child. If parents had to set a perfect example for their children, very few would be qualified to be parents at all. But faith can compensate for our lack of perfection.

When you pray fervently and compassionately that your loved ones will practice Buddhism earnestly, your prayer can touch their hearts. The same principle applies to individual guidance. Your compassion for the other person and your prayer that they will resume their practice can activate their Buddha nature. If you feel challenged because of a particular member, try not to see it as a superficial problem. As a district leader, you can use these challenges as food for your own growth.

By grappling with these problems head-on, you can create good causes and accumulate good fortune, thereby changing your own destiny for the better. So keep giving guidance with conviction, so that as many of your members as possible can be awakened to the greatness of faith.

The Power of Home Visits

I OCCASIONALLY HEAR LEADERS express their frustration at their inability to offer guidance effectively. However, in the early stages, everyone faces difficulties in mastering this skill. It takes time and practice to become a master at anything, and this is especially true for giving guidance in faith. Spending months or years in the endeavor or having plenty of free time does not guarantee success. The key is to awaken your eagerness to learn and then master the fundamental principles of giving guidance in faith.

Regardless of the problem, whether it's a mother worrying about a child who refuses to go to school or a wife anxious about her husband who won't take faith, the principles of giving guidance remain the same. Once you have learned and internalized these principles, you can apply them to any situation. Giving guidance is an act of mercy, and it also helps you grow as a human being.

It's common to hear leaders express their struggle to give guidance. But just like any skill, giving guidance requires practice and eagerness to learn. Mastery does not come overnight, nor does it come from simply spending time practicing. What's important is that you awaken your eagerness and learn the fundamental principles of giving guidance in faith.

Whether it's a mother worried about her child's schooling or a wife anxious about her husband's lack of faith, the principles of giving guidance remain the same. Once you understand these principles, you can apply them to any problem. Giving guidance is an act of mercy that also helps you grow as a human being.

However, it's important to remember that you can't grow in faith just by receiving guidance. You need to accumulate your own experiences. It's like teaching your child to ride a bike. No matter how much you explain the technique, they won't truly learn until they get on the bike and practice, even if they fall down a few times. Similarly, helping your members tackle and resolve their own problems will give you valuable experience that you can apply to other similar problems.

Even if only a few of your members are active, don't be disheartened. While it's important to try and awaken inactive members, it's just as important to consider how to further develop those who are already active. For example, if your group has ten members, and only three are active, you can ask each of those three to take care of one inactive member. This will give them their own roles to play and make them even more enthusiastic about activities. If the initial combinations don't work out, you can always change them around. Try any methods you can think of to strengthen your group. And remember, even members with problems are precious because they can help you change your destiny.

Occasionally, a visit to a member may not resolve problems and can leave you feeling discouraged. It can be disheartening to call on a member who has stopped practicing and receive no response. However, it is important not to carry your frustration with you to your next destination, assuming that the next person won't understand either. You must call forth your faith and dispel your sense of disappointment, determined to succeed without fail. Everyone has worries, and providing convincing guidance requires discerning the problem and giving encouragement.

In my experience, a leader who only gives guidance at meetings without making home visits risks creating ill feelings among their members due to a lack of communication. On the other hand, a leader who frequently visits and takes good care of their members will experience steady personal growth. I urge you to fully exert yourselves in your activities, praying that each of your members will advance vigorously toward the goal of kosen-rufu.

Building Unity in Your District

Unity is crucial in any organization. As a young district leader, it is your responsibility to ensure that your district remains harmonious. The first step to achieving this is to encourage the members of each group to support their respective leaders. You should not attempt to play a central role, but instead assist the group leaders in carrying out their activities. By doing so, all the group leaders, including those who are older than you, will come to unite with you at the center.

During home visits, it may be helpful to bring along a group leader or a member who is older than you, depending on the circumstances. The presence of senior members can be an invaluable asset that facilitates district activities. If you are unsure about what guidance to give a member, you can ask one of your senior leaders to accompany you. However, be careful not to depend on your senior leaders for help all the time, or you will not grow or develop your capabilities. Remember, you are the one responsible for building a firm basis for your district.

Unity is crucial in an organization, and it is the responsibility of every leader to maintain it. By encouraging group leaders and supporting them, you can help your district remain harmonious. Additionally, the presence of senior members can be helpful during home visits, but be sure to develop your own capabilities as a leader. With these actions, you can build a strong foundation for your district and ensure its continued success.

As a relatively young district leader, you must take necessary steps to ensure harmony in your district. Firstly, you should encourage group leaders to unite and support their leader. Avoid playing the central role yourself, but always assist group leaders in carrying out their activities. By doing so, all the group leaders, even those older than you, will come to unite with you at the center.

During home visits, it may be wise to bring along a group leader or a member who is older than you, depending on the circumstances. The presence of elder members is invaluable and can facilitate district activities. If you find yourself at a loss on how to guide a member, ask one of your senior leaders to go with you. But do not rely too heavily on your senior leaders for help, as it may impede your personal growth and development. Remember, you are responsible for building a strong foundation for your district.

Work in harmony with the group leaders, keeping in mind the importance of guiding members who have not been practicing and those who may harbor ill feelings toward other members. As a district leader, you should not lord it over other leaders and members. Nichiren Buddhism is an organization where members give and receive guidance, not exercise authority.

If a father tries to force his children to obey by using parental authority, they will resist him. Education specialists state that children seek a counselor, not a tyrant, in their father. Similar principles apply to personal relationships within a district. Refrain from flaunting your position as a district leader, even if your words are not overbearing. If you tend towards authoritarianism, it will show in your behavior, and some members may be difficult to convince.

Persist in giving guidance, keeping in mind that the growth of your human revolution is linked to your members' growth. Consider their respective situations and how you can make it easier for them to participate in activities and give them proper advice. By doing so, any gap between you and your members will close.

The Art of Giving Guidance

AT TIMES, MEMBERS MAY harbor negative feelings towards one another, such as resentment towards their chapter chief for being too strict or their district women's chief for being bothersome. Nobody wants to be disliked or create conflict. Instead, everyone desires to be known as a good and respectable person. If you wish to avoid criticism from your members, it is important to provide guidance in a kind and respectful manner. For example, during a visit, if a member admits to not regularly performing Gongyo due to a busy schedule, you could respond with understanding and say, "I see. Please do Gongyo whenever you have time. Goodbye." Similarly, if a member expresses a dislike for studying Buddhism, you could encourage them to try and say, "If you ever feel inclined to study, please give it a try."

While speaking in a gentle tone is important for building positive relationships with members, it is not always enough to make them happy. In order to truly benefit them, you must speak in different ways depending on the situation. Sometimes this may require a more direct approach or even stern guidance. When I first began my practice, I believed that Nichiren Buddhism had a monopoly on the theory of negative effects. However, upon closer examination,

I realized that mothers often use this theory more than anyone else. They are constantly reminding their children of the negative consequences that may result if they do not behave appropriately.

it is important to speak to members in a way that is both kind and effective. This may involve using a variety of approaches, including gentle and firm guidance. By doing so, you can create a positive and productive relationship with your members while still providing them with the guidance they need to grow and benefit from their practice.

"If you run out into the street, you'll be hit and killed by a car." "You'll have a stomach-ache if you eat so much." "Be careful of the kettle, or you'll get scalded." Looking back, we can appreciate that we survived safely because our mothers warned us against doing certain things. If we let babies do whatever they please, they won't survive. Parents scold their children because they want them to grow up to be fine people. They would never admonish them if they didn't care what became of them. However, there is a difference between reprimanding children with their well-being in mind and scolding them out of frustration or emotion. The same holds true when giving guidance.

If we lack sincere concern for our members' happiness, they will not take our guidance to heart, no matter how cleverly phrased it may be. Members will benefit if they can take their leaders' guidance not emotionally but as advice given for their own sake. When we were children, our parents probably scolded us now and then. At the time, it may have felt miserable to be a child. But as we grow older and have our own children, we begin to appreciate why our parents scolded us. This also applies to leader-member relationships. Take, for instance, members who resent their chapter chief for being too severe. They should understand that, aside from whether he expresses himself tactfully, he gives them advice because he wants them to be happy.

Although a member may feel resentful when given severe guidance by their leader, they will ultimately be more grateful when they come to fully understand the greatness of faith. It is common to view district women's chiefs as annoying, but those who eventually take on this role will come to realize how sincere their predecessors were. I, too, fiercely opposed faith before finally embracing it. However, once I recognized the greatness of Buddhism, I regretted not having joined earlier and even reproached the person who first introduced me, saying, "If only you had been more insistent, I could have joined much sooner."

To help new members understand faith, we must take good care of them, teaching them how to do Gongyo and studying the Gosho together with them. Our duty is to bring happiness to both our members and ourselves. True happiness lies in making this determination and putting it into practice. I urge you to engage in giving guidance pleasantly and confidently, always keeping your members' well-being in mind.

The Dangers of Complaining

ONCE, A MEMBER OF the men's division told me, "My illness has improved considerably, but I have not yet completely recovered." Hearing this, I told him that the word "but" is often used in complaining. I explained to him that unless he stops complaining, he will not receive any more benefits. Furthermore, if he thanks someone or praises them and then follows it with a "but," it cancels out the praise or thanks altogether.

To illustrate my point, I gave him an example. I said that if someone serves him tea or coffee and he says, "You served me a cup of tea, but you failed to give me a second cup," it would be very rude. Instead, if he says, "This is superb tea. Could I have another cup, please?" the host will gladly comply with his request. Similarly, it is impolite to the Gohonzon to follow thanks with a "but." I advised him to first thank the Gohonzon for his improvement and then pray for a complete recovery.

The man replied, "I understand. From today on, I'll never say 'but.'" I responded, "Of course, you won't. But what are you going to do about all the 'buts' you've said until today?" This is where most members seem to have difficulty understanding. I used an example of a person who steals things from others and apologizes for it, promising not to do it again. However, unless they return what they stole, their apology is not enough to compensate for their wrongdoing.

In the Gosho, it is written, "Even a minor offense will destine one to the evil paths if one does not repent of it. But even a great slander can be eradicated if one repents of it." Another passage also states, "These people seemed to have repented, but apparently they had not repented profoundly enough." Repentance alone is not enough to erase misdeeds, action and practice are also required. The law of cause and effect is uncompromising - if you steal, you must return what you took; if you mistreat others, you will receive ill treatment in return.

These are the teachings of Buddhism. It is vital that you make a pledge to the Gohonzon that from this day forward, you will do your best in every aspect of your life and remain true to your word.

Understanding the Causes of Suffering

IT'S COMMON FOR EVERYONE to have worries, whether it's troubles with spouses, children, or sickness. The purpose of faith is to address the underlying causes that bring about such suffering. Merely changing the effect won't lead to an improvement in the situation.

As the Gosho states, "If you try to treat someone's illness without knowing what the cause of the illness is, you will only make the person sicker than before." Every problem is an effect, which means there was an internal cause and an external cause that worked together to bring about that effect. An internal cause alone won't produce an effect, nor can an external cause create an effect by itself. It's like a seed that needs both the internal cause (seed) and external cause (water) to sprout.

Since worry is an effect, there must be both internal and external causes that have combined to produce that effect. However, many people fail to realize that the fundamental cause lies within themselves and instead blame others for being obstacles. For example, if you're troubled by a tyrannical husband or a defiant child, why did you marry such a man or bear such a child? It's because you have the destiny to suffer because of your husband or child. Until you understand this, you won't be able to understand Buddhism either.

The cause of your present suffering is rooted in the past. It's possible that you hurt your spouse or child in a past life (cause), which is why you are now experiencing pain at their hands (effect). This understanding is critical. Once, a senior leader gave guidance to a member who had a child with polio. Was the member suffering solely because of the child? No, the child was just the external cause. The member also had the karma, or internal cause, to have a sick child in their family. The member was the one experiencing agony and seeking release. If they strengthened their faith and practice, they could change their destiny and resolve their troubles.

I once had a woman come to me seeking guidance. Her husband had been diagnosed with cancer, and she had been fervently praying to the Gohonzon for his recovery. Unfortunately, his condition had not improved. "I suspect your husband's practice is rather weak," I told her. It's natural to want your spouse to recover, but praying for the recovery of someone who doesn't practice is like praying for someone who refuses to eat to be full and satisfied. If we could benefit without practicing, few of us would practice earnestly. We could just ask someone else to chant on our behalf.

Strictly speaking, you cannot change your husband's karma. However, you can change your bad karma that causes you to suffer because of his illness. Pray for your husband to be motivated by his illness to practice sincerely and become a person who can contribute to kosen-rufu in some way. This should be your attitude. You should earnestly pray to the Gohonzon, apologize for any past negligence, and pledge to strive even more from now on.

The correct way to practice faith is exemplified by the following story. After realizing her shortcomings in regards to her faith, a woman began offering sincere prayers to the Gohonzon. As a result of her devotion, her husband's health began to gradually improve, to the point where he could spend weekends at home. The doctor was surprised to see such significant improvement, unaware that the husband was chanting Daimoku.

The woman continued to pray sincerely and reflect on her past attitude towards her faith, leading to further improvement in her husband's condition. Within a month, he had made significant progress, and the doctor was impressed by his patient's recovery. The doctor even asked what kind of food the patient was consuming at home.

This story reminds us that the key to overcoming our problems lies in changing our own karma. We must reflect on our past actions and attitudes, and practice faith with sincerity and devotion to bring about positive change in our lives.

Inconspicuous Benefits of Faith

SOMETIMES WE MEET PEOPLE who claim, "I've been chanting, but I'm not getting any benefits." However, if we earnestly practice our faith, it is absolutely impossible not to receive any benefits. We must not evaluate the Gohonzon's power solely through our limited vision. The eyes of common mortals are unreliable because we can only see immediate benefits, and we cannot perceive the profound ones. For example, if we get into a serious traffic accident but come out with only minor injuries, we offer our heartfelt gratitude to the Gohonzon. However, when we return home safe and sound after an uneventful day, we grumble, "Nothing good happened to me today." This is how common mortals behave.

When we recover from an illness, we feel overjoyed at receiving a benefit. However, when we go five or ten years without falling ill, we forget to thank the Gohonzon. We fail to realize how blessed it is to remain healthy for such a long time.

In other words, we often overlook the Gohonzon's power unless we experience an accident, fall ill, or face some other difficulty. Which benefit is greater: to encounter misfortune and overcome it or to avoid any misfortune whatsoever? Clearly, the latter is far superior. Buddhism uses the term "conspicuous" to describe readily visible but small benefits and "inconspicuous" to describe invisible but significant benefits. Small benefits are easy to notice, but the great benefits take time before we realize their magnitude. What does an inconspicuous benefit look like? Let me offer an analogy. It may be difficult to imagine now, but I was quite attractive when I was younger. Each morning, I woke up looking the same as I had the day before.

For days, months, and years, nothing seemed to change in my appearance. However, today, I look vastly different from when I was a boy, at least regarding my head. My thick and beautiful hair did not suddenly disappear overnight. Although this anecdote illustrates the concept of inconspicuous benefits, it is not my personal example of such benefits. The point is that you should understand that great things are happening as long as you maintain your faith sincerely, even if you cannot recognize them.

By upholding pure faith for years, such as five, ten, or fifteen, you will eventually reach a state of complete happiness that you could not have previously imagined. This is the nature of inconspicuous benefits. It is common for what appears to be a disaster at first glance to turn into a significant benefit in the long run. The Gohonzon's power, the power of the Buddha and the Law, is absolute. Whether we can summon that power or not depends on our ability to practice and have faith.

Please encourage your members to persevere and never doubt the Gohonzon's power, regardless of what may happen. They should always be confident in the enormous blessings that will arise from their practice.

Supporting Each Other

To ensure that our organization maintains harmony, it is crucial to support the person in a position of responsibility. However, supporting the leader does not equate to always following their instructions. True support also means backing every member of the group. Similarly, just as in a family, harmony cannot be achieved if both parents criticize their child, take sides against each other, or if one is stuck in the middle.

Translating this to our organization, we should not side with our leader when they criticize members, nor should we take members' sides when they criticize the leader. For instance, if you hear a member criticizing your chapter leader, it is not advisable to reprimand them, saying, "If you criticize a leader, you'll receive a negative effect." It is even worse to agree with them and say, "I understand your resentment, because I feel the same way. He's impossible to get along with." It is also unproductive to worry about the situation without taking any action.

Instead, you can respond to the member by saying, "Our chapter leader may scold us too severely or have less tolerance at times. But that's his issue. If you hold a grudge against him for it, that becomes your problem. Under no circumstances should you harbor negative feelings towards any believer or member." You should then redirect them towards the task at hand and encourage them to tackle it. It is essential to maintain harmony within the organization while allowing every member to contribute to the best of their ability.

In the same way that every family member has a unique role in the family, each member of the organization has a distinct role to perform. It is essential to comprehend and complement each other's roles to achieve a cohesive and successful organization.

The Relationship Between Problems & Happiness

Everyone faces problems in their lives, and the nature of these problems varies from person to person. You don't need to ask others about their troubles to understand their state of happiness or unhappiness - their desires provide a good indicator. Everyone has desires, but the intensity and scope of these desires can differ greatly. For example, someone who cannot afford their next meal is faced with an urgent and immediate problem that consumes their thoughts and actions.

The second president of Nichiren Buddhism, Mr. Toda, had a strong desire to help unhappy people and prevent another atomic bomb from dropping on Japan. This was his greatest wish and the problem that troubled him the most. When comparing the magnitude of Mr. Toda's worry to the worry of not being able to get supper, it is clear that the former is of greater importance.

In fact, one's problems can be seen as a yardstick for their happiness. Even Buddhas face problems - they strive to make people happy, but some individuals are resistant to their teachings. This causes them worry, but it does not necessarily mean that they are unhappy.

In conclusion, problems are a natural part of life, and the intensity and scope of these problems can vary greatly. However, it is important to remember that even great individuals face problems and that the size of one's problems can be a measure of their state of life.

I am certain that some of you may have previously focused solely on your own problems, but now find yourselves working hard to solve other people's troubles as well. This demonstrates that you have grown in your state of life and have become happier than before. We tend to feel happy when our desires are fulfilled, and troubled when they are not. Therefore, the key is to possess the power to make our wishes come true. Everyone seeks happiness, but how can we achieve it?

Parents often remind their children that diligence is essential in life. While their words are valid, it is not always the case that hardworking individuals are happy. There are many who work tirelessly but still end up in debt. Married couples are another example. I do not believe that anyone intentionally selects the worst person in the world to marry, hoping to be unhappy. Each person must have married with the belief that they were choosing the best partner on earth and must have made great efforts to establish a happy marriage.

However, do all families who strive for happiness ultimately achieve it? Unfortunately, that is not always the case. Many people lament, saying, "This is not how I intended my life to be." Parents do their best to help their children grow up to be successful adults, but some are let down in their expectations. Diligence is undoubtedly crucial, and it is necessary for achieving happiness. Imagine a person saying, "I want to make money, but I hate getting up early in the morning, and I don't want to work hard because I get tired easily." Such a person will never become wealthy. Nonetheless, diligence alone is not enough. There are unseen elements, such as fortune and karma, that only faith can alter.

At the end of meetings, leaders may warn you about the risk of traffic accidents. However, can you avoid all accidents by simply being cautious? Not necessarily. In conclusion, while diligence is essential, it is not the sole determinant of happiness. It is important to remember that there are other factors at play, and having faith can help alter them.

Suppose you are driving and see a car approaching from ahead. You may start to wonder, "Is the driver drunk? Does he have a license? Is he dozing off?" However, becoming overly cautious and constantly scanning your surroundings can be even more dangerous. While you are focused on the car ahead, another vehicle may approach from behind.

As someone who travels abroad occasionally, I am always warned by my friends to be careful of the possibility of hijacking or plane malfunction. But what kind of precaution can I take? If something were to happen, I would be powerless to prevent it. Of course, there are certain unfortunate events that we can avoid by being diligent and cautious. However, there are also problems in life that we cannot evade even with our best efforts.

This is where the power of prayer comes in. Let's say you were involved in a traffic accident. The immediate cause could have been that it was late at night and you were in a hurry to get home, or that it was dark and rainy. But ultimately, it was due to your karma. This is why it is essential to pray to the Gohonzon. By doing so, we are setting ourselves apart from those who do not embrace the Gohonzon. Faith in the Gohonzon can help us change our karma for the better and develop good fortune. It can guide us towards a happier life.

Conquering Devilish Functions

THE FUNCTIONS THAT STRIVE to alleviate people's suffering and bring happiness to their lives are referred to as the "Buddha's functions." On the other hand, the functions that hinder the Buddha's functions and bring misery to people are referred to as "devil's functions." Both of these functions exist within ourselves. One part of us urges us to act positively, while the other part discourages us because it seems too demanding. You may recall how these two functions waged a battle within you before you embraced faith.

"Should I practice?" "No, maybe not." The question is, which voice will triumph? I recall a member who persisted with the internal dialogue of "Should I practice?" and "No, maybe not" for a staggering twelve years. However, does everything fall into place once you conquer the initial obstacle? Not entirely. Even after you have faith, two opposing voices will continue to speak to you. On the day of a significant gathering, one voice urges you to attend, while the other voice insists you remain at home. Meanwhile, it begins to rain, and you eventually decide not to go.

Functions that work to alleviate suffering and bring happiness to people are referred to as "Buddha" functions, while those that hinder the Buddha functions and cause unhappiness are called "devilish" functions. However, devilish functions don't introduce themselves by saying, "I am a devil sent here by the Devil of the Sixth Heaven." They are called devils because they are not immediately recognizable as such. Therefore, if you are not watchful, you might easily become a victim of these functions.

Once, a couple visited me seeking my counsel. They brought their child with them. As soon as they sat down before me, they began to argue with each other. The husband claimed that his wife was a devil, so I told him that this meant he was married to a devil, and their child was the child of a devil. Isn't that right? As expected, he was unable to respond. In this case, neither the wife nor the child was to blame for the man's unhappiness. It was his own negativity that was the root cause.

In Buddhism, we use the term "devil" to refer to negative functions that are inherent in life. These functions manifest themselves in our daily lives. However, the devilish functions stop working when we recognize them for what they are and defeat them through fervent prayer to the Gohonzon.

Deepening Faith for Effective Guidance

Several young leaders have expressed difficulty in giving guidance to their members due to their lack of experience or because their members are older than they are. However, is experience a prerequisite for giving guidance in faith? In my opinion, it is not. Although having experience is beneficial, even those without extensive experience can still provide effective guidance. Giving guidance in faith involves sharing the Buddhist perspective on the cause of a member's problem and how they can solve it through faith.

Many people tend to blame external factors for their problems without realizing that they themselves contribute to their own suffering through their karma. As a result, they struggle to find a permanent solution to their problems. To provide guidance to such individuals, a vast range of experience is not as necessary as returning to the fundamental principles of faith and deepening one's own faith.

Giving guidance is not necessarily dependent on age or experience but rather on a deep understanding of the fundamental teachings of Buddhism and a sincere desire to help others overcome their obstacles. As we continue to deepen our own faith and apply its principles to our lives, we will be better equipped to provide guidance that can bring about lasting positive change for our members.

To give guidance in faith, one does not necessarily need to have vast experience, and it is not productive to focus on one's lack of experience as it may hinder the ability to give good guidance. Giving guidance means to explain to the member, from a Buddhist perspective, where the root of their problem lies and how they can address it through faith.

Many people tend to attribute their problems to external factors, unaware that they are the ones responsible for creating their own difficulties. By failing to recognize this, they are unable to find a fundamental solution to their problems. To guide such individuals, it is essential to return to the basics of faith and deepen one's own understanding.

For instance, when a member approaches us with a medical problem, it is not our place to advise them on the course of action they should take. Instead, we can explain the Buddhist perspective on the causes of illness and how having a strong faith can improve one's condition, regardless of the quality of medical care received. The crucial point is to make the sick member understand that their suffering stems from their own life, and the only way to change it fundamentally is through chanting Daimoku and deepening their faith.

When faced with a member's complicated problem, it can be easy even for leaders with many years of faith to only see the surface and miss the fundamental cause. It is important to avoid jumping to hasty conclusions in such cases. To younger leaders who are newly appointed, I offer one piece of advice: they should think of the members who are older than them as being under their care.

I understand that most leaders recognize that it is not appropriate to view their position in terms of a superior-subordinate relationship. However, when they express difficulty in giving guidance due to a lack of experience, it may be because they feel that they are now above their members. In Nichiren Buddhism, positions indicate responsibility, not rank or power. The higher one's position, the greater the responsibility. It is crucial not to be confused about this point.

Strengthening Faith to Overcome Illness

THE SECOND PRESIDENT OF Soka Gakkai Josei Toda once said that guidance aimed specifically at curing sickness is not the role of faith leaders. It is the responsibility of physicians to cure an illness, while our role is to provide guidance in faith. Unfortunately, some senior leaders tend to focus on discussing the treatment of disease rather than advising from the standpoint of faith. This approach provides no fundamental solution to the member who came seeking guidance.

This is not only true for illnesses but also for other specific problems. The Gosho states that if one tries to treat someone's illness without understanding the cause, it will only make the person sicker than before. Therefore, it is crucial to discern the fundamental cause of a member's problem and provide them with advice from the perspective of faith.

While there are many illnesses, some can be cured by the exercise of moderation on the patient's part, while others require medical treatment. It is not wise to rely solely on faith and refuse to consult a doctor. At the same time, it is equally foolish to depend only on physicians and ignore the necessity of changing one's karma. When one's sickness is caused by the devilish workings of their own nature or by their karma, it is a problem originating in the depths of their life and cannot be cured by medicine alone.

Regardless of the cause, strengthening one's faith is necessary to overcome it and cure the sickness. It is the responsibility of faith leaders to guide their members on this path. As leaders, we must avoid engrossing ourselves in discussions about the treatment of diseases, as it provides no fundamental solution to the member who came to seek guidance.

In conclusion, our role as faith leaders is to provide guidance in faith, not to cure illnesses. We must help our members discern the fundamental cause of their problems and provide advice from a Buddhist perspective. Whether the sickness is caused by devilish functions or karma, we must encourage our members to strengthen their faith to overcome the cause and cure the sickness.

Great Misfortune Followed by Great Good Fortune

When a member faces a serious problem, how can you help them? First and foremost, you need to have full confidence in the principle taught in the Gosho, which states, "Great misfortune is always followed by great good fortune." No matter how dire the member's situation may seem, it's crucial that you believe in this principle of the Mystic Law. If you doubt this teaching due to the gravity of their problem, then you're not truly embracing this principle.

It's important to note that the passage doesn't say, "Great misfortune is always followed by great good fortune, but super great misfortune is not." As a leader, when one of your members is facing a serious issue, you must emphasize this passage and genuinely try to convince them of the Gohonzon's power. The member's victory or defeat depends on whether they can believe in this teaching. If they can have faith in it, then all they need to do is practice exactly as the Daishonin teaches.

GREAT MISFORTUNE FOLLOWED BY GREAT GOOD FORTUNE

The key to helping a member who is facing a serious problem is to believe in the principle that great misfortune is always followed by great good fortune. You must emphasize this teaching and convince them of the power of the Gohonzon. If they can believe in it and practice as the Daishonin teaches, they can overcome any obstacle.

According to the teachings of Nichiren Buddhism, there is no problem that cannot be transformed into a source of happiness or any poison that cannot be converted into medicine. Even if someone fails in their business endeavors, as long as they maintain their faith, they will eventually recover. However, it is not uncommon for someone who experiences business failure to lose their faith as well. As leaders, we must be mindful of this and provide support and encouragement to help our members maintain their faith during difficult times.

It is also crucial to discern what each member is relying on during challenging times. When a member faces serious trouble, they may be tempted to turn to someone or something else for support. As leaders, we must guide them to rely on the power of the Gohonzon and encourage them to practice diligently. With unwavering faith, any obstacle can be overcome and transformed into an opportunity for growth and happiness.

We must remind our members that even the most challenging situations can be transformed into a source of joy and fulfillment. By maintaining faith and relying on the power of the Gohonzon, any obstacle can be overcome. As leaders, we must be attentive to our members' needs and guide them to rely on the power of the Mystic Law.

The other day, a leader came to see me in distress. It was several days before a special meeting that was scheduled to be held in commemoration of some anniversary. She was on the verge of tears as she related, "Although the meeting is drawing near, my leader will not take part in activities. I visit his house every day and prod him, but he simply will not move an inch."

I pointed out to her that she had made her leader, not the Gohonzon, the basis of her efforts. She should reflect on her attitude in trying to rely on something other than the Gohonzon. Instead, she should pray to hold as successful a meeting as any other group whose leader and assistant leader are working in harmony. I reminded her that this was the core of her problem.

If any of her members had a serious problem, she should remind them that before complaining about their predicament, they should chant and chant, no matter what may occur or what difficulty may face them. She should convince them that this, in itself, will open a way to the solution of their problem.

The Dichotomy of Benefit and Loss

When it comes to practicing faith, it's important to remain steadfast and not be swayed by external influences. Unfortunately, some individuals abandon their faith when other members encounter misfortunes such as a traffic accident or a property loss due to fire. This impetuous behavior raises concerns, as it suggests that those individuals believe that someone with faith should never experience harm, accidents, or losses. If that were the case, it would create confusion and chaos within society.

For example, if Nichiren Buddhism followers truly believed that they could never have an accident or die, they might be tempted to disregard traffic signals and rules. This type of behavior would have dire consequences and undermine the safety of all individuals on the road. Additionally, imagine asking someone their age, and they respond, "three hundred and sixty-five." While aging is a natural part of life, no human can live for three hundred years. Therefore, it's important to recognize the limitations of our existence and appreciate the time we have.

We should avoid allowing external events to influence our faith and our decision-making processes. Instead, we must remain grounded in our beliefs and understand that misfortunes and accidents can happen to anyone, regardless of their faith or religious affiliation. By doing so, we can cultivate a deeper sense of resilience and appreciation for the moments that matter in our lives.

In the practice of faith, it's crucial to avoid being influenced by external factors. Some individuals leave their faith due to incidents like a traffic accident or property loss in a fire. However, is it wise to act impulsively in such situations? Such individuals seem to believe that a person with faith should not experience any harm or loss, which would create chaos in society. For instance, followers of Nichiren Buddhism may feel that they don't need to stop at red lights because they can never get into an accident or die. But, how would a person's appearance change if they lived for three hundred years? It's important to remember that such beliefs are not true.

Refrigerators wouldn't sell well if everyone believed that faith would protect them from eating spoiled food or dying of hunger. Similarly, we cannot use faith as an excuse to avoid work, which would lead to a world filled with lazy individuals. While some members may argue that faith doesn't make a difference, we cannot define incidents as benefits or losses without considering their potential outcomes. Each event has the potential for both.

Suppose someone's house burns down, we cannot determine whether it is a benefit or loss at that moment. The crucial factor is what happens after the mishap. Will they be able to live in a better home or a wretched shack? It's important to wait and observe the situation's potential outcome. Both benefit and loss are categorized as major, medium, and minor. It's advisable to accept a minor loss if it promises a significant benefit, but avoid a minor benefit that could lead to a major loss. For instance, drinking methyl alcohol might make someone feel happy, but it could lead to blindness.

As long as we maintain our faith, we can turn any poison into medicine. It's essential to stay strong and not be defeated by any adversity or influenced by external factors. Continuously strengthening our faith enables us to transform any individual or circumstance into a positive influence that can propel us towards our happiness.

Our Lives Contain The Universe

M‍IAO L‍O ONCE SAID, "You should understand that one's life and its environment at a single moment encompass the three thousand realms. Therefore, when one attains the Buddha way, one puts oneself in accord with this fundamental principle, and one's body and mind at a single moment pervade the entire realm of phenomena."

President Ikeda elaborates on this concept in the Threefold Secret Teachings. The question posed is how a life-moment, which is infinitesimally short, can contain three thousand worlds. The answer given is that "Three Thousand Words in Every Life moment" has two meanings according to the Lotus Sutra: "to contain" and "to permeate." Each life moment contains the entire universe and continually permeates it as well. It is like a particle of dust holding the elements of all worlds in the universe, or a drop of water whose essence differs in no way from the vast ocean itself.

The vastness of the universe is contained within our lives. According to Buddhism, we inherently possess the supreme, universal life-condition called Buddhahood. Our lives permeate the universe, which means that the state of our hearts and minds is crucial. Buddhism teaches that the power of our lives can permeate the universe and change our environment for the better. To permeate and to contain encourages us to reflect on our frame of mind: Is it strong or weak? Is it empowered or lifeless? Is it expanding or shrinking? Is it pure or impure?

As Buddhists, these are crucial questions for us. We strive to improve our state of life continuously and lead a valuable and worthwhile existence. The principle of ichinen-sanzen reveals the moment-by-moment interaction between the phenomenal world and the ultimate reality of life. It teaches us that all phenomena exist within each moment of an individual's life, and every life moment contains infinite potential. The Daishonin's point is that an individual's ichinen, their life at each moment, simultaneously permeates the entire universe and encompasses all the laws and phenomena of the universe. Therefore, it is coextensive with the universe. This relationship between the microcosm of human life and the macrocosm of the universe is mysterious and marvelous.

Chanting Daimoku – Fueling the Engines Of Our Lives

NICHIREN DAISHONIN EXPLAINS THAT the Lotus Sutra is a powerful sword, but its strength depends on the one who wields it. Gongyo, a daily practice, serves as a way to purify and prepare our hearts and minds for the day ahead. It's like grooming ourselves before setting out for the day. Some people have strong engines, while others have weak ones, and the strength of our engine significantly impacts our achievements in life. By diligently practicing Gongyo and Daimoku, we can boost the power of our engine.

During Gongyo and Daimoku, our lives commune with the universe. Through our faith in the Gohonzon, Gongyo becomes an activity in which we infuse the microcosm of our individual existence with the life force of the macrocosm of the entire universe. By engaging in this practice regularly each morning and evening, we can strengthen our life force, our engine.

In his writings, Miao lo says, "Wise men can perceive the cause of things, as snakes know the way of snakes." This means that those who are wise can understand the root cause of things, just as snakes instinctively know how to navigate their surroundings.

Nichiren similarly said, "When the skies are clear, the ground is illuminated." This means that when we have a clear understanding of Buddhism, we can comprehend the meaning behind all worldly affairs. Buddhism then becomes evident in society. We can say that Buddhism is the "true entity," and society represents "all phenomena." In the same way, faith is the "true entity," and our daily life is "all phenomena." Therefore, the principle of faith manifesting itself in daily life is the principle of the true entity of all phenomena.

The essence of Buddhism lies in its application in the real world. Nichiren Daishonin, quoting T'ien-t'ai's words, "No affairs of life or work are in any way different from the ultimate reality," emphasizes that true wisdom comes not from practicing Buddhism in isolation from worldly affairs, but from fully comprehending the principles by which the world is governed. In other words, "secular matters are the entirety of Buddhism."

The term "ultimately" here means "just as they are." In other words, secular matters, just as they are, represent the essence of Buddhism. It is only in the real world that the true value of Buddhism can be demonstrated. Just as the sun instantaneously illuminates the earth, those who uphold the Mystic Law must also have a thorough understanding of secular matters. Faith ignites the sun of wisdom in our hearts, which allows us to clearly see what we need to do in order to triumph. One of the Buddha's 10 honorable titles is "Understanding of the World." The Buddha had a profound understanding of all secular affairs.

Excuses and Complaining

THE COMMON TENDENCY OF mortals is to criticize others while being oblivious to their own faults. To illustrate this point, I would like to share an example of a woman who was not very enthusiastic about her practice. She made countless excuses for her inactivity, blaming her parents for not caring enough about her education, getting married, having children, her children growing up, and having to babysit her grandchildren. She also cited her own ill health due to overwork and her husband's low salary, which required her to work to pay for their children's school fees. It is easy to criticize others for their lack of commitment, but it is important to examine our own faults and take responsibility for our own actions.

The story of a woman I once heard about illustrates a common tendency among mortals to criticize others while failing to see their own faults. This woman never showed much enthusiasm for her practice, and came up with countless excuses for her inactivity. She blamed her lack of education, her marriage, her children, their schooling, her job, and her health, among other things. Even after her children had grown up and left home, she found new excuses, such as babysitting her grandchildren.

She never realized that these reasons were all the more reason for her to pray to the Gohonzon fervently and take part in activities. She had been a young woman when she first took faith, and now she was a grandmother. Despite her excuses, she told other members that they would never accumulate good fortune if they complained. She was a classic example of someone who couldn't see their own shortcomings.

When individuals fail to pass an examination, they often attribute their failure to a lack of time to study or to the exam not covering the materials they studied. The same mindset can be observed in leaders in Nichiren Buddhism, such as senior leaders. Upon being appointed to such a position, leaders must care for many members. However, if their attitude is one of complaint, thinking "Oh, what a hard time I'm going to have," their faith is not being practiced correctly. It's unlikely that any leader joined Nichiren Buddhism specifically to become a leader. Rather, most probably joined to solve a particular problem. However, when their mission requires them to become a leader, they must pray earnestly to the Gohonzon to fulfill their responsibility, even if they feel unequipped for the task. This is the correct attitude toward faith.

People who get caught up in the past tend to complain. However, no matter how much they complain, they cannot attain enlightenment in this lifetime or achieve their human revolution. Therefore, instead of complaining, if one has spare time, it is much wiser to devote that time to chanting to the Gohonzon. With this attitude firmly established, one can lead a life full of fulfillment, shining with the glory of their human revolution. I sincerely hope that each one of you will continue your faith in the spirit of "start from now" throughout your lives.

Becoming Someone Your Husband Can Trust

I WOULD LIKE TO share with you a story about a man who was terrified by the sight of a withered tree. Walking through the darkness of night, he mistook a tall, swaying tree for a ghost and was struck with fear. However, it was his own timidity that caused his fear, and he was both the attacker and the victim. The tree had no inherent power to frighten people, and suing it would be useless. This story illustrates that solving your problem with your husband depends on your own determination.

While you feel that your husband's lack of faith is preventing you from taking part in activities, it is important to recognize that there is an internal cause within yourself. According to the principle of karma, you have the bad karma to suffer on account of your husband. To change your situation, you must face it head-on. Strengthen your faith and pray to the Gohonzon so that you can do activities together with your husband as soon as possible.

You mentioned that your husband is strong in his obstinacy, but this means that you are weak. I do not suggest that you become equally obstinate in arguing with him, but rather that you be strong in your determination to challenge your own destiny. Do not bear a grudge against your husband; become someone he can trust. By taking responsibility for your family's happiness and exerting yourself toward realizing your human revolution, your husband will eventually come to recognize the great power of the Mystic Law and take faith in it.

In conclusion, remember that your ability to solve your problem depends on your own determination. Grapple with it squarely and change your own karma. I hope this advice helps you in your journey.

Breaking Free from Negative Cycles

When people come to me for guidance, many of them express their unhappiness and tend to blame others, such as their husbands, wives, in-laws, children, leaders, or anything and everything except themselves. Rarely do they admit that their suffering is their own fault. However, every problem, regardless of its nature, is a result of a combination of internal and external causes. For instance, let's take this glass of water with sediment at the bottom. If you stir the contents, the water will become dirty. In this example, the sediment is the internal cause, and the act of stirring is the external cause.

Similarly, suppose there is a couple who constantly fights and blames each other for their problems. Each person insists that the other is to blame, just like saying that stirring the water made it dirty. However, no matter how hard you stir the water, it will remain clear if there is no sediment. Unfortunately, people often fail to recognize the internal cause and simply accuse others of stirring up the water.

In essence, many people seek guidance and express their discontent with their lives, but often place the blame on external factors such as their spouses, in-laws, children, leaders, and so on. However, they fail to recognize that the root cause of their unhappiness lies within themselves. A problem is a result of a combination of an internal and an external cause. It is akin to stirring up sediment in a glass of water; the sediment represents the internal cause while the stirring is the external cause.

In quarrels, both parties tend to blame each other, without taking responsibility for their own role in the matter. It is rare for someone to admit, "It's my fault." In a story about a woman who complained about her mother-in-law, the President of the organization pointed out that the fundamental source of the problem was not the mother-in-law, but the woman herself. Once the woman realized this, her mother-in-law's attitude towards her improved significantly.

To solve problems, one must change their bad karma. This is the essence of faith. Merely complaining about others will not solve anything. Instead, one should reflect on why they are being hurt by others. For instance, if a child is a delinquent, it is because the parent has bad karma and negative causes from the past. It is also because the parent has not taken responsibility for their own role in the situation and has been blaming the child. By changing one's bad karma and taking responsibility for their own happiness, others around them will change as well.

it is crucial to recognize that one's own bad karma causes unhappiness and to pray for it to be changed. This is the key to solving problems and leading a fulfilled life.

The Gosho teaches us that even a minor offense can lead to the evil paths if one does not repent, while even a great slander can be eradicated if one repents. Thus, it is crucial to face your problems head-on and chant sincerely to the Gohonzon, taking responsibility for any offenses or slanders you may have committed in this or previous lifetimes. However, mere chanting is not enough. You must also take action and practice to overcome your challenges. By doing so, there will be no destiny or karma that cannot be changed.

Suppose you have a debt of a million yen, and you have little money to repay it. In such a situation, you might think that it's impossible to pay off the debt. However, if someone offers to cancel the remaining debt if you pay back only a small portion, say 30,000 or 50,000 yen, then the repayment becomes relatively easy. This illustrates the principle of lessening one's karmic retribution. You must return what you have borrowed, as you are responsible for the causes you create and must receive their effects. Yet, through the blessings of your faith, you can experience the effects of your bad karma much more lightly. No matter how serious your karmic retribution may be, you can overcome it and enter the happiest state of life.

The Significance of Posture in Gongyo

THE WAY WE POSITION ourselves during Gongyo is a reflection of our faith in the Gohonzon. It is crucial to maintain a dignified and solemn posture. Keep your back straight, and express gratitude through your eyes as you gaze at Nam-myoho-renge-kyo, which is inscribed at the center of the Gohonzon. During silent prayers, bow your head naturally while keeping your palms joined. Gongyo and chanting are the foundation of our faith and the key to achieving our goal of human revolution and attaining Buddhahood in this lifetime. Therefore, it is essential to observe Gongyo with the utmost respect and sincerity. Remember this and make a conscious effort to improve your Gongyo practice.

When multiple people practice Gongyo together, it is vital to recite the sutra and chant Daimoku in complete harmony with the person leading the session. This is in line with the principle of itai-doshin (many in body, one in mind). Suppose your family practices morning Gongyo together, and your child joins in the middle of the session. In that case, they don't have to start from the beginning. The power of the Gohonzon complements the part that they missed, thanks to the fervent prayer of the parent. However, if the child develops a habit of joining in late, it would be appropriate to correct them. If they are still very young, they only have to do the remaining part and end it with the others. However, if they are in high school or older, they should follow the others until they have finished and then start from the beginning or chant Daimoku a little longer to compensate for the part they missed.

Chanting for Personal Happiness

I AM CERTAIN THAT every one of you has something that worries you. Worry usually arises when our desires and wishes are not met, and we find happiness when they are fulfilled. Conversely, we feel troubled when they are not. I recall a leader once admonishing a member, telling them not to pray for personal wishes while facing the Gohonzon. Instead, one should pray single-mindedly for the attainment of kosen-rufu. Later, the member approached me to inquire about the correctness of the guidance. Here's my take on the matter. It is true that some individuals are solely concerned with their personal wishes and desires.

However, it is essential to remind such individuals that one should pray not only for personal matters but also for the realization of kosen-rufu. Some members take a rather casual approach to their daily lives, believing that their personal problems will be automatically solved if they pray for the attainment of kosen-rufu. Such people often harbor doubts and ask, "I am always praying for kosen-rufu, why are my problems not going away?"

Perhaps you have asked yourself, "Why doesn't my personal situation improve?" A senior leader used to teach us by saying, "Suppose you put rice and water in a pot and then chant to the Gohonzon that it will cook. No matter how long you chant, you'll never get boiled rice." This was a way of refuting the mistaken idea that benefits will come to us automatically if we only chant Daimoku and make no further effort.

We chant to gain wisdom, the kind that tells us to light the stove first and to adjust the amount of water and the strength of the fire so that we can boil rice that is neither too hard nor too soft. It is true that we should sincerely pray for kosen-rufu. However, as long as we take an easygoing attitude, thinking that things will improve automatically, they rarely will. If we are to work for kosen-rufu, we must establish our own lives on a firm foundation, which we must do our utmost to construct.

It is necessary that we pray both for the attainment of kosen-rufu and for the solution of our own personal problems when we face the Gohonzon. Remember, we should not solely rely on our prayers to make our wishes come true. We need to make efforts, too, and take action to achieve our goals. By doing so, we can transform ourselves and inspire others to do the same.

The Law of Cause and Effect

KARMA IS A FUNDAMENTAL concept in Buddhism that explains our destiny. Originally, karma referred to action. Over time, it came to be understood as the destiny we create through our actions. In other words, every thought, word, and deed is a cause that creates an effect.

For instance, if we work, we get paid, and if we exercise, we become fit. Therefore, Buddhism teaches that our fate is not arbitrary or imposed by supernatural forces, but rather, we create our own destiny. As Nichiren Daishonin put it, "If you want to understand the causes that existed in the past, look at the results as they are manifested in the present. And if you want to understand what results will be manifested, look at the causes that exist in the present."

However, the workings of cause and effect are not always immediately obvious, and life may seem unfair at times. For instance, how can a selfish business person become rich, or why would a kind woman down the road have cancer? Why are people born into such different circumstances, even when they have had no chance to make the causes for it? The concept of karma is based on the understanding that life is eternal, and thus, the circumstances of our birth are determined by causes made in previous lifetimes.

While it may be difficult to accept at times, the concept of karma ultimately empowers us to take responsibility for our own lives and make the causes for a better future. By understanding the causes we have made in the past and present, we can work to create a brighter destiny for ourselves and for those around us.

The law of cause and effect is a precise and inescapable principle that governs our lives. Although we may evade societal laws, we cannot elude this fundamental law of causality, which is ingrained in our existence. It is not an unfair concept; rather, it elucidates the various circumstances of our birth. In essence, it is an optimistic philosophy since it empowers us to shape our destiny. While this law may appear moralistic, it is much more intricate than a straightforward moral code. Scientifically, cause and effect are acknowledged, but it is also understood that the effect of a cause cannot be predetermined. The outcome of a specific cause relies on numerous other factors, and it is impossible to categorize effects as either positive or negative. The woman who contracts cancer down the street may be a compassionate individual who helps others. However, she may also be intensely worried, and in her case, this anxiety may have led to the manifestation of cancer. It is, therefore, fallacious to label effects as either good or bad. Individuals who develop a fighting spirit and appreciate life more after being diagnosed with cancer are shaping their destiny through their outlook and determination. This spirit embodies the teachings of Nichiren Daishonin's Buddhism. Westerners may view karma as fatalistic and unalterable, but the opposite is true. We are empowered to seize our destiny and improve it because we bear full responsibility for our actions and, thus, their consequences.

The Nine Consciousness in Buddhism

BUDDHISM PROVIDES A COMPREHENSIVE understanding of the layers of consciousness, which plays a fundamental role in shaping our lives. There are nine layers of consciousness in Buddhism, each with a unique function. The first five levels are the senses of sight, hearing, touch, taste, and smell. These senses collect information about the world around us. The sixth level is the thinking mind, which integrates the information collected from these senses to create a cohesive understanding of our environment.

The seventh level of consciousness is where we make judgments and decisions based on the information gathered from the previous six levels. This level is where motivation and intention arise, often on a subconscious level. The eighth level of consciousness, known as alaya consciousness, is the storehouse of our karma. It is the accumulation of all our experiences, filtered through the initial seven layers of consciousness, and stored as an unconscious memory. Alaya consciousness influences our reactions and behaviors, based on our experiences, including those from previous lifetimes.

Repetitive patterns in our behavior, such as finding ourselves repeatedly getting angry at the same person or encountering the same problems in our relationships, can be attributed to the influence of alaya consciousness. However, the doctrine of nine layers of consciousness also provides hope for change. By becoming aware of these patterns and understanding how they are stored in alaya consciousness, we can take steps to change our behavior and create a brighter future for ourselves. Buddhism teaches that we have the power to transform our karma and ultimately shape our destiny.

The doctrine of Buddhism defines nine layers of consciousness that explain how karma is stored and perpetuated. The first five consciousnesses correspond to the five senses of sight, hearing, touch, taste, and smell. The sixth level is the thinking mind that integrates information from these senses. The seventh level is where we form judgments and discern value, while the eighth level is the storehouse of our karma, where all experiences are filtered and stored as unconscious memories of our previous actions and reactions. These stored experiences can influence our behavior, perpetuating patterns of behavior that can be difficult to change.

Karma is not just an individual matter, as patterns of behavior are also perpetuated in family groups. Research has shown that people whose karma is similar are drawn together in families, and those who have suffered abuse may be more likely to abuse their own children. This is where the doctrine of karma provides clarity on why people behave in these repeating cycles. While psychology recognizes the existence of conditioned responses, it may not always be enough to change deeply ingrained karma, as it lies deeper than the rational mind.

To change our karma fundamentally, we need to transcend the influence of our karma and reach the realm of the ninth consciousness, which is pure and free of karmic impurities. Although understanding and self-awareness can help us understand our behavior, they may not be enough to change it. Therefore, it is essential to delve deeper into our consciousness to achieve genuine transformation.

The ninth consciousness, according to Nichiren Daishonin, is defined as Nam-myoho-renge-kyo, which represents the universal law of life. By chanting Nam-myoho-renge-kyo, we express our Buddhahood and gradually become aware of our karmic tendencies that limit us. With increasing confidence, we can challenge these tendencies and establish a new direction in our lives based on our emerging Buddhahood.

As Nichiren Daishonin stated, "The Buddha discovered a mystic law which simultaneously contains cause and effect and designated it as myoho-renge. The single law of myoho-renge is perfectly endowed with all phenomena in the universe. Therefore, those who practice this law simultaneously gain the cause and effect of Buddhahood." By embracing this law, we gain the ability to transform our lives and become more aligned with the universe's underlying principles.

Simultaneity of Cause and Effect: Understanding the Lotus

Nichiren Daishonin's teachings reveal that negative karma can be conquered in a single lifetime, which goes against the traditional belief that it would require numerous lifetimes. He uncovered the principle of simultaneity of cause and effect expressed in renge, which means lotus flower. As the lotus flower produces flowers and seeds simultaneously, it illustrates that the effect happens at the same time as the cause. This may be challenging to grasp because we often witness cases where a wealthy person has attained success by mistreating others, evading cause and effect. In response, Nichiren Daishonin suggests that "hell exists in the heart of a man who inwardly despises his father and disregards his mother, just like the lotus seed, which contains both flower and fruit simultaneously. The Buddha also dwells inside our hearts." Therefore, genuine happiness depends on the contents of our hearts. No matter how much we may materially gain by manipulating others, if we are hating or disrespecting them, we are suffering and creating the cause for future suffering.

Buddhist theory explains that there are two effects: the manifest effect, which is visible and may take time to appear, and the latent effect, which is invisible and felt immediately. While the manifest effect may take time to materialize, the latent effect is immediate. For instance, a wealthy man who exploits others may experience the manifest effect in his next lifetime, such as being born into a poor family. However, he is already suffering internally in the present, and the latent effect is immediate. There are two causes: one is internal, arising from our karma, while the other is external, which refers to everyday events to which each of us reacts differently based on our particular internal cause stored in our karma.

However, by basing ourselves on the Buddha state, the ninth consciousness, we can free ourselves from our past conditioning and habits, breaking free from our karma. Devotion to the Gohonzon and chanting Nam-myoho-renge-kyo enables us to change our destiny for the better, according to Josei Toda, the second president of the Soka Gakkai.

The doctrine of karma implies that we cannot blame anyone else for our suffering. While others may be accountable for their actions, they will reap their rewards. Our suffering arises from within us, not outside. Although this may seem strict, it is exceptionally liberating because we cannot change others; the only way to change them is to change ourselves by altering the way we relate to them.

By chanting Nam-myoho-renge-kyo and opening our Buddha nature, we can react to others with wisdom and compassion instead of anger or greed. Consequently, people will respond to us differently. With Nichiren Daishonin's Buddhism, we do not need to go through stages. We can experience Buddhahood immediately due to the simultaneity of cause and effect expressed in renge of Nam-myoho-renge-kyo. While external effects such as overcoming poverty or illness may take time to appear, we can feel supreme joy immediately. This joy is different from physical desires' satisfaction because it is the joy of freedom. Simultaneously, we can be confident that our physical and material circumstances will improve. Practising Buddhism does not mean we avoid the effects of our karma; we find that hidden things causing us to suffer surface. This happens because we are tapping into the ninth consciousness under the storehouse of karma. The flaws come to the surface for purification, much like forging iron. Although this can be unsettling and challenging, there is no karma we cannot overcome.

In difficult times when we wrestle with the effects of our karma, it is crucial to remember that the causes we made in the past are not as important as the ones we create now. By practising Nichiren Daishonin Buddhism, we become stronger and better equipped to deal with challenges. We feel joy and gratitude because we can fundamentally revolutionize our lives. Karma is not just about oneself, but it is also shared with our families, communities, and society at large. Different revolutions such as the industrial and class ones have been attempted to improve society. However, without revolutionizing our own lives, we cannot hope to achieve lasting peace and a constructive society. If we cannot overcome our anger, for instance, how can we stop war? Overcoming our karma starts a chain reaction that changes the karma of our families, communities, and the world. "We, living beings, have dwelt in the sea of the sufferings of birth and death since time without beginning. But now that we have become votaries of the Lotus Sutra, we will without cannot attain the Buddha's entity which is as indestructible as a diamond, realizing that our bodies and minds that have existed since the beginning-less past are inherently endowed with the eternally unchanging nature, and thus awakening to our mystic reality with our mystic wisdom."

Choosing a Marriage Partner

THE MOST IMPORTANT THING for you now is to be clear in your own mind about why you are getting married. Many people marry in search of happiness and strive, each in his or her own way, to attain it. Then do they all become happy? Everyone knows the answer is no. Why? To answer this question, we must first recognize the fundamental cause which prevents people from becoming happy. Otherwise, we will make the mistake of not seeing the forest for the trees. A man and woman join hands in marriage not just for the sake of being married but because they want to be happy. From this standpoint, consider if you can make a valid decision only based on whether the other party is a Nichiren Buddhism believer. Some members marry non-members because they cannot find anyone suitable among the believers. Sometimes, they later experience difficulty in this account. Not that, however, that you must choose your spouse from among the members. But some seniors say to their junior members, "Because that person is not a believer, he (or she) is not a suitable marriage partner" and this knowing nothing about that person! Many young members also seem to be caught up in the simplistic idea that they must marry no one but a believer. To say simply, "I won't marry anyone but a believer," is just a reverse way of saying, "I will marry anyone who is a believer." But is just any Nichiren Buddhism member a suitable marriage partner? Let's examine this question. Once a member of the young women's division came to me for advice. A man who was not a member had proposed to her.

He himself had no intention of taking faith but wanted to marry her) anyway. Each time he had asked her, she rejected him for the simple reason that he was not a believer. Her suitor, however, would not give up. At her wits' end, she sought my guidance. "You won't marry him because he is not a member," I said to her. "Then would you take just any man for your husband as long as he chants to the Gohonzon?" No, of course not," she replied. I pointed out to her the pitfalls in her way of thinking. Suppose a man who is not a member proposes to a woman who believes in Nichiren Buddhism. She persists in rejecting his request because he is not a believer, so strongly that he finally consents to taking faith.

Relieved and overjoyed, she immediately marries him. But wait just a moment! Such a suitor often turns out to be an untrustworthy person. He may have professed faith only as an expedient in order to marry her. He may only want her money, not her herself. Or he may try to get a good job through her family connections. There may be some ulterior motive involved when a man becomes a member under such circumstances. In a nutshell, the purpose of getting married is to be happy. It is relatively easy to marry but quite difficult to marry happily. Some people find happiness after marriage, others do not. There are several conditions which work to ensure a fortunate marriage. Faith is fundamental, but it doesn't exclude all the others. The ideal course for you to take is first to let this man practice Buddhism, if it seems at all possible. Then wait and see for a year. If you judge him to be trustworthy, feel a liking for him, and if your parents and seniors approve, then you may decide for yourself whether you should marry him. If you have taken all these steps, your marriage is far less likely to end in failure. Here, after receiving my guidance, the member of the young women's division met her suitor and said to him, "It would be easy to accept your proposal. But if we are not happy after our marriage, that will be against your interests and mine. Marriage is meaningless unless the couple can be happy.

In order for us to be happily married, I hope you can see your way clear in taking faith in Nichiren Buddhism. Then, when a year or more has passed, if I am convinced that you are the right man for me, I will accept your proposal. But if I don't feel convinced, I won't. I would rather remain single than be unhappily married. The man was impressed with the logic of her words, and sometime later became a believer in Nichiren Buddhism. He attended meetings of the young men's division and was eventually appointed as a leader. All the people around the girl approved of the match, and she herself was quite willing to accept him as her husband.

So they became husband and wife and are now happily married. Some members take an easy-going view of marriage. They seem to believe that as long as they maintain their faith, they will meet somebody wonderful and automatically live happily ever after. This is hardly the case, however. Marriage is not always synonymous with happiness. Seniors must advise their junior members on this very point. Generally speaking, a fortunate marriage does not depend on whether one gets married early or late in life. You must first be distinctly aware of the purpose of marriage. No matter how fervently you may wish to marry immediately, should your marriage fail, your wishes will have been in vain. You should instead pray to the Gohonzon for a fortunate marriage. Young people are apt to rely on their immediate feelings in choosing a mate. It is only natural that, being young, they may sometimes feel uneasy about the future and vacillate what course they should take. Choosing a marriage partner in this insecure emotional condition often leads to an unhappy marriage. This is where the advice of seniors becomes important. Whenever someone seeks my guidance about marriage, I am reminded anew how many members there are who misinterpret the teaching, "No prayer will go unanswered." They must correct their erroneous thinking. Let me explain the reason. Suppose you are attracted to a certain person and pray to the Gohonzon to marry him. If he will truly make you happy, your wish will be fulfilled. If not, your prayer will go unanswered.

Prayers of this kind sometimes resemble the many demands a child makes of His mother according to the whim of the moment. The mother, after pondering the situation, either gives or refuses her child what he wants. The child may resent her briefly for not giving him what he demands, but it is her duty to give or refuse, as she deems appropriate for her child's welfare. This is true parental love, isn't it? The ultimate aim of our faith in the Gohonzon is to become happy. Therefore, those wishes are not fulfilled, which would eventually work against us.

The Significance of Reciting Gongyo

LET US BEGIN BY understanding why we recite the "Expedient Means" chapter from the Lotus Sutra during Gongyo.

The wonderful Lotus Sutra, which teaches that bodhisattvas, persons of the two vehicles, and ordinary people are all capable of attaining Buddhahood, begins with the "Expedient Means" chapter in the first volume. The Sutra of True Requital: THE spirit of the Expedient Means (Hoben) chapter 37 expresses a profound form of humanistic education through these passages. Buddhism recognizes each person's infinite potential and teaches the means by which people can awaken to and draw forth the supreme treasure of Buddhahood in their lives.

When we recognize this treasure in our own lives, we begin to see it in others and treat our fellow human beings with genuine respect. Our actions naturally spark the same awareness in others. The first part of Gongyo, known as the Hoben pon, is an excerpt from the second chapter of the Lotus Sutra, which emphasizes the importance of making such efforts. Through these actions, the treasure in our own lives is polished, and we develop even more confidence in our innate potential and dignity. Buddhist practice is, therefore, the path of limitless self-improvement.

Let us now explore the significance of reciting the Life Span chapter of the Lotus Sutra in Gongyo.

The Lotus Sutra is considered the essence of all of the Buddha's teachings, and the verse section of the Life Span chapter is believed to be the heart of the twenty-eight chapters of the sutra. The Buddha of the three existences regards this chapter as his life, and the bodhisattvas of the ten directions view the verse section as their eyes. According to Nichiren Daishonin, the Lotus Sutra is the scripture that enables all people to become happy, and it is in the Life Span chapter that Shakyamuni reveals the great law that can lead all people to happiness after his passing. This is the law of Nam-myoho-renge-kyo, which is implicit in the depths of the Life Span chapter.

The Daishonin explains that in the Latter Day of the Law, the provisional and theoretical teachings cannot help people overcome the sufferings of life and death. Only the essential teaching of the Life Span chapter can enable them to do so. Overcoming the sufferings of life and death means gaining liberation from the fundamental sufferings of existence, and this is the teaching that enables people to develop a state of happiness arising from the depths of their being. The Life Span chapter explains the concept of "eternal life" from which all lives fundamentally spring.

What is the benefit of hearing the Life Span chapter expounded? The Distinctions in Benefits (17th) chapter of the Lotus Sutra explains, "Hearing that the Buddha's life is immeasurable, all beings are filled with joy." Understanding the eternity of life fills people with joy from the depths of their being. This joy is the power of the Mystic Law that can dispel any suffering, no matter how deep-seated.

Of course, this benefit refers to the power of Nam-myoho-renge-kyo hidden in the depths of the chapter. As Nichiren Daishonin states, "Nam-myoho-renge-kyo is the greatest of all joys." President Toda described the inner state of those who embrace the Gohonzon, saying, "From the depths of their lives, they feel total peace of mind, and to live is itself a joy." Nam-myoho-renge-kyo is the great law that fundamentally illuminates the lives of all people. It is the great beneficial medicine that can fundamentally save all people of the Latter Day who are steeped in the sufferings of life and death.

The Strategy of The Lotus Sutra

NICHIREN DAISHONIN'S WRITING STATES, "It is the heart that is important. No matter how earnestly Nichiren prays for you, if you lack faith, it will be like trying to set fire to wet tinder. Spur yourself to muster the power of faith. Regard your survival as wondrous. Employ the strategy of the Lotus Sutra before any other. All others who bear you enmity or malice will likewise be wiped out." These words are as relevant now as they were when they were first written.

The heart of strategy and swordsmanship derives from the Mystic Law, and it is our profound faith that allows us to manifest this power. We must chant with conviction, even when we are facing problems and worries. Nichiren Daishonin emphasizes the importance of mustering the powers of our faith and practice, and to "employ the strategy of the Lotus Sutra before any other." By doing so, we can dispel the dark clouds of our negative karma and transform our state of life through the power of Nam-myoho-renge-kyo.

In moments of deep despair, we can elevate our life condition through the power of our prayers to the Gohonzon. This transformation can turn inner sufferings into joy and appreciation, changing poison into medicine in the depths of our lives. If we persevere, our circumstances will eventually reflect this same state of joy, like a mirror reflects an image. However, we must remember that we are still common mortals bound by delusion. The only thing that can transform delusion into enlightenment is faith, and faith alone.

The Three Proofs

IN THE QUEST FOR absolute happiness, the three proofs serve as the criteria for determining the correct teaching. Nichiren Daishonin's Buddhism satisfies these three proofs, making it possible for all people in the Latter Day of the Law to attain Buddhahood in this lifetime.

The three proofs are:

#1. Documentary proof:

This proof requires that a religion's doctrines align with its foundational scriptures. Nichiren Daishonin emphasizes the importance of accepting only what is clearly stated in the text of the sutras, discarding any arbitrary interpretations or opinions. Therefore, all doctrines in Buddhism must have the support of the sutras or the teachings expounded by Shakyamuni.

#2. Theoretical proof:

Theoretical proof, or proof of reason, requires that a religion's doctrines and assertions align with reason and logic. In Nichiren Daishonin's Buddhism, reason is highly respected and valued, as Buddhism itself is rooted in reason. Therefore, irrational arguments or interpretations should not be accepted.

#3. Actual proof:

Actual proof requires that the belief and practice of a religion's doctrines produce positive results in one's life, daily affairs, and society. A religion is not merely an abstraction, but it exerts a powerful influence on people's lives. The merits of a religion can be judged by examining its actual impact. In Nichiren Daishonin's Buddhism, practicing its doctrines can lead to positive transformation in one's life and society as a whole.

Nichiren Daishonin placed great importance on the concept of actual proof as the highest form of proof when judging the merit of Buddhist doctrines. In his own words, "And even more valuable than reason and documentary proof is the proof of actual fact." This is because the ultimate goal of Buddhism is to enable people to attain genuine happiness. A religion or philosophy that lacks any of the three proofs - documentary, theoretical, and actual - is not truly credible.

To illustrate this point, consider the example of a medicine. For a medicine to be considered safe and effective, it must have a list of ingredients and their effects (documentary proof), a sound theoretical basis for its effectiveness (theoretical proof), and most importantly, demonstrate actual results in relieving the ailment it is meant to treat (actual proof). Similarly, the value of a religion or philosophy must be judged by whether its teachings are supported by documentary and theoretical proofs, as well as whether its practice leads to positive outcomes in one's life and society as a whole.

Finding Happiness through Faith, Practice, and Study

THERE ARE VARIOUS APPROACHES to religion, with some placing great emphasis on faith, while others prioritize acts of kindness or philosophical inquiry. Nichiren Buddhism, on the other hand, encourages a dynamic balance of faith, practice, and study, as emphasized by Nichiren Daishonin in his writings. He states, "Exert yourself in the two ways of practice and study. Without practice and study, there can be no Buddhism. You must not only persevere yourself; you must also teach others. Both practice and study arise from faith."

In Nichiren Buddhism, faith is not simply a passive belief in a higher power, but rather a belief in one's own potential for unshakable happiness and the limitless potential of all people. This belief is expressed through the practice of chanting Nam-myoho-renge-kyo, the Mystic Law, which is the fundamental Law that permeates our lives and the universe. Nichiren Daishonin faced numerous persecutions and hardships while establishing his teachings, yet he triumphed in every instance. He inscribed the Gohonzon, a mandala of the Mystic Law, as an expression of his winning state of life, so that future generations could manifest the same life condition. He writes, "I, Nichiren, have inscribed my life in sumi ink, so believe in the Gohonzon with your whole heart."

Nichiren Buddhism emphasizes the importance of faith, practice, and study in a dynamic balance. Through the practice of chanting Nam-myoho-renge-kyo and studying the teachings, practitioners can tap into their own potential for unshakable happiness and ultimately achieve their goals.

The foundation of Nichiren Buddhist practice is the profound belief that by chanting Nam-myoho-renge-kyo to the Gohonzon, every individual can reveal their inherent Buddhahood. Through chanting with faith, we integrate our lives with the Mystic Law and unveil the wisdom, courage, compassion, and all other qualities essential to conquer any challenge and help those around us do the same. Nichiren teaches us that we should never seek the Gohonzon or enlightenment outside our own lives.

Hence, having faith in the Gohonzon implies having faith in the enormous power and nobility that exist within our lives and the lives of others. Our faith is fortified by studying and practicing Buddhism, and the stronger our faith, the greater the benefits and growth we will attain from our efforts.

Practice for Oneself and Others

FAITH IN BUDDHISM OFTEN starts with the hope that it can bring positive change to one's life. With continued practice, this hope gradually transforms into unwavering conviction. In Nichiren Buddhism, practice is divided into two categories: practice for oneself and practice for others. These two are likened to the two wheels of a cart, both necessary for steady progress. Practice for oneself involves daily chanting and recitation of sutras to establish a higher life condition that leads to lasting happiness. Practice for others entails sharing Nam-myoho-renge-kyo with others, teaching them how to practice Buddhism, and empowering them to create fulfilling lives.

Nichiren Daishonin wrote: "Single-mindedly chant Nam-myoho-renge-kyo and urge others to do the same; that will remain as the only memory of your present life in this human world." Practicing for the sake of others and spreading the humanistic philosophy of Nichiren Buddhism is an integral part of this practice. The joy that we create through chanting Nam-myoho-renge-kyo is eternal and transcends the limitations of birth and death. By consistently practicing and teaching others, we can overcome negativity and achieve absolute happiness.

Through diligent practice, we continue to strengthen and develop ourselves, creating a path towards a life full of joy and fulfillment.

The Power of Buddhist Study

IN NICHIREN BUDDHISM, THE pursuit of knowledge is an essential aspect of spiritual practice. Study is the process of delving into Nichiren's writings, to gain a deeper understanding of the Buddhist teachings, and to apply them more effectively in our daily lives.

Through study, we can strengthen our confidence and conviction, and learn how to practice correctly. Nichiren himself stated that "both practice and study arise from faith. Teach others to the best of your ability."

By continually studying and seeking the correct Buddhist teachings, we can avoid the pitfall of forming shallow views based on personal opinions or incorrect interpretations. Being misled by such things can prevent us from fully bringing forth our Buddha nature and enjoying the true benefits of our practice.

Therefore, we also study the words and examples of the three. Throughout our lives, we will undoubtedly encounter difficulties and may question why we still face problems despite practicing

Buddhism. However, as we deepen our faith through study, we come to see the opportunities within problems and obstacles and fortify our ability to overcome them. Buddhist study provides us with a profound philosophy that serves as a compass to navigate through the stormy and perilous seas of life.

The more we learn through our Buddhist study, the stronger our faith will grow. By deepening our understanding of Nichiren Buddhism, we can resolve our doubts and continue to establish a state of unshakable happiness. Therefore, let us continue to study diligently and share the wisdom we gain with others.

Managing Your Karmic Bank Account

EVEN INDIVIDUALS WHO POSSESS a limited understanding of Buddhism are likely to have heard of karma, a term that has become part of everyday language, albeit often used without a complete comprehension of the concept. At its core, the theory is straightforward, much like the translation of its Sanskrit origin: 'action,' yet its simplicity is also incredibly profound. According to Buddhism, every utterance, thought, and action is recorded in our existence. These are the causes that will, one day, produce noticeable effects. To some degree, this is something most people are aware of: the cigarettes we smoke today will negatively impact our health at an unknown time, in ways we cannot predict (be it heart issues, respiratory problems, or cancer), but there will be consequences. Similarly, the thirty minutes of exercise we completed has no immediate impact, but we understand that with consistent exercise over time, we will experience changes in our fitness and body shape.

Buddhism goes even further, stating that our lives are also shaped in the same manner by everything we do during each day, and even our physical appearance, personalities, and circumstances can be explained by the karma accumulated over countless past lives. Daisaku Ikeda succinctly summarizes this perspective as follows: "The late Arnold Toynbee interestingly compared the human karmic situation to a banking account in which entries are always being made in the debit and credit columns to alter the balance, which is the fate of the individual life at any given moment." Buddhists believe that what Dr. Toynbee termed the karma balance sheet persists after death and into future lives.

Buddhism further asserts that we have the power to alter our karma, much like managing a bank account. Just as cutting down on expenses and making an effort to deposit more money can put our account into a healthy credit balance, making positive changes in our lives, in how we interact with others, and in our relationship with the world at large can create 'good' karma that can transform our destinies. Nichiren Daishonin, in his work 'The Opening of the Eyes,' cites the Contemplation on the Mind Ground Sutra to emphasize this point powerfully, "If you want to understand the causes that existed in the past, look at the results as they are manifested in the present. And if you want to understand what results will be manifested in the future, look at the causes that exist in the present."

According to Daisaku Ikeda, most people in the West understand that effort (causes) produces rewards (effects). In essence, the Buddhist law of causes and effects aligns with what humans everywhere experience in practical application. While demonstrating actual karmic links can be challenging, an awareness of the degree of connection between our actions and their outcomes can inspire us to strive to be and do better.

It is essential to note that our Buddhist practice significantly increases our potential to change our karma. For example, consider a water pipe that has not been used for an extended period; it will rust, and the initial water running through it will become turbid. Similarly, the turbid water is likened to the unhappy life condition of human beings, which is bound by negative karma. However, by chanting to the Gohonzon every day with a strong faith, and sending clean water into the water pipe, which is our life, we can fundamentally change our karma without fail, just as the water eventually becomes clear.

When we focus solely on external solutions, we forget the limitless potential we have to transform our destiny for the better. Unfortunately, our Buddhist practice can sometimes feel like an "endless, painful austerity" instead of the boundless source of joy it should be.

Nichiren Daishonin was clear that external solutions cannot provide indestructible happiness. Instead, true happiness comes from manifesting joy in every moment through our Buddhist practice.

We cannot find lasting happiness if we simply try to escape unpleasant situations. Rather, when we have the courage to face reality and actively change it for the better through chanting Nam-myoho-renge-kyo, we chart a correct course toward a happy life.

The Two Types of Happiness

According to Nichiren, "There is no greater happiness for human beings than chanting Nam-myoho-renge-kyo." However, in order to fully understand the significance of this statement, we must first consider the two types of happiness: relative and absolute.

Relative happiness is dependent on external circumstances, such as professional success, material possessions, good health, and social status. While these things can bring temporary joy and satisfaction, they are vulnerable to change and do not provide a stable foundation for lasting happiness. When we rely solely on these external factors for our happiness, we become subject to the whims of our environment.

On the other hand, absolute happiness is derived from the awakening of our Buddha nature and our commitment to helping others do the same. It is an unshakeable joy that is not dependent on external circumstances. Chanting Nam-myoho-renge-kyo with faith in the Gohonzon allows us to tap into this source of absolute happiness and develop an indestructible confidence and joy.

While relative happiness has its place, it is important to recognize that it is fleeting and not a reliable source of lasting happiness. By prioritizing our practice and deepening our understanding of the teachings of Nichiren Buddhism, we can cultivate a sense of absolute happiness that transcends the limitations of our external circumstances.

The ultimate goal of our Buddhist practice is absolute happiness, which exists on a completely different plane from relative happiness. Unlike the latter, which is dependent on external circumstances such as professional success, material possessions, and good health, absolute happiness cannot be attained through worldly means. It arises from our awakening to our own Buddha nature and our commitment to helping others do the same.

What makes absolute happiness so special is that it is indestructible. It comes from the eternal Mystic Law, and no matter how challenging our circumstances may be, it cannot be taken away from us. By chanting Nam-myoho-renge-kyo with faith in the Gohonzon, we can develop an unshakable sense of confidence and joy.

As Nichiren once said, "There is no greater happiness for human beings than chanting Nam-myoho-renge-kyo." It's important to remember that any happiness we experience by comparing ourselves to others or feeling better off than them is fleeting and transient. True happiness can only be found within ourselves through our Buddhist practice.

Life Changing Experience

In June 2012, I discovered Nichiren Buddhism, thanks to a colleague who introduced me to the practice during a period of deep depression. At the time, my marriage was breaking down, and I felt completely hopeless, crying for months on end. As advised by my senior leaders, I began chanting for the happiness of my husband and three-year-old son, but I faced daily challenges and felt weak and victimized. My work performance suffered, and I was plagued with negativity as new information about my marriage came to light. My husband repeatedly suggested we mutually divorce, but I was hurt and felt betrayed. Finally, I found the courage to leave my husband's house with my son, moving to my parents' home in another city where I joined the local Soka Gakkai community.

My leader taught me to pray for my high life condition, and I began to chant for long hours, hoping to rebuild my relationship with my husband on the basis of self-respect. I blamed him for my pain, which created negativity in me and left me with deep wounds in my heart. However, as I prayed for my Buddha nature to emerge, I began to study and take part in kosen-rufu activities, developing an acceptance that my environment is a mere reflection of my karma.

The concept of cause and effect gave me power, and I began to take responsibility for my problems and my own life.

Through daily practice of Gongyo and abundant Daimoku, I regained calmness and courage, and my deep-rooted sorrows began to vanish. Years of pain disappeared, and I grew stronger, no longer affected by every little thing. My faith strengthened, and I felt blessed and fortunate to have this Buddhist practice with me.

In November of that year, I found a job exactly as I had prayed for, and my faith grew even stronger. Then in February 2013, my husband presented me with a mutual consent divorce paper, which my family agreed to, but my determination to work on our relationship for my son's future remained strong. I prayed to overcome my fundamental darkness and undergo my human revolution, and mystically, the next day, my father refused the divorce, and I began to feel powerful.

Although our relationship was still plagued by negativity, I was determined to change this poison into medicine. I earnestly chanted for his happiness and prayed to overcome my fundamental darkness. Within weeks, all negativity was gone, and I was fearless and compassionate enough to talk with my husband. In May 2013, we had a series of healthy dialogues, and we worked on our relationship for the future of our son. I returned to my husband's house in June 2013, and our relationship is much better than ever.

Throughout my journey, I am grateful to my senior leaders and friends in Soka Gakkai for their support with prayers and guidance. I learned to identify problems for what they truly are, opportunities to grow and make life better. I have accomplished my human revolution, changed my karma, and fulfilled my various wishes. I want to share some key lessons I learned during my struggle: we must accept and handle our own problems, and earnestly pray until the end. Some problems take more time to change, but through our prayers, life will always unfold in the best possible way. The combination of faith, study, and practice is essential to achieving our goals.

Using Bad Karma for Good Fortune

NICHIREN DAISHONIN EMPHASIZED THE uniqueness of the Lotus Sutra as compared to other sutras. While other sutras require the accumulation of good causes before one can become a buddha at a later time, the Lotus Sutra enables immediate attainment of enlightenment. As Nichiren put it, picking up the sutra or chanting its title immediately leads to Buddhahood, just as the moon's reflection appears in the water as soon as it rises from behind the eastern mountains or a sound and its echo arise simultaneously.

In essence, chanting Nam myoho renge kyo to the Gohonzon is the cause that brings forth the innate Buddhahood within us as the effect, which is the key to transforming our negative karma. Rather than fretting over making good or bad causes, which can lead to further suffering, Nichiren Daishonin taught that the purification of the inner spirit that drives our actions is vital. The way to accomplish this is to practice Buddhism by chanting Nam myoho renge kyo to the Gohonzon and tap into our inherent Buddha nature.

Chanting to the Gohonzon is essential for the development of our Buddhahood. It is akin to weightlifting for a bodybuilder; as our Buddha nature becomes more apparent, and our dominant life tendency moves towards Buddhahood, we increasingly make causes that flow from this highest aspect of ourselves.

Despite becoming enlightened, we may still have bad karma stored in our lives. However, as our Buddhahood grows stronger, we can use this bad karma to create good fortune for ourselves and others. Problems and desires motivate us to chant, rather than simply suffer, and the act of chanting not only reveals and strengthens our Buddhahood immediately but also lays down further good fortune in our eighth consciousness. This good fortune must be revealed in the future, further strengthening our Buddhahood.

Turning Poison into Medicine

I RECENTLY WATCHED A play where one of the characters shared a powerful story. She had once come across a butterfly struggling to break free from its cocoon. Feeling sorry for the creature, she decided to help it out and gently released it from its confinement. However, upon unfurling its wings, the butterfly dropped to the ground. What she didn't realize was that the struggle to break free of the cocoon was actually what gave the butterfly the strength it needed to fly.

This lesson can be applied to people as well. Let's say a man's business fails, causing him to lose his family. Instead of taking responsibility for his mistakes, he blames external factors like the economy, the government, and even his wife. He chalks it all up to bad luck or fate, refusing to acknowledge his own shortcomings.

The man then starts over, with a new business and a new relationship. However, when these also fail, he is forced to take a closer look at himself. He realizes some of the mistakes he made in his previous endeavors, but ultimately falls back into his old habits when faced with similar challenges. He becomes frustrated and angry, unable to change his life or his negative attitudes. These attitudes have become his cocoon, trapping him in a cycle of suffering.

Nichiren Daishonin taught us how to break free from these deep-seated attitudes and reveal the wisdom, courage, compassion, and life-force necessary for change.

By consistently chanting Nam-myoho-renge-kyo, we can reveal our Buddhahood and make it the dominant state in our lives. When we look at our problems and obstacles from the perspective of our Buddhahood, we can see them as opportunities for growth, which will lead us to greater happiness than before. This principle is called "turning poison into medicine," and it is not simply a matter of putting on a brave face or ignoring our problems. Rather, it is a vigorous philosophy of challenging our problems and using our struggles to strengthen ourselves.

For instance, when faced with the news of their redundancy, some people may see it as the end of their working life and fall into despair, while others may see it as an opportunity to start afresh or take early and active retirement. Our usual reaction to problems may be to shrink and waste our energy on blaming others or finding a solution. However, finding a solution without acknowledging the underlying causes that created the problem may only deal with the immediate situation, without addressing the root of the problem.

As demonstrated in the example of the man whose business failed, the underlying causes of our problems are within us, and the answers to our problems can also be found within ourselves. By viewing our problems as opportunities to deepen our understanding of ourselves and our circumstances, we can use them as a springboard to greater happiness.

Daisaku Ikeda, President of the SGI, reminds us that some may suffer sickness or face trying circumstances in business or activities for kosen-rufu. But when going through a difficult situation, we are actually in the best position to change our destiny and open a road to great benefit. Although failures are inevitable as we continue to practice, setbacks can be likened to the valleys encountered by a traveler crossing foothills towards a mountain. Although the traveler may occasionally move downwards, the overall journey is upwards as long as we continue to practice correctly.

By focusing our minds on seeking the Buddhahood within us while we chant, we can reveal the qualities of wisdom, courage, and compassion. These qualities can help us find the best solutions to our problems for ourselves and those around us.

However, concentrating our minds on this thought can be challenging. It is a battle we must win to gradually train ourselves to overcome other challenges in our daily lives. These battles may seem small, but successfully completing even minor tasks can strengthen us for more significant challenges. By sticking to a budget, making a difficult phone call, or keeping our space tidy, we can conquer obstacles and change our attitudes and direction. It is in these everyday moments that we turn poison into medicine.

Each time we face a new obstacle and choose to challenge it, we discover strengths we didn't know we possessed. These strengths can help us break free of even the tightest "cocoon" and transform our lives.

The Illuminating Effect of Daimoku

Daimoku is often compared to light, just as the Daishonin stated, "a lantern lighting up a place that has been dark for a hundred, a thousand, or ten thousand years." This means that by offering prayers based on Daimoku, the darkness in our lives is dispelled, as the principle of the simultaneity of cause and effect takes effect. At the very moment we offer our prayers, our prayers are answered in the depths of our lives.

The inherent cause of a deep prayer simultaneously produces a latent effect. Although it may take some time for this effect to become visible in our lives, our prayers are realized instantly. Therefore, light shines forth as a result. This principle is illustrated by the lotus (renge), which blooms and produces seeds at the same time.

Thus, it is vital that we offer our prayers with confidence, as the powers of the Buddha and the Law are activated in direct proportion to the strength of our faith and practice. Strong faith is akin to high voltage, which can illuminate our lives.

Although prayers are invisible, if we pray with unwavering determination, we can rest assured that they will eventually manifest tangible results in our lives and surroundings. The Lotus Sutra teaches us to have complete faith and aspire to be born in the presence of the Buddhas in our next life.

To illustrate this point, consider the example of a person who cannot climb up a tall embankment. Someone on top of the embankment offers a rope and promises to pull the person up to the top. In the same way, we must have faith that our prayers will be answered and that we will attain enlightenment.

According to the principle of the simultaneity of cause and effect, Daimoku is like a light that can dispel the darkness in our lives. As Nichiren Daishonin said, it is like a lantern illuminating a place that has been dark for a hundred, a thousand, or even ten thousand years. When we offer prayers based on Daimoku, the inherent cause of our deep prayer simultaneously produces a latent effect. Although it may take some time for this effect to manifest in the depths of our lives, our prayers are immediately answered. Therefore, it is crucial to offer prayers with great confidence, activating the powers of the Buddha and the Law in direct proportion to the strength of our faith and practice. Strong faith is like a high voltage that turns on a brilliant light in our lives.

Even though prayers are invisible, they can undoubtedly bring clear results to our lives and surroundings if we pray steadfastly. As Nichiren Daishonin said, one should have complete faith in the Lotus Sutra and look forward to being born in the presence of the Buddhas in one's next life. To illustrate this point, imagine a person standing at the foot of a tall embankment who cannot ascend. If someone on top of the embankment lowers a rope and says, "If you take hold of this rope, I will pull you up to the top of the embankment," the person at the bottom has two options. If they doubt the other's strength to pull them up or wonder if the rope is too weak and, therefore, refuse to put forth their hand and grasp it, they will never make it to the top of the embankment. However, if they follow the instructions, put out their hand, and take hold of the rope, they can climb up.

Similarly, if we doubt the strength of the Buddha, suspect the rope held out by the Lotus Sutra, or cannot chant the Mystic Law, it will be impossible to scale the embankment of enlightenment. Thus, we must trust in the power of the Buddha, have faith in the Lotus Sutra, and chant the Mystic Law to attain enlightenment.

Embracing Nam-myoho-renge-kyo

Nichiren once said, "Never seek this Gohonzon outside yourself. The Gohonzon exists only within the mortal flesh of us ordinary people who embrace the Lotus Sutra and chant Nam-myoho-renge-kyo."

Despite the fact that Nam-myoho-renge-kyo exists within us, it can be challenging to manifest it in our lives. As mere mortals, we may struggle to bring it forth. So how can we do this?

The answer is simple: by vocalizing Nam-myoho-renge-kyo. We experience different types of life conditions by seeing or hearing various things. For instance, the beauty of cherry blossoms, the moonlight, or the disgust of seeing a cockroach. We use our ears to enjoy music or motivational speeches. Similarly, vocalizing Nam-myoho-renge-kyo connects us to our Gohonzon, bringing forth our Buddhist life force.

As the Gosho explains, your voice has the power to bring out Buddhahood. So, as long as you chant Daimoku, your Buddhahood will emerge from within you. If someone wrongs you or if you are robbed, you will feel anger, and if you are experiencing suffering, worries, or poverty, you may feel like giving up. But if you chant Nam-myoho-renge-kyo, you can overcome your problems and transform your life.

Nichiren Daishonin's Doctrine of Changing Destiny

THE NIRVANA SUTRA CONTAINS teachings on lessening one's karmic retribution. It explains that if one fails to expiate their heavy karma during their lifetime, they will suffer in hell in the future. However, if one endures extreme hardship in this life due to the Lotus Sutra, the sufferings of hell will instantly disappear.

This letter was written by Nichiren Daishonin on the fifth day of the tenth month in 1271, just three weeks after he narrowly escaped execution at Tatsunokuchi. He sent it to his three leading disciples: Ota Saemon, a prominent government official, the lay priest Soya Kyoshin, and the Dharma Bridge Kimbara.

It is possible that one of these disciples visited Nichiren Daishonin during his detention for exile at the residence of Homma, the deputy constable of Sado Island, in Echi after the failed execution. This letter may express gratitude for their visit and concern for Nichiren Daishonin's safety.

The Gosho, "Lessening One's Karmic Retribution," teaches that the power of the human spirit is limitless. Regardless of what fate may bring, we have the ability to overcome it and find happiness. Nichiren Daishonin's Buddhist teachings on changing karma are an unparalleled principle of triumph in life, giving hope, courage, and confidence to all people. It embodies a philosophy of supreme humanism, showing that every individual inherently possesses the power to weather any destiny.

In this passage, we witness Nichiren Daishonin's profound life-state of regarding great hardships as an opportunity to attain Buddhahood. He illuminates the fundamental truth of Buddhism and human existence, emphasizing that hardships are an integral part of life and that we should not be disheartened by them. Specifically, he refers to the principle of lessening one's karmic retribution, underscoring its significance in relation to karma, a subject that resonates with all individuals. The reality is that there is no life without obstacles, and adversity is essential to achieving genuine peace in life.

However, without recognizing our innate resilience to withstand hardships, we risk falling into a trap where one problem leads to another, ultimately crushing us under their weight. Nichiren Daishonin's writing explains the essential power that dwells within us, empowering us to endure hardships. He exemplified this strength by enduring intense persecution himself.

During Nichiren Daishonin's time, the prevailing belief regarding karma was that if a person had accumulated such severe offenses in past lives that they could not expiate all of their negative karma in their current lifetime, they would have to endure hellish sufferings in future lives before their retribution could be concluded. However, the principle of lessening karmic retribution that Nichiren Daishonin expounded held that even the most severe negative karma from past lives could be expiated by experiencing retribution in a lighter form in the present lifetime.

The theory of karma in Nichiren Daishonin's Buddhism is a transformative teaching that has the power to renew people's lives. It reveals that there is no negative karma, no matter how weighty, that cannot be transformed for the better. In this writing, the Daishonin's doctrine of changing karma or destiny is discussed through the lens of the principle of lessening one's karmic retribution.

There are two key points concerning lessening one's karmic retribution that the writing highlights. The first point concerns the Daishonin's statement that "the sufferings of hell will vanish instantly." He asserts that even heavy karma that leads to hellish retribution can be expiated immediately, in the present moment—not gradually at some distant point in the future. The principle of mutual possession of the Ten Worlds enables this possibility. Karma is created by past causes and manifested as present effects, meaning that there is a time lag between cause and effect; they do not occur simultaneously. However, the Daishonin's Buddhism teaches that karma can be transformed through the manifestation of the Buddhahood that already exists within us. Just as the countless stars in the sky disappear when the sun rises, the vast store of negative karma in our lives can be erased when we awaken to the life-state of Buddhahood.

The second point, which holds significant importance, is that reducing karmic retribution serves as the gateway to achieving Buddhahood in this lifetime. By lessening karmic retribution, we can directly pave the way for attaining Buddhahood. However, it is crucial to note that reducing karmic retribution does not simply mean balancing out negative karma, but it encompasses a significant transformation in our lives. It involves a shift from a negative path to a positive one, leading to genuine goodness and an upward ascent towards happiness. The power of Mystic Law allows us to convert negativity into something constructive and turn poison into medicine.

In Daishonin's Buddhism, the doctrine of lessening karmic retribution is the fundamental principle for redirecting our lives towards happiness in the present moment. Hence, this moment of struggle is of utmost importance. As Daishonin stated in "The Opening of the Eyes," understanding our past causes can help us comprehend the present results, and examining present causes can shed light on future outcomes. Our present moment represents the effect of our past causes, but it also serves as the cause that shapes our future. The present encompasses the past, present, and future, all in this instant.

The most crucial aspect is our ability to alter our attitude or inner resolve in the present moment. We possess the power to shape our future freely by our determination and actions in the current instant.

Daishonin's teachings on changing karma hold immense significance as they pave the way for a bright revolution of hope. They liberate individuals from the prevailing, gloomy, and deterministic perception of karma or destiny.

Nichiren Daishonin's Call to Kosen-rufu

NICHIREN DAISHONIN WROTE IN Gosho, "Now at the beginning of the Latter Day of the Law, I, Nichiren, am the first to embark on propagating, throughout Jambudvipa (the entire world), the five characters of Myoho-renge-kyo, which are the heart of the Lotus Sutra and the eye of all Buddhas." It is noteworthy that, in the 2,200 years since Buddha's passing, even great Buddhist figures such as Mahakashyapa, Ananda, Ashvaghosha, Nagarjuna, Nan-yueh, T'ien-tai, Miao-lo, or Dengyo have not propagated these teachings. Therefore, Nichiren called upon his disciples to join him and surpass even the most respected figures in Buddhism.

The letter was written in 1276 and addressed to the lay nun Konichi, also known as Sage Konichi. She was a widow living in Awa, which was Nichiren's native province. Konichi's son, Yashiro, had earlier converted to the Daishonin's teachings, and through him, Konichi and her husband became disciples of Nichiren. Unfortunately, after her conversion, Konichi lost both her beloved son and her husband. Nonetheless, through Nichiren's continuous and wholehearted encouragement, she overcame her deep sorrow and remained a sincere believer in Nichiren's Buddhism until the end of her life.

The Gosho entitled "The Actions of the Votary of the Lotus Sutra" is a personal account written by Nichiren Daishonin that covers a significant period in his life, beginning with the arrival of a delegate from the Mongol empire in 1268 and culminating in his retirement to Mount Minobu. This autobiographical writing includes his struggles and persecutions throughout the nine years, from the Tatsunokuchi Persecution to his exile on Sado Island, in great detail.

In this Gosho, Nichiren Daishonin reveals that Nam-myoho-renge-kyo, the heart of the Lotus Sutra, is the teaching that must be propagated throughout Jambudvipa, the entire world, in the Latter Day of the Law. According to him, this Mystic Law is a great teaching that has never been propagated before, not even by the remarkable teachers of the Former and Middle Days of the Law.

Mahakashyapa and Ananda were direct disciples of the Shakyamuni Buddha and were considered the Buddhist teachers who had correctly propagated Hinayana teachings for the first 500 years of the Former Day of the Law. Ashvaghosha and Nagarjuna, on the other hand, spread the teachings of Mahayana Buddhism in the second half of the Former Day of the Law in India. Meanwhile,

Nan-yueh, T'ien-tai, Miao-lo, and Dengyo were Buddhist teachers who appeared in China and Japan during the Middle Day of the Law and propagated the theoretical teachings of the Lotus Sutra. Despite their contributions, none of them have ever propagated the Mystic Law of Nam-myoho-renge-kyo before Nichiren Daishonin.

All of the individuals mentioned in the previous passage propagated teachings that were appropriate for their time and age, but none of them spread Nam-myoho-renge-kyo, which is the essential teaching hidden in the depths of the Lotus Sutra. Nam-myoho-renge-kyo is the fundamental source of Buddhahood that has led all Buddhas to enlightenment, which is why the Daishonin referred to it as the "eye of all Buddhas." He also called it the "heart of the Lotus Sutra" because its teaching is found in the depths of the Lotus Sutra.

It was Nichiren Daishonin who first spread the fundamental teachings of the Mystic Law in the Latter Day of the Law, which the Buddhist teachers of the Former and Middle Days did not propagate. For this reason, the Daishonin is revered as the original Buddha of the Latter Day of the Law. The Daishonin opened the way for kosen-rufu in the current age of the Latter Day while enduring life-threatening persecutions.

Based on the Buddhist principle of "Many in body, one in mind," we must strive to develop and maintain a direct connection with Nichiren Daishonin and practice faith in exact accordance with his teachings throughout our lives. In this passage, the Daishonin calls to us, "My disciples, form your ranks and follow me." The Daishonin is teaching us that the quintessence of faith is to advance on the path of kosen-rufu opened by the Daishonin in the same mind and spirit as him.

Empowering Others: The Essence of Compassion

According to the Lotus Sutra, compassion is often mistaken for pity, but it's much more than that. While pity may have condescending undertones, compassion springs from a sense of equality and interconnectedness of life. Genuine compassion entails empowering others, helping them to discover their inner strength and courage to overcome their challenges.

All individuals desire to live happily, yet human society is plagued by forces that undermine this basic aspiration. From rampant violence and environmental destruction to structural inequalities, exploitation, and oppression, the realities of the world often frustrate our desires for happiness.

Buddhism provides insights into the inner workings of human life that lead to these undesirable outcomes. One of the most pervasive and powerful desires in human existence is the desire for power and control over others. This urge to dominate and subjugate others is deeply ingrained in our ego and often manifests in destructive ways, disregarding the needs and wellbeing of others in our quest for personal gain.

Buddhism uses the Devil King of the Sixth Heaven as a symbolic representation of the exploitative, authoritarian impulse that plagues human existence. Its influence is pervasive in our world, as evidenced by the widespread violence, inequality, and oppression that pervade society. Nichiren, the founder of Nichiren Buddhism in the 13th century, saw the world as the devil king's domain, with all people living under his rule.

Despite this dark reality, human nature also provides the solution to our most pressing global problems. Compassion, the countervailing force to the destructive aspect of human nature and the suffering it causes, is the heart and origin of Buddhism. Compassion arises from a sense of solidarity with others, with all life, and a desire for mutual happiness and growth.

In Sanskrit Buddhist texts, compassion is described using the words maitri and anukampa. Maitri reflects a sense of fellowship with others, while anukampa signifies a deep empathy that arises from encountering suffering and motivates action to alleviate it. In essence, Buddhist compassion is a desire to relieve suffering and bring joy.

While compassion may be misconstrued as pity, it is fundamentally different. Compassion springs from a sense of the equality and interconnectedness of all life and is rooted in respect for the inherent dignity of life, both our own and that of others, with a desire to see that dignity triumph.

Authentic compassion is not just about resolving difficult situations for others. It is about empowering them to tap into their inner strength and courage to overcome their challenges. Sometimes this may involve taking a firm stance, which could be misunderstood as being stern or contradictory. For instance, resolving someone's problem for them may seem compassionate, but if it leaves them weaker and less self-reliant, it does not contribute to their actual happiness in life. Empowerment is the essence of compassion.

The effort to offer effective encouragement tailored to an individual's specific circumstances gives rise to wisdom. Compassion and wisdom are closely intertwined, and even small acts of kindness require courage.

Nichiren, the founder of Nichiren Buddhism, introduced the practice of chanting Nam-myoho-renge-kyo as a practical means for people to unlock the strength and rich potential of their humanity and live with confidence and joy. For Nichiren Buddhists, sharing this practice with others is the most critical act of compassion.

The transformation of society can only happen through a change in people's hearts. Living a life grounded in compassion entails having unwavering faith in the unrealized potential of ourselves and others. It's effortless to give up on ourselves and others when we face failure and foolishness. Unfortunately, losing faith in humanity is a pervasive trait in our troubled world today. Nichiren Buddhism's philosophy is anchored in continuing to have faith in and promoting the inherent goodness and potential of our own and others' lives.

The belief in the untapped potential of humanity is also the foundation of a strong optimism that serves as a base for all people's actions towards creating positive change in our world.

The Key to Increasing Good Fortune

IN THE GOSHO, NICHIREN writes, "Appreciation and gratitude increase good fortune. Complaint and negativity erase it." This statement underscores the importance of cultivating a positive attitude and outlook towards life.

Recently, I had an encounter with a woman who was working hard and doing everything right, but she was resentful about it. She was angry that her work was not being acknowledged and appreciated by the people around her. Her situation reminded me of a bird that charges ahead with all its power but repeatedly bumps into a window.

This encounter made me reflect on the experiences of people I know who have worked tirelessly on their duties, invested countless hours in Daimoku, and engaged in a lot of kosen-rufu activities. While they have accomplished a lot, the relationships in their lives remain unchanged, and the bulk of the work continues to fall on them. They feel unappreciated, and people around them seem to make their lives tougher rather than easier. This stubborn cause could be due to karma or mission, but it could also be attributed to their attitude, which is infused with resentment, arrogance, and anger.

Transforming resentment into compassion and complaints into gratitude is crucial to increasing good fortune. When we resent others, we create negative karma, which brings misfortune into our lives. On the other hand, when we cultivate a compassionate attitude towards others, we create positive karma, which brings good fortune into our lives. Likewise, when we complain and focus on the negative aspects of our lives, we attract negativity, but when we express gratitude for what we have, we attract positivity.

Cultivating a positive attitude towards life requires introspection and self-reflection. It entails looking within ourselves to identify the root cause of our resentment, anger, and complaints. We need to develop empathy towards others, recognize their contributions, and express gratitude for them. When we cultivate gratitude, we become aware of the blessings in our lives, and our perspective shifts towards positivity.

In conclusion, transforming resentment into compassion and complaints into gratitude is essential to increase good fortune in our lives. Cultivating a positive attitude towards life requires introspection, self-reflection, and empathy towards others. When we express gratitude and cultivate compassion, we create positive karma, which brings good fortune into our lives.

The transformation of resentment into compassion is an essential aspect of personal growth. Without this change, we may spend our entire lives looking in the wrong direction. The key to making this transformation is compassion. When we have compassion for ourselves and others, it becomes easier to see things from a different perspective. This is because when we look in the mirror, the image that we see will bow back to us. Similarly, if we express hatred or resentment towards others, we may find that they reciprocate these negative emotions.

We may do everything right and work hard, but if our hearts are not in the right place, people will respond to our negativity. To make this change, we should pray to transform all resentment into compassion. This is in line with Daishonin's teachings, which encourage us to pray for positive and protective forces to enter our lives and the lives of those around us, including all members.

Gratitude is another essential aspect of personal growth. When we have gratitude for the things we have and express it frequently to those who support our lives, our good fortune increases manifold. Therefore, we should always express gratitude for the things we have, including our relationships, work, and material possessions. By doing so, we can improve our lives and the lives of those around us.

The Relationship between Knowledge and Wisdom

THE FUNCTIONING OF WISDOM in our lives enables us to overcome our habitual thinking and attain a fresh and holistic view of a situation. It broadens our perception of facts and helps us identify the essence of an issue, guiding us towards happiness. By dispelling our delusions of separateness, wisdom awakens a sense of empathetic equality towards all living beings.

Buddha is renowned for his profound wisdom, which is a central concept in Buddhism. However, wisdom can be elusive and challenging to define, making it difficult to attain. Can we actively develop wisdom, or do we have to wait for it to come with age? The vagueness of the concept might be why wisdom has lost its value in modern society, which focuses on information and the acquisition of knowledge.

Despite the difficulty of defining wisdom, its value is immeasurable. It empowers us to see beyond our limited understanding and break free from the confines of our habitual thinking. Wisdom allows us to make informed decisions, navigate challenges, and discover a greater sense of purpose. It helps us cultivate a more profound connection with others and the world around us.

To develop wisdom, we need to cultivate the habit of reflection and self-examination. We can start by questioning our beliefs and assumptions, seeking to broaden our perspective and challenge our understanding of the world. By reflecting on our experiences, we can gain insights into ourselves and the world, deepening our understanding of life's intricacies. We can also learn from the wisdom of others, seeking out mentors and role models who embody the qualities we aspire to cultivate.

In conclusion, wisdom is a fundamental aspect of personal growth and development. It allows us to overcome our habitual thinking and attain a fresh and holistic view of the world. Although wisdom might be elusive, we can actively cultivate it by reflecting on our experiences and seeking out the wisdom of others. By doing so, we can develop a deeper connection with ourselves, others, and the world around us.

In his critique of modern society, Josei Toda, the second president of the Soka Gakkai, identified the confusion between knowledge and wisdom as a major failing. The astonishing progress of technology in the last century exemplifies this confusion. While science and technology have made some progress in alleviating human suffering, they have also been responsible for great destruction.

Toda likened the relationship between knowledge and wisdom to that of a pump and water. A pump that doesn't produce water (knowledge without wisdom) is of little use. This is not to diminish the value of knowledge. However, knowledge can lead to both extreme destructiveness and profound good.

Wisdom, on the other hand, is the force that guides knowledge toward good and the creation of value. It is the ability to discern what is truly beneficial and constructive in the long term, beyond the immediate gain or short-term advantage. In this sense, wisdom is the ultimate goal of human learning and growth.

The dynamics of wisdom and its various manifestations are described and analyzed in Buddhist teachings, including the concept of the five kinds of wisdom. When wisdom is active in our lives, it enables us to transcend the limited perspectives of our habitual thinking and gain a fresh, holistic view of a situation. We can assess the facts broadly, grasp the essence of an issue, and steer a confident course toward happiness.

Buddhism compares wisdom to a clear mirror that perfectly reflects reality as it is, including the interconnectedness and interdependence of all living beings. This wisdom dispels our illusions of separateness and awakens within us a sense of empathetic equality with all things. The term "Buddha" refers to someone who freely manifests this innate wisdom, which is fueled by compassion.

According to Buddhism, the universe and life itself embody compassion, which is the interweaving of interdependent phenomena that give rise to and nurture life in its diverse and wonderful forms. While knowledge is important, wisdom is the force that directs knowledge toward good and the creation of value, as it is capable of generating both great destruction and profound good.

The teachings of Buddhism suggest that the purpose of human life is to actively participate in the compassionate workings of the universe and enrich its creative dynamism. Thus, our life is brought into accord with the universal life force and our inherent wisdom is manifested when we act with compassion. Through encouraging and sharing hope with others, we awaken to a larger and freer identity beyond the narrow confines of our ego. Wisdom and compassion are inextricably linked.

Self-mastery is a central tenet of Buddhist practice, as it involves becoming the master of our minds. By developing an altruistic spirit, we can arouse the wisdom of the Buddha within us and direct all aspects of our being towards creating happiness for ourselves and others. This includes our knowledge, talents, and unique character.

Daisaku Ikeda, the SGI President, once commented at Tribhuvan University in Nepal that being the master of one's mind entails cultivating the wisdom that resides in the inner recesses of our lives. This wisdom wells forth in inexhaustible profusion when we are motivated by a compassionate determination to serve humankind.

To redirect human history from division and conflict towards peace and an underlying ethic of respect for the sanctity of all life, human beings themselves must change. The Buddhist understanding of compassionate wisdom can serve as a powerful foundation for such a transformation.

From Basic Needs to Spiritual Fulfillment

Nichiren Daishonin once said, "As you crave food when hungry, seek water when thirsty, long to see a lover, beg for medicine when ill, or as a beautiful woman desires powder and rouge, so should you put your faith in the Lotus Sutra? If you do not, you will regret it later."

It's interesting to note that when we feel hunger or thirst, the urge to eat or drink arises from within us without anyone prompting us to do so. Similarly, when we are in love, that person becomes the center of our thoughts, and when we're sick, getting well is our top priority. People with illnesses often spend all their resources searching for a cure, while those blessed with good looks want to enhance their appearance.

In the same way, Nichiren Daishonin urges us to put our faith in the Lotus Sutra. Just as we satisfy our physical needs, we should satisfy our spiritual needs by putting our faith in the teachings of the Lotus Sutra. If we neglect to do so, we may come to regret it later. So let us heed Nichiren Daishonin's words and cultivate a strong faith in the Lotus Sutra.

A great beauty may spend hours in front of a mirror, carefully choosing the perfect makeup to enhance her looks. Nichiren Daishonin teaches us through this example and others the ideal attitude we should have towards faith. Ideally, we should be able to turn to the Gohonzon wholeheartedly, spontaneously, and immediately, without anyone's prompting.

This passage also shows that we can confidently pray to the Gohonzon for the fulfillment of any desire. "As you crave food when hungry, seek water when thirsty" represents our basic needs for survival. "Longing to see a lover" represents our emotional, spiritual, and physical needs. "Begging for medicine when ill" represents our problems that need resolution, and "as a beautiful woman desires powder and rouge" represents our desire to fulfill our potential and enhance the meaning of our existence.

Thus, Daishonin teaches us that faith in the Gohonzon can benefit us in every aspect of life, no matter how big or small or what it may concern. The Gohonzon's beneficial power knows no bounds.

The Gohonzon: A Blueprint of Inner Potential

NICHIREN BUDDHISM STANDS OUT from other Buddhist teachings in its belief that all people have the potential to manifest Buddhahood in their current lifetime, regardless of their background or circumstances. To help practitioners bring forth their inherent Buddhahood, Nichiren inscribed the Gohonzon, a scroll containing Chinese and Sanskrit characters.

The Gohonzon is a representation of the sublime life condition of Buddhahood, based on a scene from the Lotus Sutra known as the Ceremony in the Air. In this scene, a magnificent tower adorned with precious gems emerges from the earth, and beings from across the universe gather to hear the Buddha preach the law.

Nam-myoho-renge-kyo, the central phrase of the Gohonzon, is flanked by the names of various buddhas, bodhisattvas, and living beings that represent the Ten Worlds, or the different inner states of life. This inclusion signifies that all living beings have the potential to reveal their inherent enlightened nature when they are illuminated by the wisdom and compassion of

Nam-myoho-renge-kyo, which represents the entity of the eternal Buddha.

The term "Gohonzon" can be translated as "object of devotion." Practitioners of Nichiren Buddhism typically have altars in their homes where they enshrine the Gohonzon and offer their prayers and devotion. By chanting Nam-myoho-renge-kyo while facing the Gohonzon, practitioners can tap into their inherent Buddhahood and manifest their full potential in their daily lives.

Nichiren Buddhists practice a daily ritual of chanting Nam-myoho-renge-kyo and reciting portions of the Lotus Sutra while facing the Gohonzon. Through this practice, they reaffirm and respect the sanctity of their lives and all life.

Chanting Nam-myoho-renge-kyo to the Gohonzon activates the Buddha nature inherent in one's life, resulting in a surge of wisdom, courage, compassion, and life force. This empowers individuals to confront and overcome life's various challenges, illuminating their lives as they are.

The Gohonzon represents the limitless potential of our inner lives and is not a symbol of something we lack or need to gain from an external source. It also embodies a world where all the problems of our troubled age have been resolved.

In the Lotus Sutra's Ceremony in the Air, the Bodhisattvas of the Earth suddenly appear in vast numbers, pledging to uphold the Buddha's teachings in the era after his passing. They aim to eliminate the suffering and conflict of the age and bring happiness to all people.

Chanting Nam-myoho-renge-kyo to the Gohonzon is, at its core, an awakening to one's mission as a Bodhisattva of the Earth. Nichiren's followers strive to inherit the spiritual legacy of Shakyamuni and Nichiren by actualizing a peaceful and happy world for all beings. They seek to manifest their Buddhahood in their everyday lives and assist others in doing the same.

Human Revolution: Path to Inner Transformation

DAISAKU IKEDA ONCE SAID, "Human revolution is the work of transforming our lives at the very core. It involves identifying and challenging those things which inhibit the full expression of our positive potential and humanity." This statement captures the essence of Nichiren Buddhism, which emphasizes the possibility of inner transformation and bringing forth our full human potential.

Some people believe that such transformation requires ideal circumstances that are not readily available to most. However, Nichiren Buddhism teaches that it is only by facing the challenges that confront us amidst the harsh contradictions of society that we can change our own lives and the world for the better.

The term "human revolution" describes the fundamental process of inner transformation in Nichiren Buddhism. It involves breaking through the shackles of our "lesser self," which is bound by self-concern and ego, and growing in altruism toward a "greater self" capable of caring and taking action for the sake of others and ultimately, all of humanity.

Many theories, religions, and publishing empires have attempted to answer the question of how to change in a positive direction. While self-discipline and effort can enable us to make positive changes, such as exercising regularly, they are often difficult to maintain. This is because we may not have addressed the underlying causes of our behavior.

Human revolution is a vital concept in Nichiren Buddhism that can lead to profound inner transformation. It requires courage, self-reflection, and a willingness to face the challenges that arise in our lives. By doing so, we can break through our limitations and bring forth our full potential, ultimately contributing to the betterment of society as a whole.

Human revolution entails a profound transformation of our lives from the core. It requires identifying and confronting those aspects that hinder the realization of our full positive potential and humanity.

Nichiren Buddhism is founded on the conviction that an inherent condition of pure, positive, and enlightened life exists equally within all people. This state of "Buddhahood" is characterized by the qualities of compassion, wisdom, and courage, which enable us to derive value from any situation. Nichiren discovered that the most profound process of change and purification occurs when we bring forth this state within ourselves, and he advocated the practice of chanting "Nam-myoho-renge-kyo" as a direct and immediate means of accessing and experiencing it.

The expression of our Buddha nature takes concrete form in several ways. Firstly, we gain the conviction that our life is limitless in its possibilities, and we possess a profound sense of our human dignity. Secondly, we develop the wisdom to comprehend that what we previously considered impossible is, in reality, achievable. Finally, we acquire a robust vitality that enables us to approach our challenges with a sense of inner liberation. As a result, we are empowered to undertake our own human revolution, striving to improve our "self" from yesterday to today and making the "self" of tomorrow even better.

The interpretation of the law of cause and effect in some Buddhist traditions can lead to a focus on negative past causes, where life's obstacles and challenges are seen as requiring lifetimes of effort to overcome. However, Nichiren Buddhism and the Lotus Sutra emphasize that Buddhahood, our highest and most enlightened state of being, can be attained through faith and practice in the present moment.

This enlightened wisdom enables us to recognize that seemingly unfortunate circumstances, such as incurable illness or bereavement, can actually provide the best opportunities for personal growth and tackling our human revolution. When we shift our focus from personal concerns to taking action for the sake of others, this process is strengthened and accelerated, and previously burdensome experiences can become the key to discovering the purpose of our lives.

The individual process of human revolution is critical in bringing about global change, as a great human revolution in one individual can ultimately change the destiny of a nation and all humankind, as noted by Daisaku Ikeda. By taking responsibility for transforming our own lives, we can lay the foundation for a human society that values compassion and respect for the dignity of all people's lives.

Nichiren's Controversial Message

NICHIREN REJECTED THE PREVAILING belief that Buddhism could only offer hope for comfort after death and that the best attitude towards life was patient endurance. In his treatise, Rissho Ankoku Ron, which he presented to the political ruler of the day in July 1260, he passionately advocated for a return to the original purpose of Buddhism: securing the peace and happiness of the people.

Buddhism holds a fundamentally positive view of human life, with its core message emphasizing the infinite dignity and potential of every individual. The Lotus Sutra, recognized in the Nichiren tradition as the highest and most complete teaching of Shakyamuni, uses the image of a jewel-decked treasure tower to illustrate the beauty, dignity, and preciousness of life. If we recognize human life as the most valuable treasure, we will appreciate the value of our own lives and the lives of others, making the prevention of violence and the elimination of suffering the highest priorities of humanity. Those who care for life, such as parents, nurses, doctors, and teachers, should be treated with the utmost respect.

However, humanity's common curse is an inability to fully believe in or appreciate the value of our own lives and those of others. Even if we accept this in theory, it can be challenging to put it into practice. In moments of bitter interpersonal conflict, we may experience poisonous thoughts of jealousy and hatred, wishing to harm others or remove them from our way. The UNESCO Constitution recognizes that "since wars begin in the minds of men, it is in the minds of men that the defenses of peace must be constructed." Similarly, Buddhism teaches that only through an inner transformation, from the deepest level, can we strengthen our compassion and move beyond our egotistical desire to dominate or use others.

Buddhism offers teachings and tools that enable us to undergo this type of transformation at our core.

Buddhism perceives life as a contest between good and evil. Good, according to this doctrine, embodies the creative and compassionate nature that exists within each person, which seeks personal happiness and helps others in their pursuit of contentment. Evil, on the other hand, represents anything that separates and weakens our sense of connectedness, leading to a fear-driven competition to control and dominate others before they can do the same to us. In the 13th century Japan, during the lifetime of Nichiren, a string of natural disasters such as earthquakes, floods, pestilence, and fire had caused widespread devastation. The suffering of the people was unbearable. Nichiren's mission to uncover the fundamental cause of this misery motivated him to study and analyze the underlying belief structures of society.

Despite the abundance of Buddhist temples and priests in the country, their prayers and actions appeared ineffective in providing peace or security for the people. Nichiren was convinced that the chaos prevailing in the world mirrored the chaos within human beings. As he wrote, "In a country where the three poisons [of greed, anger, and foolishness] prevail to such a degree, how can there be peace and stability? Famine occurs because of greed, pestilence because of foolishness, and warfare because of anger." He believed that only Buddhism could equip people with the strength to overcome these spiritual poisons in their lives. However, after extensive research, he realized that Buddhism, as practiced in his time, encouraged passivity, leaving people vulnerable to the influence of these poisons, instead of empowering them to conquer them.

Nichiren dismissed the prevalent belief that Buddhism could only offer the hope of comfort after death and that people should patiently endure the challenges of life. He was deeply convinced that Buddhism, in its original form, had a lot more to offer, such as the possibility of joy and fulfillment in the present life, and that it could provide people with the power to turn human society into a peaceful and ideal land. His most significant treatise, the "Rissho Ankoku Ron," which he presented to the political ruler of that era in July 1260, was an impassioned call for a return to the original purpose of Buddhism: to ensure the peace and happiness of the people.

At that time, one of the primary roles of Buddhist priests was to pray for the protection of the nation's rulers. In contrast, Nichiren's focus was on the ordinary citizens. For instance, in the "Rissho Ankoku Ron," the Chinese character he chose to write "land" had at its core the character for "common people" rather than the more commonly used characters that represented the king or the armed protection of the domain.

Nichiren's treatise is a powerful reflection of the turmoil he witnessed around him. He noted that "over half the population has already been carried off by death, and there is hardly a single person who does not grieve." It was his deep empathy for the people's plight that motivated him to take action. As someone who had taken a vow to lead himself and others to happiness, he believed that it was crucial to awaken and empower people to challenge their own destiny.

Nichiren's outspoken determination to help the people earned him a controversial reputation, which persists to this day. He believed that it was his duty to speak out on this matter, stating, "I cannot keep silent on this matter...I cannot suppress my fears." In practical terms, Nichiren urged the political leaders of his day to cease official patronage of favored sects and instead encouraged open public debate on the merits of different schools of Buddhism. On a personal level, he called on leaders to "reform the tenets that you hold in your heart." Today, this means transforming ourselves and our most deeply held beliefs about life.

Nichiren believed that the function of any religion or philosophy should be to give people the courage and hope needed to transform their sufferings. He believed that we need to develop the strength to engage successfully in a struggle against the forces of division and destruction within our own lives and in the larger social realm. Unless we empower ourselves and others, we cannot resist and overcome the negative influences within our own lives and their environment.

To create an age of peace in which life is given supreme value, it is vital for us to have a philosophy that reveals the wonder, dignity, and infinite potential of life. When we base our actions on this belief and act out of compassion for others, the result is a pure joy that motivates us to further action. Empowering ourselves from within, our sphere of compassion becomes wider and wider, encompassing not only ourselves, our own families and nations, but the whole of humanity.

By developing the wisdom and compassion to reject and resist all acts that harm or denigrate life, we can create an inner sense of security and a peaceful society that prioritizes protection for the vulnerable. Nichiren's message is clear: we must challenge our own beliefs, empower ourselves and others, and act with compassion to create a better world for all.

Living Confidently in the Present Moment

THE CONCEPT OF THE nine worlds and the world of Buddhahood coexisting within our lives is a fundamental teaching in Buddhism. This is vividly symbolized by the lotus plant, which produces flowers representing the state of the common mortal and fruit representing the state of Buddhahood simultaneously.

In Buddhism, the principle of cause and effect underlies all phenomena. This means that positive thoughts, words, and actions will lead to positive effects and happiness in life. Conversely, negative thoughts, words, and actions that undermine the dignity of life will lead to unhappiness. This is the general principle of karma.

In traditional Buddhist teachings, the path to Buddhahood is often viewed as a gradual journey of transformation. Over many lifetimes, the imperfect common mortal gradually molds and transforms themselves into a state of perfection through accumulated positive causes and the avoidance of negative ones.

However, in Nichiren Buddhism, the attainment of Buddhahood is governed by a deeper principle of causality revealed in the Lotus Sutra. This principle emphasizes that the ultimate cause of Buddhahood already exists within the lives of all individuals. It is a matter of bringing forth and manifesting this inherent Buddha nature through the practice of chanting Nam-myoho-renge-kyo and the study of the Lotus Sutra.

In essence, Nichiren Buddhism teaches that the path to Buddhahood is not a gradual journey of transformation but rather a process of revealing our inherent Buddha nature through the activation of the law of cause and effect within our lives.

The perspective offered by the Lotus Sutra on human nature and the attainment of Buddhahood is vastly different from traditional Buddhist teachings. According to the Lotus Sutra, delusion and enlightenment are two inherent aspects of life that are equally present, and life itself is neutral. While it may be common for humans to exist in a state of delusion, the attainment of Buddhahood does not require a fundamental change in our nature. In fact, the idea that Buddhahood is separate from our ordinary reality is itself a delusion.

This difference between the pre-Lotus Sutra and Lotus Sutra's views of enlightenment is also reflected in the concept of the Ten

Worlds. The Ten Worlds describe our inner state of life at any given moment, ranging from hell to Buddhahood, and are constantly in flux depending on how we direct our lives and respond to our environment. In traditional Buddhist teachings, practitioners move from the nine worlds of cause towards the world of Buddhahood, which then replaces the nine worlds. However, the Lotus Sutra reveals that both the world of Buddhahood and the other nine worlds are eternally inherent possibilities of life at every moment. Buddhahood is brought forth by faith and practice, and both delusion and enlightenment are present simultaneously.

The view of enlightenment presented in the Lotus Sutra is radically different from the conventional understanding. To explain this difference, an analogy can be made to a video game. In the conventional view, the process of enlightenment is akin to a video game character gradually accumulating powers and tools as they progress through the game's levels. However, in the Lotus Sutra's view, the character already possesses all the necessary powers and tools from the beginning; they just need to find a way to unlock them.

The practice of Nichiren Buddhism focuses on manifesting the potential of Buddhahood in the present moment. By chanting Nam-myoho-renge-kyo with faith in our inherent Buddhahood, we can activate the "code" that unlocks this potential. Once we bring forth our enlightened nature, characterized by courage, wisdom, compassion, and life force, we become equipped to engage fully with life's challenges and work to change reality for the better. Instead of seeing problems as obstacles, we can view them as opportunities to show the strength and reality of our enlightened nature and inspire others to do the same.

In Buddhism, living confidently and expansively in the present moment is key, and this is rooted in our faith in our inherently enlightened nature. This revolutionary perspective on "attaining" Buddhahood is expressed through the concept of simultaneity of cause and effect. The lotus plant, which bears flowers symbolizing the common mortal and fruit symbolizing Buddhahood at the same time, symbolizes the coexistence of the nine worlds, representing cause, and the world of Buddhahood, representing effect, in our lives.

Activating the Inherent Buddha Qualities

NICHIREN WROTE IN A letter to a follower that the ultimate reality exists within the depths of every individual's life. He emphasized that there is no treasure tower or ultimate reality outside of the figures of men and women who embrace the Lotus Sutra. In Nichiren Buddhism, the Lotus Sutra is considered to be the teaching where the Buddha reveals the complete truth of his enlightenment. It is an allegorical description of the Buddha interacting with a large gathering of disciples, and at a pivotal point, a magnificent "treasure tower" suddenly appears from the earth, adorned with seven kinds of treasures. "Tower" in this context is a translation of stupa, a dome-like structure constructed to house the Buddha's relics.

As the gathering of disciples gazes in amazement, a voice speaks from inside the tower, praising Shakyamuni and testifying to the truth of his teaching. Shakyamuni opens the tower, revealing the Buddha Many Treasures, who lived and died in the distant past beyond calculation. Shakyamuni clarifies that this treasure tower appears anywhere in the universe where the Lotus Sutra is being preached. He then enters the tower and takes a seat beside Many Treasures. The tower and the entire gathering are lifted up into space, where incredible events occur during "the Ceremony in the Air."

All of this is a symbolic representation of the Buddha nature, which is unfathomable and inherent within the lives of all individuals.

In Buddhism, the Buddha is the embodiment of human development and perfection. Shakyamuni, with his wisdom, courage, and great compassion, became a role model for his followers. However, after his death, Buddhism became cloaked in mystique, and the ideal of Buddhahood became an almost unattainable goal divorced from everyday reality.

Nichiren's teachings, on the other hand, are founded on the Lotus Sutra's principle that the world of Buddhahood is an intrinsic part of every individual's life, and we can manifest it as we are. The emergence of the treasure tower explains the actual relationship between the rarefied ideal of Buddhahood and everyday life.

Nichiren interpreted the treasure tower as a symbol of the ultimate reality, which he identified as Nam-myoho-renge-kyo. The Buddha Many Treasures represents the eternally enduring world of Buddhahood, which has always existed but only manifests under certain conditions. Shakyamuni Buddha represents a mortal Buddha, or Buddhahood that is active and present in this transient, actual world. Shakyamuni's decision to sit beside Many Treasures indicates that these two aspects of the Buddha – the eternal and the transient – are the same.

In a letter to one of his followers, Nichiren explained the location of ultimate reality. He stated that it resides in the depths of every person's life, saying, "No treasure tower exists other than the figures of the men and women who embrace the Lotus Sutra."

The qualities and attributes of the Buddha are already present within each individual's life. The purpose of the Lotus Sutra and the mission of those who practice it is to activate the inherent Buddha qualities within and bring them to the surface. Nichiren developed the practice of chanting Nam-myoho-renge-kyo as a means of practicing the Lotus Sutra and enabling the treasure tower to emerge within our lives. He also inscribed a mandala, the Gohonzon, which represents the Ceremony in the Air and depicts the Buddha nature present in all things.

Nichiren describes the seven treasures adorning the treasure tower as the virtues of "hearing the correct teaching, believing it, keeping the precepts, engaging in meditation, practicing assiduously, renouncing one's attachments, and reflecting on oneself." These qualities are not only for an exalted Buddha-like figure, but also for those striving to attain Buddhahood. It is through effort and striving that the qualities of the Buddha nature inherent in our lives become manifest.

Seeing the treasure tower means recognizing our inherent Buddha nature and upholding the great dignity of life, both our own and others. Faith in the inherent Buddha nature distinguishes a "Buddha" from a "common mortal."

As Daisaku Ikeda, President of SGI, notes, "The 'tower adorned with the seven treasures' is the grand and dignified original form of our lives."

The Oneness of Body and Mind

In Buddhism, life is not seen as a dichotomy between the physical and the spiritual. Instead, it is considered to be the unity of both. According to the Nichiren tradition, all things, whether they are material or spiritual, seen or unseen, are manifestations of the same ultimate universal law or source of life - Myoho-renge-kyo.

This perspective differs greatly from the beliefs of materialists, who assert that the physical or material world, which can be quantified and touched, is the only "reality." In contrast, certain spiritual traditions view the physical world as an inherent illusion, something corrupt that must be transcended in order to access the ultimate truth of the spiritual realm.

Buddhism regards the physical and spiritual aspects of life as completely inseparable and of equal importance. This concept is conveyed in the Japanese expression shikishin funi. The term shiki refers to all matter and physical phenomena, including the human body, while shin refers to all spiritual and unseen phenomena, including reason, emotion, and volition. Funi, which translates to "two but not two," signifies the indivisible relationship between the physical and spiritual realms.

This perspective on life can have profound implications for individuals and societies. By recognizing the unity of the physical and spiritual, we can develop a deeper appreciation for the interconnectedness of all things and the sanctity of life. We can also work towards a more harmonious and sustainable world by addressing issues that affect both the material and spiritual realms, such as environmental degradation and social inequality.

In a letter to one of his followers, Nichiren expressed that a person's physical aspect reveals their spiritual aspect, stating, "A person can know another's mind by listening to his voice. This is because the physical aspect reveals the spiritual aspect. The physical and the spiritual, which are one in essence, manifest themselves as two distinct aspects."

A person's emotional state is often conveyed through their physical appearance. When someone is happy and optimistic, their face may reflect their positive mood and their step may be light. Conversely, someone suffering from emotional pain may appear weighed down with drawn features and a painful gait, communicating their inner turmoil even from a distance.

Moreover, our inner mental state also has a significant impact on the physical functioning of our bodies. The physical expressions of laughter and tears are visible signs of our inner emotions. Stress from mental or psychological factors has been linked to a range of illnesses, from skin disorders, allergies, asthma, and ulcers to cancer. Feelings of depression and hopelessness can lower our body's resistance, making us susceptible to various afflictions. Conversely, a positive determination to overcome illness can inspire our organs and individual cells toward better health.

Daisaku Ikeda elaborates on this point, stating that "when our determination changes, everything will begin to move in the direction we desire. The moment we resolve to be victorious, every nerve and fiber in our being will immediately orient itself toward our success. On the other hand, if we think, 'This will never work out,' then at that instant, every cell in our being will be deflated and give up the fight."

The importance of both physical and spiritual well-being for true health and genuine happiness cannot be overstated. SGI members have shared experiences of improved health, physical and material conditions through the practice of chanting Nam-myoho-renge-kyo. They have come to realize that the spiritual and physical aspects of their lives are inseparable. This realization leads to both physical well-being and a growing clarity and purity of the mental and perceptive processes. Buddhist practice offers "conspicuous benefits" that primarily relate to the physical and material planes, but the "inconspicuous benefits" are the most crucial in the long term. They include increased self-awareness, wisdom, and compassion for others.

However, the ultimate inconspicuous benefit is enlightenment. According to Buddhism, a living being is made up of the harmonious coming together of the "five components." These components include the physical aspects of life and the senses, perception, conception, volition, and consciousness. Life is the energy that keeps these components functioning as an integrated whole.

Modern medical science is only beginning to explore the subtle interconnections between body and mind, between the physical and spiritual aspects of life. Buddhism views both physical and spiritual aspects as vital manifestations of the life force that is inherent in the cosmos itself. Nichiren wrote that life at each moment encompasses both body and spirit, self and environment of all sentient beings in every condition of life, as well as non-sentient beings like plants, sky, earth, and even the smallest particles of dust. Life at each moment permeates the universe and is revealed in all phenomena.

The Middle Way in Buddhism

THE MIDDLE WAY IS a concept deeply ingrained in Buddhist philosophy, and it carries significant meaning. At its core, the Middle Way suggests a balanced approach to life, where one regulates their impulses and behaviors, similar to Aristotle's "golden mean." This approach means that every virtue is a mean between two extremes, both of which represent a vice.

While the term middle may denote balance, the Middle Way should not be mistaken for passivity or compromise. To follow the Middle Way requires ongoing effort and a conscious effort to maintain balance in one's life.

In the broadest sense, the Middle Way refers to the correct view of life that the Buddha taught, and it encompasses the actions or attitudes that promote happiness for oneself and others. Buddhism itself is sometimes referred to as "the Middle Way," as it seeks to transcend and reconcile opposing views and extremes.

Shakyamuni, the founder of Buddhism, exemplified these ideas through his own life story. Born a prince, he enjoyed all the physical pleasures and comforts of life. However, he was dissatisfied with the pursuit of fleeting pleasures and sought a deeper, more enduring truth. He embarked on a period of extreme ascetic practice, depriving himself of food and sleep, which brought him to the brink of physical collapse. Realizing the futility of this path, he turned to meditation and worked tirelessly to understand the truth of human existence, which had eluded him in both a life of asceticism and luxury. It was through this path that Shakyamuni awakened to the true nature of life, its eternity, and its profound wellspring of unbounded vitality and wisdom.

Later, to guide his followers toward the Middle Way, Shakyamuni taught the eightfold path, a set of eight principles including right conduct and right speech by which individuals can regulate their behavior and develop true self-knowledge.

Throughout the history of Buddhism, scholars have attempted to clarify and define the true nature of life. In the third century, Nagarjuna developed a theory on the non-substantial nature of the universe, explaining that there is no fixed basis to reality behind the constantly changing phenomena of life. For Nagarjuna, this view represented the ultimate perspective on life, which he called the Middle Way.

T'ien-t'ai further developed Nagarjuna's ideas in sixth-century China. According to T'ien-t'ai, all phenomena are manifestations of a single entity, life itself. This entity exhibits two aspects: a physical aspect and a non-substantial aspect. Ignoring or emphasizing either of these aspects distorts our understanding of life. T'ien-t'ai thus clarified the indivisible interrelationship between the physical and the spiritual, which gave rise to Buddhist principles such as the inseparability of the body and mind, and of the self and the environment.

Nichiren, in turn, gave practical form to these often abstract arguments. Based on the teachings of the Lotus Sutra, Nichiren defined the Middle Way as Nam-myoho-renge-kyo, and taught that by reciting this phrase, one can harmonize and energize the physical and spiritual aspects of one's life, and awaken to the deepest truth of one's existence.

From this perspective, life is the vital energy and wisdom that permeates the cosmos and manifests as all phenomena, transcending and harmonizing apparent contradictions between the physical and the mental, even between life and death. SGI President Daisaku Ikeda shares this view, stating that life gives rise to DNA, rather than the other way around.

In Buddhism, individuals and societies tend towards either a primarily material or spiritual perspective on life. The negative consequences of materialism, which permeates modern industrialized societies, are evident at all levels of society, from environmental degradation to spiritual impoverishment. However, merely rejecting materialism outright constitutes idealism or escapism, and hampers our ability to respond constructively to the challenges of life.

The historian Eric Hobsbawm dubbed the 20th century "The Age of Extremes." The violence and grotesque inequalities of that time illustrate the importance of finding new ways to peacefully reconcile apparent oppositions. In order for humanity to discover a Middle Way towards a creative global society in the 21st century, it is crucial to develop a new appreciation and reverence for the inviolable sanctity of life.

The Optimistic Philosophy of Buddhism

The concept of "turning poison into medicine" is a transformative practice of Nichiren Buddhism followers, who use their Buddhist practice to change negative, difficult or painful situations into positive experiences. From a Buddhist perspective, suffering can be viewed as an opportunity for self-reflection, courage, and compassion, leading to a deeper experience of happiness. Inherent in all negative experiences is the potential for profound positivity.

The phrase "changing poison into medicine" refers to the transformation of deluded impulses into enlightenment. According to the Treatise on the Great Perfection of Wisdom, the Lotus Sutra is compared to a great physician who turns poison into medicine, as it opens the possibility of enlightenment to people who have scotched the seeds of Buddhahood due to arrogance and complacency. This principle suggests that there is no one beyond redemption.

Nichiren further elaborates on this idea in his writing "On First Hearing the Teaching of the Supreme Vehicle," by emphasizing the power of the Mystic Law of Nam-myoho-renge-kyo. He suggests that through this law, one can transform the three paths of deluded impulses, karma, and suffering into the three virtues of the Buddha, which are the Dharma body, wisdom, and emancipation. This means that any unfavorable situation can be changed into a source of value. Ultimately, it is through overcoming difficult circumstances that we can grow as human beings.

The way we react to life's inevitable sufferings is crucial. Negative and painful experiences are often necessary to motivate us towards seeking the truth. According to one Buddhist scripture, illness can awaken the desire to seek the truth. Similarly, many people have been inspired to devote their lives to peace and justice after experiencing war and injustice.

Transforming poison into medicine begins with our approach to difficult experiences. By reflecting on ourselves and developing our courage and compassion, we can turn negative experiences into sources of growth, vitality, and wisdom. From the Buddhist perspective, all negative experiences possess profound positive potential, and suffering can serve as a springboard for a deeper experience of happiness. However, if we are defeated by suffering or respond to challenging circumstances in negative and destructive ways, the original "poison" remains poison and is not transformed.

Buddhism teaches that suffering is a result of karma, the causes that we have created ourselves. The Buddhist concept of karma emphasizes personal responsibility, and we are responsible for transforming our sufferings into value-creating experiences. Even deeply ingrained karmic patterns can be transformed, and the Buddhist view of karma is not fixed or fatalistic.

By using difficult situations such as illness, unemployment, bereavement, or betrayal to deepen our sense of personal responsibility, we can gain self-knowledge and develop our inner strength, wisdom, and compassion. According to Buddhism, self-knowledge leads to awareness of our infinite potential, also known as our "Buddha nature." The phrase "to turn poison into medicine" originally refers to this level of self-knowledge.

The chapter "Belief and Understanding" in the Lotus Sutra recounts the response of the Buddha's long-time disciples, including Subhoti and Shariputra, to the prophecy that Shariputra would attain ultimate enlightenment. The disciples, having long given up on becoming Buddhas themselves, were moved by the teaching of the Lotus Sutra to renounce their previous resignation and spiritual laziness. They were filled with joy and their minds were transformed. This transformation is likened by Nagarjuna and T'ien-t'ai to a good doctor turning poison, in this case the disciples' laziness and resignation, into medicine, a sincere aspiration for the ultimate enlightenment of Buddhahood.

The teaching of profound transformation in Buddhism is a source of deep optimism. This optimism motivates Buddhists to seek to transform negative and destructive tendencies in their own lives as well as in society and the world at large.

The Power of Interconnectedness

OUR EXISTENCE IS ONLY meaningful when we recognize the extent of the myriad interconnections linking us to all other life. Buddhism teaches us that all life is interrelated, and that nothing exists in isolation or independent of other life. This concept of "dependent origination" - engi in Japanese - means that all beings and phenomena exist or occur only because of their relationship with other beings or phenomena. Everything in the world arises in response to causes and conditions; nothing can exist in absolute independence of other things or arise of its own accord.

Shakyamuni used the image of two bundles of reeds leaning against each other to explain this deep interconnectedness. He described how the two bundles of reeds can remain standing as long as they lean against each other. In the same way, because this exists, that exists, and because that exists, this exists. If one of the two bundles is removed, then the other will fall. Similarly, without this existence, that cannot exist, and without that existence, this cannot exist.

Therefore, we must recognize that our existence only becomes meaningful through interaction with and in relation to others. When we acknowledge and appreciate the interconnectedness of all life, we can cultivate a greater sense of compassion, empathy, and understanding towards others, leading to a more harmonious and fulfilling life for ourselves and those around us.

Buddhism teaches that our lives are constantly evolving, dynamically influenced by both the internal causes within our own lives (such as our personality, experiences, and outlook) and the external conditions and relationships around us. Each individual existence contributes to creating the environment that sustains all other existences, forming a living cosmos, a single living whole.

As we become aware of the myriad interconnections that link us to all other life, we come to realize that our existence only becomes meaningful through interaction with, and in relation to, others. By engaging with others, we develop, establish, and enhance our identity. We then understand that building our own happiness on the unhappiness of others is impossible. We also see that our constructive actions affect the world, as Nichiren wrote, "If you light a lamp for another, your own way will be lit."

There is an intimate mutual interconnection in the web of nature, in the relationship between humankind and its environment, and also between individuals and society, parents and children, and husbands and wives.

If we embrace the view that "because of that, this exists," or in other words, "because of that person, I can develop," we can avoid pointless conflicts in human relations. For instance, a young married woman's present existence is in relation to her husband and mother-in-law, regardless of their personalities. Someone who realizes this can turn everything, both good and bad, into an impetus for personal growth.

According to Buddhism, we "choose" the family and circumstances into which we are born to learn, grow, and fulfill our unique role and mission in life. We are connected and related not only to those physically close to us, but also to every living being. If we can realize this, feelings of loneliness and isolation, which cause so much suffering, vanish, as we understand that we are part of a dynamic, mutually interconnected whole.

An understanding of the interconnectedness of all life can lead to a more peaceful world, as Daisaku Ikeda has written:

"We are all human beings who, through some mystic bond, were born to share the same limited life span on this planet, a small green oasis in the vast universe. Why do we quarrel and victimize one another? If we could all keep the image of the vast heavens in mind, I believe it would resolve conflicts and disputes. If our eyes are fixed on eternity, we come to realize that the conflicts of our little egos are really sad and unimportant."

The Heart of Buddhist Practice

NICHIREN EMPHASIZES THAT SHOWING respect towards others, as embodied by the actions of Bodhisattva Never Disparaging, is the fundamental essence of Buddhist practice and the correct way for human beings to behave. However, this respect is not a passive recognition of others' worth; rather, it is an active engagement of our humanity.

The human heart is capable of both great nobility and terrible brutality. Our ability to direct the orientation of our hearts is what sets us apart from other animals. Instances of human nobility can be found in the selfless actions of a parent sacrificing their comfort for their child or a spontaneous act of kindness between strangers. However, the same heart can also be consumed by the dark forces of rage, prejudice, resentment, and self-deprecation. The atrocities of war are a stark reminder of the extent of these impulses within us.

Ultimately, the direction of our hearts determines whether we create societies characterized by joy and dignity or crippled by conflict, fear, and despair. Buddhism explains that all people possess an enlightened Buddha nature that gives rise to limitless positive potential and can bring wonder to our experience of living. However, an equally fundamental reality in the life of each person is delusion or ignorance, which gives rise to evil. Delusion makes it difficult for people to acknowledge their own capacity for either profound virtue or evil.

To direct our lives towards positive, value-creating potentials, we must focus on the core questions of religion and ethics. How can we cultivate respect for others and foster the nobility of the human spirit? How can we transcend delusion and ignorance and awaken to our true potential? These are the critical questions that should guide our pursuit of a fulfilling life.

The essence of Buddhist practice and the correct way for human beings to behave, as Nichiren clarifies, is to respect others, as exemplified by the actions of Bodhisattva Never Disparaging in the Lotus Sutra. Such respect is not passive but a bold engagement of our humanity.

The human heart is capable of both great nobility and violent brutality, and it's our ability to direct the orientation of our heart that distinguishes us from other animals. We see examples of the noble possibilities of the human spirit in everyday instances such as a parent's willingness to sacrifice personal comfort for the sake of a child or in a sudden act of kindness between strangers. Yet, the same heart can also seethe with the dark currents of rage, bigotry, resentment, and self-deprecation. The horrific extent of these impulses within us becomes apparent in the experiences of ordinary people caught up in the all-too-pervasive hell of war.

Ultimately, the simple orientation of our hearts determines whether we create societies characterized by joy and dignity or crippled by conflict, fear, and despair. Buddhism analyzes the dual potentialities of life, teaching that all people possess an enlightened Buddha nature that gives rise to limitless positive potential and which can bring wonder to our experience of living. An equally fundamental reality in the life of each person, however, is delusion or ignorance, which gives rise to evil. It is delusion that makes it difficult for people to acknowledge their capacity for either profound virtue or evil.

The Lotus Sutra, regarded by Nichiren Buddhism as the teaching that encapsulates the essence of the Buddha's enlightenment, offers a seemingly simple response to how we direct life towards its positive, value-creating potentials. This response is conveyed in the story of Bodhisattva Never Disparaging. Despite facing violence and abuse, Never Disparaging bowed in reverence to everyone he met and praised their inherent Buddha nature. His persecutors' reactions never upset his convictions, and he would retreat to a safe distance and repeat his obeisance, honoring the potential for good within them. Over time, his humanity shone, and those who had despised him were moved to become his disciples and enter the path of attaining Buddhahood themselves. The sutra reveals that Never Disparaging was the Shakyamuni Buddha himself in a previous existence, implying that his past-life behavior as Never Disparaging is the original cause of Shakyamuni's enlightenment.

Nichiren Buddhism regards the Lotus Sutra as the teaching that encapsulates the essence of the Buddha's enlightenment. In the Never Disparaging chapter, Nichiren finds the heart of the practice of the Lotus Sutra. Bodhisattva Never Disparaging's profound respect for people signifies the purpose of the appearance in this world of Shakyamuni Buddha, the lord of teachings, lies in his behavior as a human being.

While Buddhism is often considered an abstract philosophy, it is far from abstract in practice. The Buddha nature is not described in theoretical terms, but in the behavior of this humble bodhisattva. A Buddha is not an extraordinary being but a person who is deeply conscious of the positive potential within him or herself and within all others and who strives to help others bring forth this potential.

Nichiren clarifies that respecting others, as exemplified by the actions of Bodhisattva Never Disparaging, constitutes the essence of Buddhist practice and the correct way for human beings to behave. This respect is not limited to a passive regard for others but is a bold engagement of our humanity. While simple in its formulation, in practice, such an attitude represents the most challenging path. The effort required, however, is precisely that fundamental energy that can bring about the positive transformation of society. As SGI President Ikeda writes, "The key to the flowering of humanity of which Buddhism speaks is a steadfast belief in people's goodness and dedication to cultivating this goodness in oneself and others."

Beyond Cause and Effect: Karma and Choice

THE CONCEPT OF KARMA is constantly in flux, much like everything else in our lives. Our choices in each moment create our present and future, and this understanding empowers us to become the protagonists in the unfolding drama of our lives.

However, even in Asia, where the concept of karma has a long history and is incorporated into various cultures, it is often misunderstood. Many view karma negatively and backward-looking, using it to encourage disadvantaged members of society to accept their situation in life as a consequence of their own past actions. This mindset can lead to a sense of powerlessness and resignation, which is a distortion of the original meaning of karma in the Buddhist tradition.

To accept the idea of karma is not to live in guilt and vague anxiety, unsure of the negative causes we may have made in the past. Instead, it means being confident that we have the power to transform our destiny for the better at any moment.

Karma, which means actions, is the universal operation of a principle of causation, similar to that upheld by modern science. Science assures us that everything in the universe exists within the framework of cause and effect, and "for every action, there is an equal and opposite reaction" is a familiar principle. The difference between the materialistic causality of science and the Buddhist principle of karma is that the latter includes the unseen or spiritual aspects of life, such as the experience of happiness or misery, kindness or cruelty.

In 1993, SGI President Ikeda delivered a speech in which he discussed different approaches to the Buddhist concept of causal relations. According to him, this concept differs fundamentally from mechanistic causation, which modern science holds sway over the natural world - a world divorced from subjective human concerns. In the Buddhist view, causation is more broadly defined and encompasses human existence. For instance, assume an accident or disaster has occurred. A mechanistic theory of causation can pursue and identify how the accident happened, but it is silent on why certain individuals find themselves caught up in the tragic event. The mechanistic view of nature requires the deliberate forestalling of such existential questions.

Conversely, the Buddhist understanding of causation seeks to address these poignant questions. The Sanskrit word karma originally meant work or office and was related to verbs that simply mean "do" or "make." According to Buddhism, we create karma on three levels: through thoughts, words, and actions. Acts have a greater impact than mere words. Likewise, when we verbalize our ideas, this creates more karma than merely thinking of them. However, since both words and deeds originate in thoughts, the contents of our hearts - our thoughts - are also of crucial importance.

Karma can be viewed as the essence of our personality, the profound tendencies that have been etched into the deepest layers of our lives. The most profound cycles of cause and effect extend beyond our present existence, shaping the manner in which we begin this life, including our specific circumstances from birth, and will continue beyond our passing. The purpose of Buddhist practice is to transform our fundamental life tendencies to achieve our full human potential in this lifetime and beyond.

An ancient Buddhist text offers this wisdom: "If you wish to understand the causes that existed in the past, look at the results that are manifested in the present. And if you wish to understand what results will be manifested, look at the causes that exist in the present."

As such, karma is in constant flux, just like everything else. Our choices in each moment shape our present and future. Therefore, the doctrine of karma does not encourage resignation but instead empowers us to become the central characters in the unfolding story of our lives.

Manifesting Buddhahood in Everyday Life

THE PRACTICE OF THE bodhisattva involves a wholehearted commitment to personal development while also seeking to alleviate the suffering of others and promote their happiness and well-being. This principle is central to Nichiren Buddhism, which asserts that anyone can achieve enlightenment or Buddhahood during their lifetime. However, what exactly does Buddhahood or enlightenment signify?

The historical founder of Buddhism, Shakyamuni, earned the title of Buddha due to his exceptional ability to comprehend people's suffering, help them recognize their inner resources for overcoming challenges, and inspire them to envision a greater potential for themselves. His character was a powerful source of inspiration for all. Nevertheless, as time passed, the notion of Buddhahood portrayed in Shakyamuni's example became increasingly abstract and remote. The Buddha was seen as a being from another realm, creating an insurmountable divide between himself and ordinary people.

Although the goal of Shakyamuni's teachings was to "make all beings equal to me," some Buddhist schools regarded him as a one-of-a-kind entity, and spiritual attainment became about achieving stages of enlightenment that were less comprehensive than Buddhahood. For others, Buddhahood was an exceedingly remote objective that could only be achieved after many lifetimes of hard work, which was beyond the capacity of all individuals.

In Nichiren Buddhism, the concept of Buddhahood is not a static endpoint that is attained in the future. Rather, the qualities of Buddhahood are already present within all individuals. The practice of Buddhism is centered on manifesting these qualities - such as compassion, wisdom, courage, and creative life-force - amidst the challenges of everyday life.

The key to consistently manifesting Buddhahood lies in bodhisattva practice, which involves practicing for oneself and for the benefit of others. Bodhisattvas, as described in Mahayana Buddhist sutras, are followers of the Buddha who have devoted themselves to Buddhist practice and have developed various qualities and characteristics to aid people in need. These qualities and the bodhisattvas themselves represent the limitless ways in which Buddhahood can manifest in the lives of all individuals.

Bodhisattva practice requires a strong commitment to self-development while simultaneously seeking to alleviate the suffering of others and promote their happiness and well-being. This practice provides a practical connection between the abstract ideal of Buddhahood and the realities of our everyday lives. Ultimately, the way of life of the bodhisattva is the same as that of the Buddha himself, making it a tangible and achievable path for all individuals.

The Buddha's life was characterized by an unceasing pursuit of self-development and active involvement in people's lives and their predicaments. This engagement was founded on the Buddha's unwavering belief in the inherent worth and dignity of each person's life. A Buddha is someone who continuously endeavors to awaken people to their innate potential to overcome any difficulty, inspiring them to utilize challenges and hardships as a catalyst for growth and achieve an unassailable state of happiness.

Ultimately, it is through our interactions with others that we can awaken the Buddha within us. By aiding others and being influenced by positive role models and friends, we can elevate our life condition to the exalted state of Buddhahood, as SGI President Daisaku Ikeda has described it. Performing altruistic acts reinforces, nurtures, and strengthens the Buddhahood inherent in our own lives. As our Buddhahood grows stronger, we can inspire others to lead even more fulfilling lives.

The path to human revolution lies in this ongoing process of self-development and helping others do the same.

Funi: The Idea of 'Two, but Not Two'

THE BUDDHIST PRINCIPLE OF the oneness of self and environment (esho funi) asserts that life (sho) and its environment (e) are indivisible (funi). Funi conveys the idea of "two, but not two," implying that although we may perceive our surroundings as distinct from ourselves, there exists a dimension of our lives that is united with the universe. In fact, at the most fundamental level of existence, there is no division between ourselves and our environment.

According to Buddhist philosophy, everything in our surroundings, including our relationships with colleagues and family, is a reflection of our inner selves. Our individual state of mind shapes our perception of the world around us, and consequently, our circumstances alter accordingly. Therefore, if we transform ourselves, our surroundings will inevitably change as well.

Nichiren, an influential Buddhist monk, once wrote that life manifests itself in a living subject and an objective environment. He claimed, "Life at each moment encompasses... both self and environment of all sentient beings in every condition of life and insentient beings–plants, sky and earth, on down to the most minute particles of dust."

"Life" refers to the subjective self that experiences the effects of past actions and can create new causes for the future. The environment is the realm where the karmic effects of life take shape. Each living being has their own unique environment. For instance, a person whose inner life is in a state of hell may perceive the environment of a crowded subway train as being hellish, while a person in the state known in Buddhism as bodhisattva might feel compassion and a sense of camaraderie with the other people pressed around them.

Individuals also create physical environments that reflect their inner reality. For example, someone who is depressed may neglect their home and personal appearance. In contrast, someone who is secure and generous creates a warm and attractive environment around them.

Buddhism teaches that everything around us, including work and family relationships, is a reflection of our inner lives. We perceive everything through ourselves and our inner state of life can alter our perception of the world. Therefore, if we change ourselves, our circumstances will inevitably change as well.

This concept is liberating because it means that there is no need to seek enlightenment outside ourselves or in a particular place. We can bring forth our innate Buddhahood, wherever we are and in whatever circumstances we find ourselves. This transformation can turn our experience of our environment into "the Buddha's land" - a joy-filled place where we can create value for ourselves and for others.

Nichiren, wrote, "If the minds of the people are impure, their land is also impure, but if their minds are pure, so is their land. There are not two lands, pure and impure in themselves. The difference lies solely in the good or evil of our minds." In this context, "evil" refers to self-centered and short-sighted tendencies based on greed, arrogance, fear, and aggression.

This concept is evident in the state of the natural environment in different societies. In some rural areas, indigenous peoples show deep respect for their natural surroundings, taking only what they need and preserving the riches of nature. As a result, the environment provides protection and sustenance in return. However, in developed areas where materialistic greed predominates, the environment has frequently been exploited and degraded, resulting in catastrophic effects.

The most positive action we can take for society and the land is to transform our own lives, so that they are no longer dominated by anger, greed, and fear. When we manifest wisdom, generosity, and integrity, we naturally make more valuable choices and find that our surroundings are nurturing and supportive. While it may be difficult to foresee the long-term results of our actions, Buddhism teaches that through the oneness of self and environment, everything is interconnected.

As we come to believe that our actions make a difference, we can make an even greater difference. Through our individual choices, we can positively impact the world around us, contributing to a healthier and more harmonious environment for all.

From Hell to Buddhahood: Exploring the Ten Worlds

Have you ever experienced a range of emotions, from anger to sadness, from hopelessness to elation? Have you ever been so absorbed in an activity that it felt like a teacher, guiding you through an experience you couldn't quite put into words? Or have you felt another person's pain, even that of a stranger, as if it was your own?

These are some of the inner states described in the Buddhist concept of the Ten Worlds. Even when we're feeling good, something can quickly knock us out of that positive state, while something else can lift us out of a negative one.

The Ten Worlds represent ten different conditions of life that everyone possesses and experiences from moment to moment. Most people spend the majority of their time moving between the first six conditions, from Hell to Rapture, which are highly vulnerable to changing circumstances and governed by external influences.

The Chinese Buddhist T'ien-t'ai developed a system for classifying human experience into these ten states or "worlds," based on his reading of the Lotus Sutra in the sixth century. Nichiren adopted and expanded upon this Ten Worlds teaching, emphasizing the inner, subjective nature of these states.

As Nichiren stated, "Hell and the Buddha may exist in different places according to some sutras, but upon closer examination, both exist within our five-foot body." This highlights the fact that our internal states shape our experience of the world, regardless of external circumstances.

What are the Ten Worlds?

They are ten conditions of life that we all experience from moment to moment. These worlds, ranked from the least to the most desirable, are as follows:

1- Hell: a condition of suffering where one is devoid of freedom and has very little life force. Without experiencing Hell, we could never truly appreciate happiness, and the fear of falling into this condition can motivate us to make positive changes in our lives.

2- Hunger: a condition characterized by an insatiable desire for food, power, wealth, fame, pleasure, and other material things.

While hunger can drive human activity, it can also lead to negative consequences such as greed and selfishness.

3- Animality: a condition in which one is governed by instinct and has no sense of morality. The positive aspects of animality include intuitive wisdom and the instinct to protect and nurture life.

4- Anger: a condition in which one is dominated by the selfish ego, competitiveness, and the need to be superior. Anger can also fuel passionate energy and a burning desire for justice.

5- Humanity (or Tranquility): a tranquil state marked by the ability to reason and make calm judgments. However, it is an unstable state that can be easily disrupted.

6- Rapture (or Heaven): a temporary state of pleasure experienced when one's desires are fulfilled. This state is easily disrupted by changes in circumstances.

The remaining four worlds must be revealed from within one's own life:

7-Learning: a condition in which one seeks self-improvement and lasting truth through the teachings of others.

8- Realization (or Absorption): a state in which one discovers a partial truth through one's own observations, efforts, and concentration. People in these states can become arrogant and self-centered.

9- Bodhisattva: a condition in which one aspires not only for personal enlightenment but also devotes oneself to relieving the suffering of others through compassionate and altruistic actions. However, this state can also have negative aspects such as self-sacrifice and acting out of a sense of duty or resentment.

10-Buddhahood: the highest state of life, where one has achieved complete enlightenment and embodies the highest wisdom, compassion, and courage.

Buddhahood is considered to be the ultimate state of the Ten Worlds, a state of pure and indestructible happiness that is not influenced by one's circumstances. It is a state of absolute freedom, marked by limitless wisdom, courage, compassion, and life force.

Each of the Ten Worlds encompasses all ten worlds and has the potential to reveal any of the others at any given moment. Therefore, we can reveal our Buddhahood from the very first moment we start chanting. As we continue to practice, we make Buddhahood the dominant state of our lives, acting as a filter that reveals the positive aspects of the other nine worlds, from Hell to Bodhisattva.

Throughout the day, we experience different states in response to our environment. However, each of us has one or more worlds that our activities usually center on, and to which we revert when external stimuli subside. This is called one's basic life tendency, established by prior actions. The purpose of Buddhist practice is to elevate this basic life tendency and ultimately establish Buddhahood as our fundamental state.

Establishing Buddhahood as our basic life tendency does not mean that we rid ourselves of the other nine worlds. All of these states are necessary and integral aspects of life. Without experiencing the sufferings of Hell, we could not feel genuine compassion for others. Without the instinctive desires represented by Hunger and Animality, we would forget to eat, sleep and reproduce, and soon become extinct. Even after establishing Buddhahood as our fundamental life tendency, we will still experience the joys and sorrows of the other nine worlds.

However, these worlds will not control us, and we will not define ourselves in terms of them. Based on the life tendency of Buddhahood, our nine worlds will harmonize and function to benefit both ourselves and those around us. The purpose of Buddhist practice, particularly for Nichiren Buddhists who recite the phrase Nam-myoho-renge-kyo, is to bring forth the life-state of Buddhahood that illuminates our lives and enables us to forge lasting value from our eternal journey through all the Ten Worlds.

A Path to Buddhahood

THE FAMOUS QUOTE BY Nichiren Daishonin states, "Suffer what there is to suffer, enjoy what there is to enjoy. Regard both suffering and joy as facts of life and continue chanting Nam-myoho-renge-kyo, no matter what happens. Then you will experience boundless joy from the Law."

In this passage, the phrase "Suffer what there is to suffer, enjoy what there is to enjoy" pertains to the realm of relative happiness, whereas "joy derived from the law" means absolute happiness. Both joys and sorrows are integral to life, and we should not allow ourselves to be swayed by either, whether it be doubting and despairing in times of trouble or becoming complacent during times of prosperity. As Nichiren Daishonin teaches, we should persist in chanting Nam-myoho-renge-kyo, regardless of what happens.

During times of good fortune, we should chant Daimoku in gratitude. During adversity, we should chant Daimoku to transform poison into medicine. If we can use all the experiences, both positive and negative, to reinforce our connection with the

Gohonzon, we can purify and elevate our life-condition, gradually establishing Buddhahood as our fundamental tendency. As we do so, we will experience an unquantifiable happiness that transcends circumstances - the "boundless joy from the Law."

Printed in Great Britain
by Amazon